D1516800

Screen Process Printing

Screen Process Printing

Second edition

John Stephens

BLUEPRINT
An Imprint of Chapman & Hall

London · Glasgow · Weinheim · New York · Tokyo · Melbourne · Madras

Published by Blueprint, an imprint of Chapman & Hall, 2–6 Boundary Row, London SE1 8HN, UK

Chapman & Hall, 2–6 Boundary Row, London SE1 8HN, UK

Blackie Academic & Professional, Wester Cleddens Road, Bishopbriggs, Glasgow G64 2NZ, UK

Chapman & Hall GmbH, Pappelallee 3, 69469 Weinheim, Germany

Chapman & Hall USA, 115 Fifth Avenue, New York, NY 10003, USA

Chapman & Hall Japan, ITP-Japan, Kyowa Building, 3F, 3-2-1 Hirakawacho, Chiyoda-ku, Tokyo 102, Japan

Chapman & Hall Australia, 102 Dodds Street, South Melbourne, Victoria 3205, Australia

Chapman & Hall India, R. Seshadri, 32 Second Main Road, CIT East, Madras 600 035, India

First edition 1987

Second edition 1996

© 1987, 1996 John Stephens

Typeset in 10½/12 Sabon by WestKey Ltd, Falmouth, Cornwall
Printed in Great Britain by Alden Press, Oxford

ISBN 1 85713 009 X

A catalogue record for this book is available from the British Library

Library of Congress Catalog Card Number: 95–78834

Contents

Colour plates appear between pages 200 and 201.

Foreword

The screen printing industry is characterized by its diversity. The range of applications, products and services it provides is unique. No other printing process can yet match the versatility of the screen printing process – and every year the quality of print and diversity of application seems to increase. This makes the industry one of the most dynamic and exciting areas of printing in which to be involved. There is so much to learn and there is always something new and innovative going on.

Of course, these characteristics do not occur as a simple corollary of the process. They are there because the process attracts people who have the creative intelligence, the vision and the entrepreneurial flair to perceive the potential of the process and to create the new and innovative within it. Indeed, it might be argued that the second most significant characteristic about the industry is that it tends to attract very special people with these qualities, so valued in this time of rapid technological development and change.

It is a very good thing that the industry does attract such talented people, as they are needed now perhaps more than ever, for the industry faces many important challenges. The development in communications technology and electronic media is influencing the way we live and work. Its effects are already apparent in many areas of the industry and this trend will continue to gather in momentum and force, changing the nature of our work, the way we do it and our attitude to it, providing new opportunities for us to apply those valuable qualities we have.

Concerns for the environment and the laws which control the impact of industrial processes and operations also provide important challenges for the future of the industry and its workforce. Managing the way the industry impacts upon the environment and the way we conform to the new and rapidly developing legislative framework will be a matter of increasing concern. It is a matter which we ignore at our peril.

So, how best can we meet these and other challenges which are only just around the corner? Firstly, we should not attempt to meet them on our own. We are part of a larger industrial community, which includes the manufacturers and suppliers of the products we use. Collectively we have considerable power, not only in the political arena, through representations made by the Screen Printing Association and the Federation of European Screen Printers, but as a body of creative and innovative industrial practitioners who from necessity must begin to approach the problems of this age of change with a collective intelligence, rather than in isolated and vulnerable self-interest. We must begin to make effective use of the industry of which we are part.

How is this to be done? The first step is to join the professional bodies and technical associations which exist to promote the interests of the industry. I make no excuses for promoting the body I represent, the Screen Printing Association UK Ltd (SPA), as I firmly believe that its role in the development of the industry is becoming more vital with every passing day. Other organizations with a specialist interest in the technical developments of the industry are the Screen Printing Technical Association (SPTA) and the Printing and Publishing Research Association (PIRA), and also the Screen Printing and Graphic Imaging Association International (SGIA), which represents developments in the industry on a truly international scale.

These organizations provide invaluable information resources, dealing with economic, legal, technical and training matters. They provide lectures and seminars on a wide range of industry-related topics. As this book quite rightly points out, our future will be shaped by our ability to access and interpret relevant information, for this is indeed the 'information age'.

Lastly, and most importantly, I come to the topic of education and training. Having access to information is important, but being able to interpret it and apply it is what really matters. Information on its own is of little use. If we cannot make use of it, it is worthless. In industry and commerce application is everything. In order to make effective use of information we must be able to understand it, to analyse it, to evaluate its relevance to our needs, and finally to be able to learn from it by applying it and assimilating it within our knowledge base. And this requires intelligence and skill.

As the processes of screen printing become more critically linked to technological change, the need for a well informed and technologically literate workforce will become more and more apparent. As the author rightly points out, the industry is emerging from its craft traditions. Many of its more senior personnel, conditioned by the craft culture from which they came, have a strong tendency to resist the new, and to approach its advance with reluctance, even fear. The majority of these people will have received little or no formal training and will therefore have no experience which allows them to place a value upon it. The problem is that even the most sentimentally inclined have to acknowledge that commercial screen printing is now more a technology than it is a craft. If we are to move on in the industry we have to acknowledge this fact and that we must have a workforce which is ready and intellectually able to accommodate change.

In short we must have a workforce which is not only competent to carry out a complex of operations but also has the ability to learn quickly and to approach new tasks and operations with a positive and engaging attitude. The valuable human attributes and qualities which have made the industry what it is need to be refocused within a structured training programme that provides standards of competency for the industry and seeks to promote a change at the roots of our industrial culture.

As the industry lead body, the SPA, together with the City and Guilds of London Institute (CGLI), has produced just such a training scheme. Approved by the National Council for Vocational Qualifications (NCVQ), the scheme provides a set of training standards which measure operational competence in the processes of screen printing. Achievement of these standards leads to the award of a National Vocational Qualification (NVQ) in Screen Printing. NVQs are now widely accepted as the standard vocational qualification for operatives in almost all industrial occupations, and have currency in the UK and the European Union.

The scheme provides a very flexible approach to training, which can be conducted wholly in-company or in association with an authorized assessment centre, such as local colleges and universities or training centres like Europrint in Barnsley.

The Europrint training centre is a new and much needed development which has been established specifically to answer the need for up-to-date training in the fast-moving environment of the screen printing industry. By providing custom-made residential courses, giving access to a wide range of advanced machinery and computer-based design, production control and management information systems, the centre is able to respond to specific sectorial and individual company training needs.

Good training needs a sound knowledge base, which brings me to my final point: the purpose and function of this book. As the lead body for the industry we most warmly welcome the second edition of what has proved to be a most important book. In both its scope and its detailed treatment of screen process technology, it provides a long awaited and most valuable supporting text for the NVQ training scheme. For new entrants to the industry it will serve as an essential core reference, and for those already acquainted with the squeegee and the screen it will, I am sure, provide much that is both instructive and thought provoking.

To its author, our thanks for his careful diligence in so clearly and comprehensively presenting the intricacies of the process and our thanks also for his perceptive insights, gathered from many years experience both in the industry and in education. I commend the book to you.

Michael Turner
Director
Screen Printing Association (UK) Ltd.

Preface

The first edition of *Screen Process Printing* was published in 1987. It was written to satisfy the need for an authoritative textbook on a diverse and rapidly developing area of the printing industry. Its focus was on commercial and industrial screen printing as opposed to the purely craft-based approach with which other publications dealt. The intention was to reflect an already established change in the development of the process and within the screen printing industry away from the craft culture of subjective empirical judgements toward a more analytical approach facilitated by developments in the technology of the process.

This is not to say that the industry has no place for craft skills or that these are in some way devalued by advances in technology. Technology is not a replacement for the experience and knowledge gained through skilled practice. How many companies have fallen for the seductive marketing of the 'user friendly' sales pitch, which promises everything from the man and woman in the street, only to find out to their cost that there is no substitute for knowledge – especially where quality and price are the masters of the game, as they are indeed today? No: modern technology is only as effective as those who have the knowledge and experience to make the most effective use of it. What is changing is the nature of the skills required and the intellectual and attitudinal frame of reference needed for the application of these new skills.

The advances of the technological age are of course reflected throughout the whole of the printing industry. The consequent problems of capital investment and training are evident in all sectors, not least in the screen printing industry, which continues to develop at an increasing pace. However, unlike the other areas of the printing industry, screen printing is singular in that it appears to have one foot firmly planted in the past whilst the other is trying to march bravely if somewhat unsurely into the future. This in my view was clearly the case in 1987. A good example of this is the slow and rather lame-footed take up of the advances and opportunities made available by the introduction of UV screen printing inks some 15 years ago.

Happily, this innate conservatism, a tendency to be always looking over the shoulder, is beginning to disappear. The positive response to new materials and innovations in pre-press technology is now more generally evident. The industry has always attracted individuals with innovative and entrepreneurial flair. The difference now is that there would appear to be more of them around than before. Perhaps it is a condition of the time in which we live: the 'information age' – it is becoming more and more imperative to have access to the relevant information. To have access to information is one thing but to be able to interpret it, to understand it fully and to be able to make effective use of it is quite another. As I began to put this new edition together, the fundamental importance of these concepts began to shape the work in hand.

What was said in 1987 about the process is just as true today, perhaps even more so because of the speed at which change now appears to take place. Screen process is still the most versatile method of printing that has yet been devised. Recent developments in inkjet printing have caused ripples of anxiety to pass through the industry. There are certain sectors where the versatility and flexibility of digital colour printing is having an impact. It is very likely that this will continue to take effect as development costs are recovered and greater market share is gained. However, before we all pack up our squeegees and turn out the light it is worth reflecting again on the huge versatility of screen process and the massively complex nature of the industry. I use the collective singular with caution, since it can be argued that there is no single screen printing industry but rather a very wide range of diverse applications, some of which may not even be regarded as printing at all. We must not forget that screen process is still the only process capable of printing on to almost any surface, of producing a range of special effects and varying ink film deposits which cannot be matched by any other process, and of providing a competitive alternative to conventional processes like offset-litho in the medium-run poster and point-of-sale print markets.

In relation to the other major printing processes, screen printing is technologically a relatively 'young' process. We are still learning how it works and how best to control it. New screen mesh materials, stencil systems, inks, innovations in pre-press systems and printing press design and new applications for the process are continuing to drive it forward into the 21st century.

My approach in writing this new edition has been firstly to produce an up-to-date text which takes account of recent developments and addresses the concerns of those involved in the process. For example, much of the recent development in ink and solvent systems, cleaning and reclamation technology has been encouraged by the growing concern with environmental protection. Recent legislation prohibiting and controlling the use of certain solvents and chemicals in the work place, and controlling the disposal of environmentally hazardous substances, has sent shock waves through the industry. The impact of these new laws has yet to be fully assessed but what is certain is that the law does not recognize ignorance. There is therefore a new chapter dealing with health, safety and the environment. Secondly, in recognition of its diversity I have broadened the focus of the book to reflect more accurately the nature of the industry. There are new chapters dealing with screen printing applications and with the art and craft of screen printing. Here the aim has been to identify the broad sectors of the industry and to outline some of the key differences in equipment, materials, processes and products and in this way to provide some insight as to the range and scope of the process.

This said, the essential purpose of the book has not changed. It has been written primarily as a practical guide for those who are studying screen printing on a formal basis, as part of a programme of education and training. Revisions to the text have taken into account the needs of those engaged on the new NVQ Screen Printing Training Scheme, administered by the Screen Printing Association UK Ltd (SPA).

A great deal has been written recently about the threats posed by digital technology and non-impact colour printing. One thing is certain: the digital world is here to stay and the electronic revolution will continue to impact upon the industry. Furthermore, the pace of its development still appears to be increasing. However, there is also a great deal of development going on in the technology of screen printing, and this combined with the many opportunities created by the electronic revolution will provide a growing market for the industry for some years to come. The greatest asset we have is our ability to adapt to change and to seek new ways of applying what we have learned. I hope that, in some small way, this book may be of service in this.

John Stephens
June 1995

The principles of screen printing 1

Screen process printing is a 20th-century invention but it has it origins in the very ancient method of image reproduction known as stencilling. In its simplest form stencilling is carried out by forcing a pigment medium through an aperture or around a shape cut from stiff paper or thin metal sheet.

Examples of stencilling have been traced back to prehistoric cultures. Deep inside caves at Cabrerets, in southern France, there are wall-paintings that bear the stencilled signatures of those who made them. They are signed with the image of the human hand, made, it is thought, by blowing coloured earth around an actual hand, placed palm down on the cave wall, very much in the manner used by the Australian aborigines in their painting and decorative art.

Stencils have been used throughout history as a simple means of graphic reproduction and decoration. They are still used today in interior decoration and for marking containers, or perhaps more commonly for tracing letters and symbols on to paper. Yet as a method of reproduction, stencilling does have certain limitations. It is suitable only for the reproduction of relatively simple images. This is because the stability of a stencil relies upon the negative areas of the image being held together. This can be best illustrated by looking at the example of stencilled letter forms in Fig. 1.

ABBCC
HDDJS

(a)    (b)

Fig. 1 (a) Paper stencil.
(b) Stencilled letter forms.

Fig. 2 Japanese 'hair stencil'.

Here one can see how the centres of the letters have to be 'tied' to the main body of the stencil to give them support. The presence of these 'ties' breaks up the letter forms and reduces their legibility. It is also quite evident that the more intricate the design, the more delicate and unstable the stencil will be.

The Japanese paper stencils exhibited at the Victoria and Albert Museum, London, are extremely intricate. But the Japanese have very cleverly provided a fine web-like structure of human hair to act as a support for the stencil. The hair support is fine enough to allow the free passage of the pigment medium, thus creating the possibility of producing stencilled images with complete continuity of design.

It is thought that screen printing was developed directly from the Japanese 'hair stencil'. The web-like support of human hair was replaced by finely woven cotton or silk gauze (bolting cloth), which, when stretched over a wooden frame to form a screen, provided a stable support structure for the stencil.

Screens made from silk bolting cloth, used in the sifting of flour, proved to be the most commercially viable stencil support material. It is from this use of silk bolting cloth that the name 'silk screen' derives. Modern screen gauze is made from synthetic materials which have far greater durability and provide the improved printing characteristics required in modern screen printing. For this reason the process is now more correctly referred to as 'screen printing' or 'screen process', since silk is no longer used, except for very specialized fine art and craft printing techniques.

Screens are made by tensioning the mesh material over the screen frame and attaching it to the edges of the frame, usually with a special epoxide resin adhesive. Here again, the demands of modern precision printing require that screens are tensioned to very closely measured levels.

Stencils are still cut by hand, using a special knife-cut film or laminate

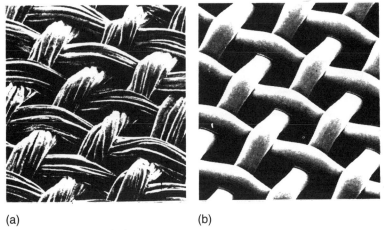

(a)   (b)

Fig. 3 (a) Silk bolting cloth.
        (b) Monofilament polyester mesh.

material. This work is usually restricted to large format line designs for posters, display and large printed sign panels. Stencils made by photo-mechanical techniques are more commonly used, since the detail that they are able to reproduce is far more intricate than could ever be cut by even the most skilled in the craft of stencil cutting.

Printing is carried out by registering the screen which carries the stencil over the printing stock. A rubber or plastic blade called a 'squeegee' is

Fig. 4 A photographic stencil.

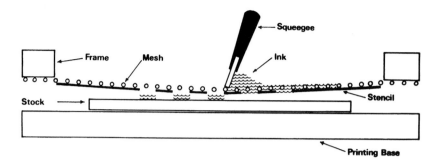

Fig. 5 Sectional view showing the elements of screen printing.

then used to draw the printing medium across the screen, forcing it through the stencil and on to the stock beneath.

Printing can be carried out manually by pulling the squeegee across the screen by hand but high volume production work is carried out on semi or fully automatic screen printing machinery. Originally the inks used in manual screen printing were very slow drying but the automated screen printing of today requires an ink which will dry quickly. For this reason most modern screen printing inks are made to dry rapidly, usually by accelerative forced air drying, or more recently with the almost instantaneous effect of UV (ultraviolet) curing.

Using the most advanced drying systems it is possible to screen print close-register multicolour work at speeds of up to 6000 copies per hour. There are multicolour flat-bed and web-fed (reel to reel) screen units that produce self adhesive labels and stickers, flexible circuits, T-shirts and printed textiles, wallpaper and floor coverings and many other mass-produced products. The range and diversity of the machinery and processes used in modern screen printing is truly amazing. Indeed it is a tribute to the ingenuity and innovative genius of those who have focused their creative intelligence in the development of this almost magical process.

Screen mesh 2

Silk was originally used for screen printing because it provided the finest possible gauze structure available at the time. As can be seen in Fig. 3, silk yarn is made by spinning a number of very fine silk filaments together to form a strong multifilament thread. The threads are then woven together to form an open gauze fabric, suitable for printing purposes. To be suitable for screen printing the mesh material must:

- provide an adequate supportive structure for the stencil;
- allow the free passage of the printing medium.

Because of its complex surface structure silk provides a very good adhesive surface for stencils, particularly the indirect type, which are fixed to the underside of the screen. Yet these same properties have an adverse effect upon the permeability of the stencil. The characteristic uneven surface of the silk thread makes the mesh openings uneven and this facilitates mesh blocking or clogging. Pigment particles are easily trapped by the rough mesh structure and very quickly cause the stencil openings to become blocked, thus causing eventual print failure.

Another major disadvantage of silk is that it is very hygroscopic, that is it absorbs moisture readily from the atmosphere. As it takes in moisture, the silk thread tends to swell and this in turn causes a reduction in the size of the mesh openings, adversely affecting the stencil's permeability.

This tendency to absorb moisture can also cause the screen to lose tension which in turn causes a loss of dimensional stability in the image-forming stencil. On multicolour work, any change in the dimensions of the stencil will cause misregistration between printings.

In addition to these disadvantages, silk meshes are very difficult to clean and reclaim after printing. Ink and stencil residue can become lodged in the mesh and cannot be removed without the aid of strong chemical cleaning agents, such as caustic and bleach. Unfortunately, even in very weak solutions, these chemicals will destroy the silk fibres in a very short period of time.

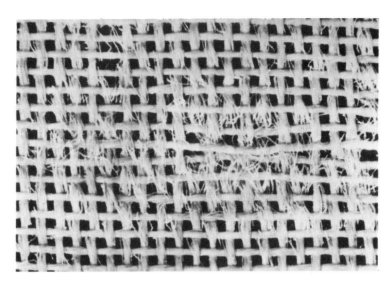

Fig. 6 Multifilament mesh damaged by physical abrasion and chemical attack.

Synthetic mesh materials Modern screen printing gauzes are made from synthetic fibres, such as polyamide (nylon) and polyester (Terylene). The main advantages provided by these so-called 'man-made fibres' can be listed as follows.

- Very fine monofilament fibres can be made, making it possible to produce finely woven meshes.
- Synthetic fibres have high tear resistance, which makes the mesh very durable under the physical stresses effected upon it during printing.
- Synthetic fibres (especially polyester) have a good resistance to extension, which makes the mesh very stable when under tension.
- Synthetic fibres have a good resistance to the chemicals used in screen cleaning and reclamation.
- Synthetic fibres can be made to very precisely controlled thicknesses and woven to provide a screen mesh with a uniform gauze structure. This improves ink passage and makes for easier cleaning and reclaiming.
- Synthetic fibres can be spun into multifilament yarns which, when woven into a screen mesh, provide improved dimensional stability and increased mesh thickness.

Mesh classification Synthetic screen meshes are classified in two ways: by mesh count and by grading.

THE SCREEN MESH COUNT

The number which is printed at intervals along the edge of the screen fabric denotes the number of single threads in the weave per linear centimetre. On some fabrics there are two sets of numbers printed: one metric, the other an imperial measure.

THE MESH GRADING

The number denoting mesh count is usually followed by the letters 'HD', 'T', 'M' or 'S'. These letters signify the thickness of the fibres which have been used to weave the mesh.

HD = heavy duty, the fibre being relatively thick
T = thick thread
M = medium thick thread
S = small diameter thread.

Screen fabrics are woven in a wide range of mesh counts. At the bottom of the scale are meshes with counts as low as 12 threads per linear

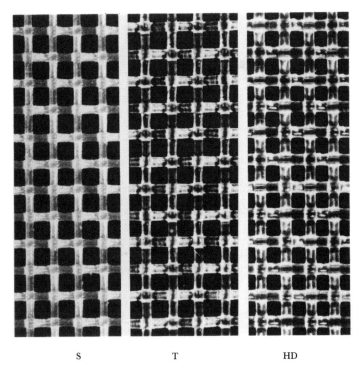

S   T   HD

Fig. 7 Nylon (polyamide), 120 threads per cm, in three grades.

centimetre, and at the top of the scale they run as high as 200 threads/cm. Only the thicker grades are used at the low end of the scale; the high mesh counts require the light fibre grades. As can be seen from Fig. 7, the thickness of the mesh thread determines the size of the mesh openings. As the mesh count rises, so the effective printing area of the gauze is reduced, until a point is reached when the fabric is no longer suitable for screen printing, as its permeability is too low and the printing medium simply will not pass through it.

Mesh selection As we have seen, screen printing mesh is made in a wide range of mesh counts, each in three or four grades. This range gives the printer a great deal of control over the quality of print that can be produced. Of course, to exercise that control the printer must be able to select the right mesh for the right job. The two major considerations which must be taken into account when selecting the right screen mesh are:

- ink film thickness requirements;
- stencil detail requirements.

INK FILM THICKNESS

The thickness of the fibres used in making a screen mesh will determine the overall thickness of the mesh, and in turn this will have a direct effect upon the ink deposit produced. The diagram in Fig. 8 illustrates this.

The mesh count and therefore the permeability of the screen, also serve to determine the thickness of the ink deposit. If a very heavy deposit of ink is required, say to obliterate an undercolour, then a screen mesh with an HD grade thread and a Iow mesh count might be selected.

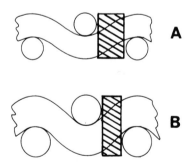

Fig. 8 Ink film thickness in relation to screen mesh thickness.
A = 90 T; B = 90 HD. The shaded area represents the ink volume produced.

Screens with low mesh counts are also used for printing inks which carry very large pigment particles, as in the case of the 'glitter inks' used in the printing of T-shirts. If, on the other hand, a very thin ink deposit is required, in order to produce a very translucent colour, then a lighter quality mesh would be used, giving a correspondingly lighter ink film. If the mesh count was also increased, it would further decrease the ink film thickness deposited by the screen.

STENCIL DETAIL REQUIREMENTS

The primary function of a screen mesh is to provide a supportive structure for the stencil. If the stencil is very intricate and made up of fine detail, the supportive screen mesh must be very finely woven.

For fine line and half-tone work, a screen printing mesh with a count of 100 threads/cm may be regarded as the general minimum requirement. Here, 'T' grade meshes are most commonly used; on the higher mesh counts 'M' and 'S' grades may be employed. With very fine half-tones, with line screens above 36 lines/cm, the closed areas of the screen mesh can seriously inhibit the reproduction of highlight detail, as is evident in Fig. 9.

As can be seen, the quality of half-tone reproduction is critically influenced by the size of the dots the screen mesh is capable of reproducing at each end of the tonal range. If we consider the influence that the mesh thread has on the reproduction of the small highlight dot stencil apertures, it can be seen that the thread diameter should not be larger than the smallest half-tone dot. Where this is the case the stencil aperture may be partially or totally blocked by the mesh thread and will fail to reproduce,

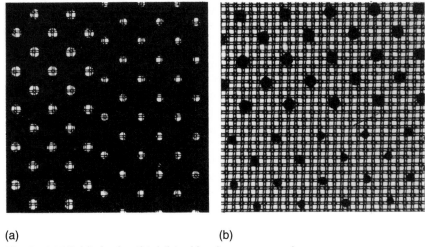

(a)   (b)

Fig. 9 (a) Highlight detail inhibited by the screen mesh.
(b) Shadow detail requires an adequate support.

causing loss in the highlight areas of the image. In the shadow areas of the image the smallest half-tone dots must find sufficient support in the mesh structure to remain intact.

As a very rough guide the mesh count to screen ruling ratio should be between 3:1 and 5:1. This ensures that there is adequate support for the small shadow dots, which is one of the most critical factors in half-tone reproduction. Without adequate screen mesh support the dots will either collapse or fall away from the screen during stencil development or in the early stages of printing, causing loss in shadow detail.

To exemplify this, if we take a half-tone screen ruling of 26 lines/cm ($26 \times 4.25 = 110.5$) we would require a screen mesh with a count of approximately 110 T threads/cm. For a screen ruling of 36 lines/cm ($36 \times 4.25 = 153$) we would select a 150 T screen mesh; and for a screen ruling of 48 lines/cm ($48 \times 4.25 = 204$) we would want to select a mesh count of 200 S.

The mesh grade and thickness of thread are also variables which have a direct critical influence on the reproduction of half-tones. Mesh thread and weave data varies from one manufacturer to another; also between one bolt of cloth and another. The table below illustrates the problem:

Variations in mesh data between one supplier and another for 110 T monofilament polyester mesh

Manufacturer	Mesh count/ grade	Thread diameter (microns)	Mesh opening (microns)	Open area of mesh (%)
A	110 T	40	56	38
A	110 M	35	62	39
B	110 T	40	47	28
B	110 M	34	53	35

It is clear from this that the application of general guidelines is insufficiently precise where fine half-tone work is undertaken. All mesh manufacturers publish tables specifying data relating to their mesh types and grades. Where screen mesh selection is critical, as it is in fine line and half-tone printing, reference to the appropriate screen mesh data tables is advised.

The quality of reproduction in half-tone printing is critically influenced by the size of the dots the screen mesh is capable of reproducing at each end of the tonal range. Further consideration of the relationship between the tonal range (screen range) parameters and screen mesh selection is given in Chapter 4.

POLYAMIDE MESH (NYLON)

Polyamide screen mesh (more commonly referred to as nylon mesh) is manufactured in all four grades and is available in mesh counts ranging from 8 to 200 threads/cm.

Due to its excellent resistance to mechanical abrasion and its elasticity, it is very suitable for printing on to uneven surfaces and shaped articles, such as plastic or glass containers.

It is produced in the very highest mesh count of 200 S, which makes it suitable for printing the very finest half-tone work. Furthermore its high resistance to wear and stress in printing satisfies screen durability requirements in high volume machine printing.

POLYESTER MESH

Sometimes referred to by the trade name Terylene, polyester mesh is made from multifilament and monofilament thread. However, due to its poor printing and cleaning properties, multifilament mesh is most commonly used for high volume applications where heavy ink deposits are required as in textile applications and printing inks containing large and abrasive particles such as glitter inks.

The smooth, wire-like monofilament threads produce a mesh with an evenly woven, regular structure, providing the printing characteristics required for precision screen printing.

Polyester has a greater resistance to extension than is the case with polyamide; it is also less hygroscopic (absorbs less water). These two properties make polyester mesh more dimensionally stable than polyamide mesh. For this reason, polyester is always used in preference to polyamide when the close registration tolerances of the print demand dimensional stability in the screen. Polyester is probably the most widely used screen mesh for graphic and general screen printing applications. Its good wear resistance makes it suitable for machine work, and its excellent chemical and solvent resistance makes it very easy to clean and reclaim.

COLOURED MESH

There are a number of coloured screen meshes on the market, both polyamide and polyester. The mesh is dyed red, orange or yellow to prevent the effects of light scatter which can occur when exposing a direct coated screen to ultraviolet light, in direct stencil making. When white mesh is used for a direct stencil, the surface of the mesh will reflect a certain amount of the actinic UV light within the mesh structure. (Actinic

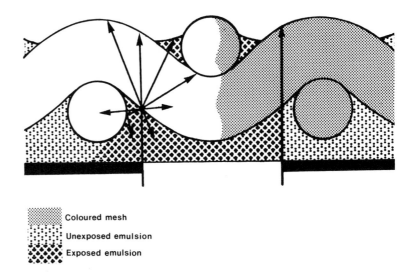

Coloured mesh
Unexposed emulsion
Exposed emulsion

Fig. 10 The effects of light scatter. Coloured screen mesh absorbs actinic UV radiation.

light is light which will produce a chemical reaction in photosensitive materials.)

This internal reflection causes areas behind the image which is being copied to expose, usually at the edges, which can result in what is known as 'image undercutting' – a slight reduction in the overall dimensions of the image reproduced on the stencil. If the image is finely detailed, such as fine line or half-tone work, this can result in substantial image loss. Using a dyed mesh helps to eliminate the image undercutting effect by absorbing the actinic wavelengths of light and reflecting only those wavelengths to which the stencil emulsion is not sensitive. When using dyed meshes, exposure times recommended for white meshes should be increased by 50–150%, depending on the screen mesh count used.

METALLIZED POLYESTER

For high precision printing, such as printed circuit work, dimensional stability is of prime importance. Stainless steel mesh is often used in such applications. However, metallized polyester mesh has very similar printing characteristics and costs somewhat less.

It is made by coating the screen mesh with nickel, after it has been woven. This effectively fuses the entire mesh structure together, increasing its dimensional stability by 50%. The nickel coating also improves the surface structure of the mesh, filling the tiny fissures which trap ink where the threads overlap. In this way the ink passage properties of the mesh are greatly enhanced. The nickel coating also makes the mesh electrically conductive. This helps to eliminate the problem of static electricity, which can be generated during printing. Both polyester and polyamide mesh have a tendency to produce static charges, created by the action of the squeegee blade passing over the screen: the friction between the blade and the screen generates a static charge, which, in certain conditions, can cause serious production problems. The electrically conductive coating on the metallized mesh can prevent the static charge from building up, since it is immediately conducted away by the nickel coating.

This property also allows the mesh to be used for printing with thermoplastic inks. These inks have to be heated during printing. The metallized mesh can be electrically heated, which makes it ideally suited for this printing application.

ANTISTATIC MESH

The problem of static charges generated during printing can be very serious, particularly in printing certain types of plastic material and where dust contamination is a problem as in the case of illuminated graphics panels. In an attempt to cure the problem, the mesh manufacturers have produced a carbonized fabric, which prevents the static charge from being generated on the mesh.

The fabric is woven partly from polyester and partly from a special carbon-coated polyamide thread which forms every alternate weft thread (cross-thread). This carbonized thread allows static electricity to be discharged from the screen before it can build up.

CALENDERED MESH

Reducing the overall thickness of the screen mesh will reduce the thickness of the ink film deposit produced. When printing conventional evaporative screen inks, only some 30% of ink that is printed remains on the stock after drying; the other 70% is the solvent which has evaporated in the drying process. However, when conventional UV inks are used there are no solvents present, since the ink becomes a solid by a photochemical reaction and not through the evaporation of a volatile solvent. Therefore, the printed ink film remains 100% solid on the stock after curing.

Although screen process printing has gained much of its popularity by virtue of the thick ink deposits that it can achieve, this becomes a handicap when printing 100% solids with UV ink. The first difficulty created by the thick ink film is that it requires a lot of energy, in the form of intense UV radiation, to dry and cure it, and this can add considerably to the printing costs. In addition to this, the ink is relatively expensive. Another difficulty arises when printing four colour half-tone work. Here the thickness of the ink film can produce a relief surface which can prevent the ink from reaching the stock on the third and fourth colour printings. This can result in shifts of colour balance and in the increased appearance of visually disturbing moiré effects, the pattern created by the superimposition of regular half-tone screen patterns (Fig. 39).

To combat this problem the mesh manufacturers have produced 'UV or calendered mesh', a screen mesh which has been flattened on one side. This is achieved by passing the mesh through heated rollers, called calendering rollers. One of the rollers spins slightly faster than the other and this flattens the mesh 'knuckles' where the threads cross one another. As a result the overall thickness of the mesh is reduced, which in turn reduces the ink film thickness that is deposited by as much as 50%.

STAINLESS STEEL WIRE MESH

Stainless steel wire has been used for many years in the weaving of specialist screen mesh for very close tolerance precision printing, such as is found in certain industrial applications. As was noted earlier, this material is used in the printing of electronic circuits. Its unmatched dimensional stability meets the high standards of print fidelity demanded in circuit work. Unlike synthetic fabric it does not absorb moisture and is therefore unaffected by changes in humidity and is less elastic than even metallized polyester.

In a 'print-on-print' test carried out by German manufacturers, Haver & Boecker, the deviation of print from forward to backward squeegee strokes was 25% less than that obtained using a polyester screen mesh. Furthermore, a stainless steel mesh will retain its tension almost indefinitely, whereas all conventional synthetic meshes show a tendency to lose tension with use, and as a result they also lose dimensional stability.

In addition to its excellent stability, the ink passage properties of stainless steel mesh are unsurpassed. This is due to the fact that the diameter of the wire used to weave the mesh is relatively small compared

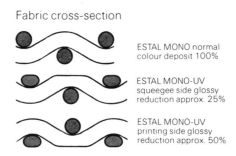

Fabric cross-section

ESTAL MONO normal
colour deposit 100%

ESTAL MONO-UV
squeegee side glossy
reduction approx. 25%

ESTAL MONO-UV
printing side glossy
reduction approx. 50%

Fig. 11 The effect of calendered screen mesh on ink film thickness.

with the threads used in weaving synthetic meshes. For this reason the permeability of stainless steel mesh is greater than a metallized polyester mesh with the same mesh count. The following examples of mesh data relating to ink passage and theoretical ink volume deposit may help to illustrate the point.

Relationship between screen mesh and ink passage and theoretical ink film deposit

	Mesh count	Wire/thread thickness (microns)	Mesh opening (microns)	% open area of mesh	Theoretical ink film deposits, cm^3/cm^2
Metallized polyester mesh	130 T	38	40	27	17
Stainless steel wire mesh	130 BC*	28	50	41	25

*BC refers to the grade of cloth, i.e. Standard Bolting Cloth; the equivalent of a 'T' grade synthetic mesh.

For this reason stainless steel mesh is used for printing very heavy deposits of ink, since the mesh will allow a greater volume of ink to be deposited whilst providing a stable support for intricate stencil structures. Typical applications will be in printing precisely controlled deposits of conductive and dielectric inks, and solder pastes in the production of thick film circuits and membrane switches. Stainless steel mesh is also used in the decoration of glass, ceramic and chinaware, where dimensional stability and resistance to the highly abrasive ceramic colours are important factors in mesh selection.

Like polyester, stainless steel screen mesh can be calendered to provide a flatter, thinner fabric, with corresponding reductions in ink film deposits. With stainless steel there is less distortion of the mesh structure and correspondingly less reduction in the mesh openings compared with calendered synthetic mesh.

Like metallized polyester, stainless steel mesh is electrically conductive and can therefore be used for printing thermoplastic inks. In this application the wire mesh is tensioned on a steel frame and insulated from the screen carriage. When connected to an electrical current the screen mesh acts as a resistor and the electrical current passing through the mesh causes it to heat up. The heated mesh causes the dry, almost friable, thermoplastic ink to melt as it passes across the screen. The heated liquid ink passes through the mesh/stencil apertures to the stock below where, without the presence of heat, it immediately fuses into a solid film.

There is of course a price to pay for such excellence in quality. Stainless steel screen printing mesh is considerably more expensive than the equivalent synthetic material; three times the cost in some cases. Unlike synthetic mesh, stainless steel has very low elasticity and this makes the screens very vulnerable to mechanical damage. Tensioning requires the use of specialist equipment. Screen frames must be constructed to provide an especially rigid and stable base for the mesh. For these reasons the mesh is only used in the very specialized applications mentioned above.

HIGH TENSION (HIGH TECH) POLYESTER MESH

In recent a years a new hybrid polyester has been developed which has improved tension properties over those of conventional polyester. This new material has been used to produce a new high tension 'high tech' mesh for the screen printing industry. The material differs from conventional polyester in several ways:

- *Higher resistance*
  The mesh threads have a higher tensile strength, offering increased resistance to extension. Consequently, much higher levels of tension can be achieved without damage to the fabric. To put this in context, consider that tension levels for conventional polyester mesh are 15–22 N/cm, whereas high tension mesh can be tensioned in excess of 30 N/cm. (Mesh tension is measured in N/cm – newtons per centimetre. A newton, derived from Newtonian laws of motion, is a unit of force: 1 N = the force producing an acceleration of 1 m/sec on a mass of 1 kg – see also Chapter 3: *Measuring mesh tension with a meter*.) In the USA, where these fabrics have found considerable favour with the garment printing fraternity, mesh tensions up to 100 N/cm have been achieved, using specially developed self-tensioning frames (see Chapter 3: *Self- tensioning frames*).
- *Reduced tension loss*
  Conventional polyester mesh loses tension fairly quickly during production. This results in poor dimensional stability and a loss in registration control. High tension mesh maintains a more constant level of tension throughout the life of the screen. In fact the mesh is said to increase in stability with use. These two features bring a number of benefits which were hitherto only accessible to those using stainless steel meshes.
- *Reduction in off-contact*
  Higher levels of tension make it possible to lower considerably the 'off-contact' distance (the gap between the underside of the screen and the stock, which promotes ink film splitting and print release). This benefits the printer in two ways: firstly it reduces the stress levels on the stencil due to lower screen deformation under squeegee pressure; and secondly it reduces the consequent excessive wear upon the squeegee blade.

- *Increased register control*
  High levels of off-contact are major contributing factors in registration failure, since they lead directly to stencil image elongation. The reduction of off-contact distance will therefore directly increase the dimensional stability of the printing process.
- *Improved print definition*
  The dynamics of ink splitting and print release at the screen/stencil interface play a critical part in controlling the quality of the printed image. High tension screens improve the dynamics by increasing the rate at which the printed film and the screen mesh part company. Consistent screen tension also provides greater consistency in ink film deposit throughout the print run, and from run to run where repeat runs are carried out.
- *Improved mesh structure*
  The lower elongation properties of high tension mesh help to reduce the problems associated with excessive mesh take-up in self-tensioning frames and the increases in tension at the mesh corners during conventional screen tensioning. The low elongation rate will also reduce distortion of the mesh structure at the corners of the screen, thus improving the geometry of the mesh openings. This makes it possible to increase the printing area of the screen. Further to this the even elongation characteristics between warp and weft threads provides greater uniformity of tension and mesh structure across the whole screen.

The advantages which accrue from this new fabric have yet to be fully evaluated and appreciated throughout the diverse areas of the industry.

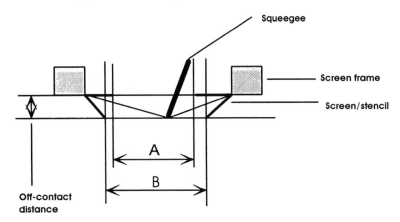

Fig. 12 The influence of off-contact distance on screen/image dimensions. A = screen/image dimensions with 0 off-contact; B = elongation of screen/image dimensions due to excessive off-contact.

The manufacturers have clearly aimed this new mesh at the market traditionally catered for by the stainless steel mesh manufacturers. The areas of immediate interest might be in the industrial sector; for use in the production of facia panels and precision instrumentation; touch panel and membrane switch technology; flexible and double-sided circuit production.

However, it is interesting to note that the area where one would have least expected the concept of high tension, high precision printing to take on is exactly where it has taken on – in the garment printing sector.

For many years this area of the industry was rather looked down upon. In the printing industry, as in many other areas of human activity, there is a certain amount of prejudice and snobbery. Perhaps this need to differentiate between groups is a singularly British trait. It operates between processes, sectors and whole sections of the industry. Traditionally screen printing has been regarded, by those in the so-called 'major' processes like offset-litho and gravure printing, as a 'Cinderella' process. 'Silk screening? Not really printing, is it? More like some kind of handicraft.' Within this intricate class hierarchy the humble garment or T-shirt printer comes pretty low down the social scale. Traditionally associated with the backyard, low skilled, self-taught, DIY operation, it has long been regarded as the province of the 'cowboy'. Most self-respecting graphic printers would laugh at the idea of associating the concepts of quality or control with the T-shirt printer, whose understanding of registration adjustment has been traditionally focused upon the weight of force exerted by the swing of the hammer head on a screen frame.

Now, seemingly, the tables are turned, for it is the garment printers who are in at the sharp end with a technology that is up in the high ether with the clean room boys of the electronics industry. There is a certain sense of poetic justice in this. It also serves to illustrate very clearly that screen printing is always full of surprises. A development aimed at one sector of the industry is taken up immediately by another. Eventually, no doubt, the benefits of high tech mesh will be enjoyed by all. At a recent exhibition one of the major machine manufacturers exhibited high tension frames on presses designed for the graphic industry.

Screen frames and screen tensioning 3

Screen printing frames come in all shapes and sizes. They can be made from wood, steel, aluminium and even plastic. However, there are two essential requirements which all serviceable screen frames should meet: rigidity and appropriate weight.

Rigidity

Rigidity is an important requirement, since the primary function of the frame is to provide a stable support for the screen mesh. When the mesh is fixed it is usually under tension, and the stress which it exerts on the frame can be quite considerable – as much as 30 kg/10 cm (66 lb/4 in). If the frame is not of a sufficiently robust construction it may be distorted when it comes under the stress loading exerted by the tensioned mesh.

Furthermore, if the material from which the frame is made is too lightweight then the frame shanks may bend under the stress loading of the mesh. This bending may be disproportionate from the long to the short sides of the frame.

Such faults as these would cause very serious problems for the printer. If a frame is warped it will most certainly mean that the mesh on it has lost its tension and its structure is no longer regular or uniform. A warped frame will present problems in off-contact adjustment and print release, both critical factors in achieving good print definition and the maintenance of production speeds. It will also mean that the screen will lose dimensional stability and the stencil will change shape/size, causing image and registration variance.

Weight

The weight of the screen frame is also an important factor. In poster printing, as in sign and display work, screen sizes can be very large, with print areas in excess of 2AO. In such applications it is important that the screen frame is light in weight, since it must be lifted on and off the machine or printing table by one operator.

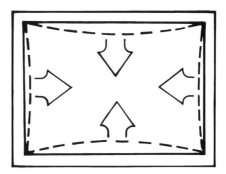

Fig. 13 Frame shanks bow when made from lightweight or small-sectioned material.

Wooden screen frames   Ideally, wooden screen frames should be made from lightweight, close-grained timber. The wood should have good resistance to the effects of moisture, since the frame will be wetted and dried repeatedly in the reclamation process. Frames made from cedar are particularly good, being both durable and light in weight. The small frames used in container printing are often made in one-piece construction, from water-resistant marine ply.

The jointing of wooden frames is important, since poorly constructed frames will distort under tension. The best frames are made with mortise and tenon joints, using a water and solvent resistant adhesive, and reinforced with dowelling or starpegs.

Wooden frames may also be protected with a coating of polyurethane varnish, which seals the timber and joints against water, solvents and chemicals.

TENSIONING A SCREEN BY HAND

Wooden screen frames were traditionally covered with mesh by fixing the fabric to two adjacent sides of the frame, usually with adhesive and tacks or staples, and then pulling the mesh tight across the frame and fixing it to the two opposite sides with a staple gun. After the frame has been covered, the mesh is secured and reinforced with adhesive.

With the increased demand for greater quality control and the improvements in screen mesh materials, it is more common practice to cover screen frames on a mechanical tensioning device. Here, the tension of the screen mesh is uniformly measured to a predetermined limit. The disadvantage of tensioning a screen by hand is that it is impossible to achieve an even degree of tension across the whole screen. Furthermore, because the mesh is pulled in only two directions to achieve tension, the gauze structure becomes distorted. Instead of square mesh openings that allow good ink flow, there are diamond shaped ones which tend to block very quickly during printing.

Steel screen frames

Steel screen frames are commonly used for precision work, where high tension screen mesh is used. They provide the robustness and rigidity required for close tolerance multicolour printing. They are made in a variety of hollow sections, which maintain rigidity and reduce weight. The frames must be constructed with watertight welding at each corner joint. They should also be protected against corrosion, either by galvanizing or by coating with an epoxide resin lacquer which is subsequently stoved to provide a very hard, scratch-resistant finish. Protection is important since the chemicals that are used in screen reclamation can be extremely corrosive.

Aluminium screen frames

Large screen frames are often made in aluminium, since it is far lighter than steel: the specific gravity of steel is 7.8, whereas that of aluminium is 2.7. Aluminium is also far less subject to corrosion than steel. Sodium hydroxide and sodium hypochlorite will cause aluminium to corrode if allowed to remain in contact for extended periods but no harm is likely to occur if the frames are thoroughly rinsed after any chemical treatment.

As is the case with steel, aluminium screen frames must be constructed with watertight welds at the corner joints. If any corrosive substance should enter the inside of the screen frame section, damage may go undetected, causing the frame to weaken and become unstable.

Self-tensioning frames

Since writing the first edition there has been somewhat of a renaissance in the use of self-tensioning frames. This has been brought about largely through the combined impact of high tension screen mesh and the missionary-like zeal of Stretch Devices of Philadelphia USA with the Newman Roller Frame. These screen frames have a built-in tensioning system. They allow the printer the flexibility to tension screens to specific working requirements – to monitor and adjust the tension of a screen at any time, even during production, tweaking registration (a forbidden practice long treasured by the decal printers).

The almost unbelievably high tensions achieved with these devices on 'work-hardened' screens has produced work (especially multicolour and four colour process work) which is of exceptionally high quality in terms of both print definition and colour fidelity. The results have to be seen to be believed. However, there is a body of expert opinion which casts doubt upon the practicality of these ultra-high tension practices. Not least amongst these doubters are the mesh manufacturers, who do not advocate the use of self-tensioning frames to achieve excessively high screen tension. Rather, they appear to recommend that printers stay within the reasonable and safe parameters of the standard recommended tension limits given in their data sheets; this being in the order of 30–40 N/cm.

Many of the problems experienced in using high tension methods are caused by a failure to recognize that far greater care is require in the handling and setting up of screens on the machine. Screen carriages must be checked to ensure that they are square and level. Off-contact and squeegee pressure adjustments must be carefully set to ensure that excessive pressure and screen stressing does not occur during printing. As high screen tension removes almost all the elasticity from the screen, the off-contact can be kept to the barest minimum – 1 mm is recommended, though this will vary depending on the size of the screen.

Most advocates admit that there is a considerable learning curve involved in using this new technology. As in most things which lead to increased quality, there is usually a price to pay. The frames are expensive. However, the benefits claimed by those who have mastered the techniques are considerable. The reduction in off-contact and squeegee pressure brings reductions in ink deposit and ink consumption; improved image definition; and less mechanical wear on the machine, the squeegee and on the screen itself. In the end it is a question of weighing the benefits against the costs of capital investment and the training of personnel.

Self-tensioning frame systems vary between one manufacturer and another but essentially they are designed on two basic principles: the floating bar and the rotating bar systems.

Floating bar systems

These frames are designed around the principle of an adjustable inner frame of 'floating bars' supported by a series of threaded bolts within a fixed outer frame. The screen mesh is fixed to the four floating bars of the inner frame with a clamping insert. The mesh is then tensioned by adjusting the bolts on which the floating bars move; as the bolts are

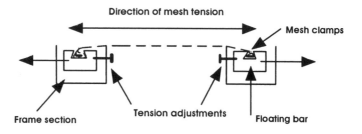

Fig. 14 Sectional view of 'floating bar' self-tensioning screen frame.

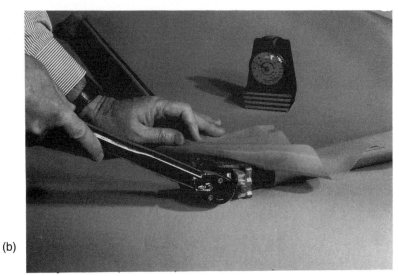

Fig. 15 The Newman Roller Frame.
(a) Inserting the mesh in the mesh clamping system.
(b) Unlocking the roller-bar for tensioning.

tightened the floating bars pull the mesh in opposite directions. Like the
Newman Roller frame in Fig. 15, floating bar frames allow mesh tension
to be increased over time as the screen becomes work-hardened.

Rotating bar systems

Roller frames are designed on the principle of the rotating bar. Here the frame consists of four round bars which can be rotated within a ratchet block at each corner of the frame. The bars are rebated to allow the screen mesh to be attached with plastic clamping slides. When the screen mesh has been securely clamped into the bar rebates on all four sides of the frame, the bars are rotated. The mesh simply wraps around the bars, gaining tension as the bars turn in opposing directions.

ADVANTAGES OF SELF-TENSIONING FRAMES

Self-tensioning frames provide a number of benefits for the printer:

- Increased autonomy and control over the quality of screens available for use, since they are tensioned in-house rather than reliant upon a frame-covering service.
- No adhesive required, improving health and safety and environmental management, whilst saving screen costs.
- An opportunity to tension screens to specific job requirements.
- Screen tension can be monitored and adjusted so that a set of screens can be tension-matched, providing greater consistency in dimensional stability and thus improved control in registration and ink film formation – in terms of both print definition and deposit.
- Possibility of tension tweaking during set-up or even during the run, to improve print register. Care must be taken in this practice, since stencil damage can result when liberties taken with the torque bar stretch the stencil beyond the limits of the screen emulsion.

There are also a number of disadvantages:

- The initial unit cost is high compared with that of the conventional 'stretch-and-glue' frame.
- Large sizes cause a handling problem – they are heavy!
- They are not suitable for tensioning mesh at angles above 15°.

PRACTICAL GUIDELINES

Most of the problems experienced when using self-tensioning frames are caused by a failure to adhere to the advice and guidance provided by the frame and mesh supplier. More often than not, screen bursts result from careless tensioning or from frame mishandling. The following guidelines should form the basis for good practice.

- Make regular frame maintenance checks, checking especially for sharp edges caused by knocks and scratches.

- Check that mesh tucking/clamping systems are effective; replace worn or damaged parts.
- Lubricate moving parts with a high tech water-repellent lubricant, but avoid getting this on the mesh.
- Check the manufacturer's recommended tension for the fabric and do not exceed this.
- The fabric should be inserted squarely in the bars on all four sides; supporting the fabric from beneath with a sponge block will help to ensure that it is inserted squarely into the clamps.
- Ensure that sufficient slack mesh is provided at the four corners of the frame to prevent overtensioning at the corners as tension is applied. Failure to observe this essential requirement is a common cause of screen bursting.
- Use of a tension meter is of course a prerequisite. Ensure that it is properly calibrated before use.
- Tension is applied systematically working alternately from opposite sides: 1–2, 3–4, 1–2, 3–4, until the required tension is reached.
- As in all tensioning the process should proceed in three stages with intervals of 15 minutes between each stage to allow for the stabilization of the mesh under tension. This relaxation period is important and should be adhered to.

Screen tensioning devices

Conventional stretch-and-glue screen frames are widely used throughout all sectors of the industry. These frames are best covered using a screen tensioning device to pre-tension the mesh evenly and accurately before it is fixed to the frame. The method of fixing the mesh to the frame, whether made of wood or metal, is to use a water/solvent-resistant adhesive.

Health and Safety Note:

In line with the legislative requirements under the Control of Substances Hazardous to Health (COSHH), manufacturers are now supplying new UV-cured, solvent-free screen adhesives, which make for a safer and more pleasant environment to work and live in. Uvifix, from Sericol Ltd, is an example. When using solvent-based and two-pack epoxy resin adhesives, refer to the manufacturer's health and safety data sheets and user instructions. Always ensure that there is adequate ventilation in the work area. Avoid inhalation of the adhesive vapours. Dispose of waste materials safely. Do not allow any solvents or adhesives to enter the wastewater system.

There are numerous screen tensioning devices on the market, ranging from the very simple mechanical tensioner which stretches the screen fabric one side at a time, to the much more sophisticated devices which allow for lateral equalization of the mesh threads during the tensioning process. However, they can be divide into two types: mechanical devices and pneumatic devices.

MECHANICAL SCREEN TENSIONING DEVICES

Mechanical screen tensioning devices vary in degree of technical sophistication. Basically they provide a method of tensioning the screen mesh over the frame by extending it in four opposing directions. The device allows the mesh to be held at a controlled degree of extension while it is fixed to the screen frame with adhesive. The Elliot Screen Tensioner is a mechanical tensioning device which has been widely used for many years. It is chosen as an example of a basic device which is well designed, robust and simple to use.

The Elliot Screen Tensioner

With this tensioner the screen frame is placed on a table-lift which can be raised to bring the frame into contact with the mesh when it is ready for adhesion. The screen mesh is clamped into the rubber-lined grooves on the four sides of the device, using special clamping battens for the purpose. When the mesh has been finally secured, the four sides of the device are simultaneously moved outwards by the action of a central tensioning gear, operated by turning a single tensioning wheel. The level of mesh tension can be easily measured by noting the percentage of mesh extension, calibrated in coloured rings on the tensioning gear shaft, behind the tensioning wheel.

Although this device may be a very good example of its kind, it does have limitations:

- The fixed dimensions limit the size of screen frame that can be economically tensioned, although multiples of small frames may be tensioned together.
- The rigid sides of the tensioner can tend to cause overtensioning of the screen mesh at the corners and prevent the threads from equalizing during tension. This can distort the mesh structure and weaken the screen, leading to an early loss of tension. Care must be taken to allow slack mesh at the corners of the tensioner to prevent excessive corner stressing.

There are more technically sophisticated mechanical and pneumatically operated tensioners which allow for the increased tension at the corners of the screen and for thread equalization across the mesh.

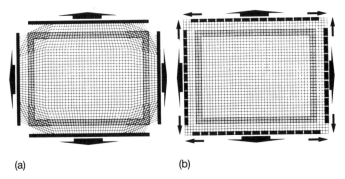

(a)   (b)

Fig. 16   (a) Stretching device with rigid sides.
(b) Yielding of clamps at corners on a pneumatic tensioner.

PNEUMATIC SCREEN TENSIONING DEVICES

These devices employ a series of pneumatically-operated mesh clamps, which are positioned around the edges of the screen frame. Each clamp operates individually, exerting a measured amount of force upon the mesh, determined by the pressure applied through the air line from a central compressor control. Because the clamps are relatively small and are able to exert force upon the mesh individually, they allow for even mesh tension along the entire perimeter of the screen frame. There are mechanical tensioners which have the same facility, and allow for lateral equalization of the mesh during tensioning, but they do not have quite the same responsiveness, as is provided by the best pneumatic screen tensioners.

SST screen stretching clamps

The Swiss mesh manufacturers, Schweiz Seidengazfabrik AG Thal, have designed a pneumatic screen tensioning clamp which allows for lateral equalization of the mesh during tensioning. As the clamps apply their tensioning force to the mesh, they are able to move laterally with the mesh, thus minimizing distortion of the mesh structure. The clamps are made with jaws measuring 267 mm and 160 mm, and are calibrated so that they can be used simultaneously to ensure an even and optimum tension on a wide variety of screen frame sizes.

The measurement of mesh tension

As has been stressed throughout this chapter, dimensional stability is a critical factor in screen printing. In the other printing processes, the dimensional stability of the image carrier (plate or cylinder) is relatively high. In screen printing the image-forming stencil is carried on a flexible screen which, depending on its composition, can be only as stable as its

Fig. 17 SST Pneumatic Tensioner.

tension will allow. If a screen is over or undertensioned it will inevitably lack the required stability. It is therefore important that the degree to which the screen is tensioned is measured very precisely. There are essentially three ways of measuring the tension of a screen:

- Measuring the extension of the mesh.
- Measuring the force applied to the mesh by the tensioning device.
- Measuring the resistance of the tensioned mesh to a force exerted vertically upon its surface.

MEASURING THE PERCENTAGE EXTENSION OF THE MESH

When using very simple mechanical screen tensioning devices the degree of tension can easily be measured by marking the surface of the mesh in the x and y coordinates with given measures. These are then carefully checked as the mesh is tensioned, measuring the degree to which they have extended.

For example, if the screen is marked with a measure of 500 mm in the two planes of extension and then the mesh is tensioned until the marks measure 515 mm, it will have extended the mesh by 3%. It is important to remember that the mesh is extended in opposite directions on all four sides, and for this reason it is necessary to measure along both x and y coordinates.

MEASURING THE FORCE APPLIED TO THE MESH

When using a pneumatic tensioner the degree of mesh tension can easily be ascertained by measuring the amount of force which is applied to the mesh through the operation of the pneumatic clamps. Each clamp is connected by an air line, supplying compressed air from a central compressor, where a gauge measures the level of pressure supplied in atm. bar (atmosphere bar, a unit of barometric pressure = 10^5 newtons/m^2). Mesh manufactures supply detailed tables with recommended atm. bar values for all grades of fabric.

The regular maintenance of a pneumatic tensioner is important, since leaks and dirt in air lines can cause fluctuations in air pressure. This can lead to irregular and inaccurate tensioning. It is also important to ensure that the clamps are set up correctly so that they bear on the screen frame evenly and squarely. Lack of care in setting up the clamps can cause accidents, resulting in screen bursting or even injury to the operator.

MEASURING MESH TENSION WITH A METER

It is also possible to measure the tension of a screen by ascertaining its resistance to further stretching, either during or after tensioning. A number of devices are designed to do this; some of them operate mechanically, others are electronic. All of them measure the degree of mesh deformation in newtons per centimetre (N/cm; 1 N = 102 g/cm).

Tension meters can give a very precise measurement of mesh tension. They should be calibrated before use, by placing the meter on a plate glass slab and adjusting the setting to zero.

To measure the mesh tension the meter is placed at various strategic positions on the screen. When screens are used for very close register work, the allowable tolerance across the screen would be between 0.5 and 1 N/cm, and for less critical work 1–2 N/cm. Again, mesh manufacturers supply tables of recommended tension values for each mesh type and grade.

The advantage of the tension meter is that it enables the printer to keep a regular check on screen tension. This is particularly useful in four colour half-tone work, where the four screens must be under equal tension in order to ensure accurate register through each printing. As all synthetic mesh tends to lose tension with use, the tension meter provides a useful way of applying quality control to a very important part of the process.

Mesh identification and preparation

When a new screen has been stretched it is important to mark its grade and count with a permanent marker, either in the screen mesh or on the frame. Where polyamide and polyester screens are in use, it is sensible to use a distinguishing mark to avoid any mistaken screen selection; a simple colour coding system is perhaps the most effective method. Such a system could also be used to identify the various grades and mesh counts that are used.

Frame colour coding

Frame colour	Mesh grade	Mesh count
BLUE	HD	90
RED	T	90
GREEN	T	120
YELLOW	S	150

Recognition tests for polyamide and polyester fabrics

Screen fabrics have identification markings printed along the selvage at metre intervals. In cases where these markings are missing, on an offcut or remnant length of fabric, it will be necessary to establish the fabric type by carrying out a recognition test. As other forms of testing involve the destruction of the fabric and present potential health and safety hazards it is recommended that the dye-stuff reagent test is the method of fabric identification to be employed.

Fig. 18 Tension meter. (Courtesy of Coates Screen and Swiss Silk Zurich.)

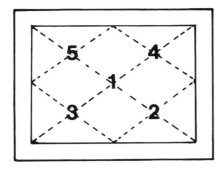

Fig. 19   The tension meter is placed at strategic positions on the screen.

THE DYE-STUFF REAGENT TEST

The test is carried out by dropping the colour reagent 'Neor- carmin MS' on to the fabric, using a small pipette. The reagent is then dried with warm air. After a reaction time of 10 minutes the treated area is rinsed with water. When dry the following colour reaction will indicate the fabric type.

Polyamide: will turn a strong yellow-green colour in the treated area, the intensity depending on the mesh count of the fabric.

Polyester: very little discolouration is likely to occur; if any, there will be a pale rose-coloured staining, according to mesh count and reaction time.

Establishing mesh count

A screen ruling scale can be used to establish the mesh count of a screen where the identification mark is missing from the frame. The scale consists of a small acetate rule with radial lines of graduating frequency printed on it. When the scale is placed on the screen mesh the radial lines cause a moiré interference pattern to occur. The pattern resembles a diamond, with points in the vertical and horizontal axes. The scale is rotated on the screen until the position of the vertical point of the diamond indices indicates the ruling at a point on the scale printed above.

Using a travelling mesh microscope allows more accurate measurement of mesh count. The device provides 100× magnification of the screen mesh. A graticule on the lens, which can be moved across the mesh by turning a small wheel, allows each thread to be counted. As the lens moves over a measured distance of 1 cm, very accurate thread counts can easily be achieved.

Fig. 20   A polyester mesh after roughening with a silicon carbide paste to increase the surface area of the mesh threads. (Courtesy of Autotype International Ltd.)

Screen pretreatment   The durability of a stencil, particularly an indirect stencil, depends very largely on the adhesive bond that exists between the stencil and the screen mesh. Synthetic fabrics are woven from very smooth, wire-like threads. The surface, although complex in structure, does not provide the optimum physical properties required for good stencil adhesion. For this reason it is always necessary to pretreat all newly tensioned synthetic screen meshes.

It is generally accepted now that the only safe method of preparing a new synthetic mesh is to roughen the stencil side of the screen with a proprietary mesh abrasive. These are usually supplied in paste form and contain a fine grade silicon carbide abrasive (number 500 or finer).

ROUGHENING A NEW MESH

1. The screen is wetted with water before applying the abrasive paste.
2. A small amount of paste is applied to the underside of the screen.
3. The paste is worked into the mesh with a wet sponge wrapped inside a piece of off-cut of mesh. The idea is to cover the entire surface of the screen with the abrasive, working in small circular scrubbing motions.

Fig. 21   Mesh damaged by scouring powder treatment. (Courtesy of Autotype International Ltd.)

The more thoroughly this is done, the better the surface will be.
4. When the entire underside of the screen has been treated the paste is rinsed away with cold running water. The screen should then be rinsed thoroughly to ensure that no abrasive residue remains on the screen.

Stencil film manufacturers recommend that screens used for capillary direct stencils should be pretreated at periodic intervals to improve stencil adhesion.

The use of chemical preteatment, such as cresylic acid, is no longer recommended as it can damage the mesh. The use of domestic scouring powders such as Vim or Ajax are also outlawed, since they cause severe damage to the mesh threads and the large particles of abrasive pumice can become trapped in the mesh, causing stencil failure and pinholes.

Degreasing a screen

All screens, new or old, whether for use with indirect or direct stencils, must be thoroughly degreased each time, before stencil application. This is necessary because the screen mesh can very easily become contaminated by handling or by dust from the atmosphere. If a screen is not thoroughly degreased prior to use stencil adhesion will be impaired, resulting in early stencil breakdown and in the development of pinholes.

A number of chemicals can be used for screen degreasing. There are also several specially formulated preparations on the market; some have a concentrated alkaline base and must be handled with caution. The recent concerns which have followed from the Environmental Protection Act and with the requirements of the Control of Substances Hazardous to Health (COSHH) legislation have encouraged manufacturers to develop safer systems for cleaning and degreasing.

In the light of this it seems no longer practical to consider using sodium hydroxide (caustic soda) solutions for screen degreasing. Some of the new biodegradable chemicals like the Degreaser Concentrate 1:10/50, from CPS Graphics, or Universal Mesh Prep, from Autotype International, and Seriprep 102, from Sericol Ltd, provide safer, environmentally sound solutions to the problem of screen degreasing. With all these proprietary systems it is essential to follow the manufacturer's instructions to the letter. Usually they require the screen to be treated on both sides and for the chemicals to be left on the screen for a prescribed reaction time. This is to allow the chemicals effectively to convert the grease and fatty acids on the screen into water-soluble substances which can be easily rinsed away from the screen. The chemicals also contain surfactants which lower surface tension on the mesh and promote thread wetting and water retention, which is especially important when working with capillary direct stencil systems. After application the screen is thoroughly rinsed with cold water.

DEGREASING WITH FRENCH CHALK

Good results can be achieved by using french chalk ($CaCO_3$) as a degreasing powder. It is a safe and (it seems) an environmentally acceptable alternative. The method of application is as follows.

1. Wet the screen thoroughly.
2. Sprinkle french chalk liberally over the surface of the screen.
3. Work the french chalk into the mesh with a sponge, using a circular scrubbing motion.
4. Repeat the process on the other side of the screen.
5. Rinse the screen thoroughly in cold running water, checking that the water wets the surface of the screen evenly in a flat film.
6. Should the water fail to wet the screen evenly and signs of water rejection become evident, then repeat the process, steps 1–5.

DOMESTIC DETERGENTS

Domestic detergents, though they may do complete justice to the advertiser's claims of cleaning those greasy spoons whilst preserving the softest skin, will do little that is good in the way of degreasing screens. At best they will put the grease and fatty acids into a nice thin solution and coat the entire surface of the screen with it. At worst they will deposit a layer of skin-softening lanolin on to the mesh threads, increasing the chances of stencil failure.

The advice is to leave domestic cleaning products where they belong, in the kitchen, doing the jobs they are designed to do. Do not use them for screen degreasing!

AFTER DEGREASING

After a screen has been degreased it should be used. If it is handled or left around it will soon become contaminated and must be degreased again before it can be used. Incorrect or inadequate screen degreasing accounts for about 70% of all stencil breakdowns. This is frustrating enough when it happens during stencil development, but when it happens on the press it is costing the company a lot of money! Remember: if a screen is not correctly prepared to receive the stencil then it will simply fail to perform its primary function of providing an effective support.

Stencil making 4

Stencils can be made by several methods but they all must function in the same way: to block the non-printing areas of the screen and to provide clear, well defined open areas to form the printed image. Looking at them in relation to their preparative techniques they form two distinct groups:

1. Autographic (handmade) stencils.
2. Photomechanically made stencils.

These groups can be subdivided as follows.

1. (a) Hand-painted stencils, produced by working directly on the screen with block-out filler and/or wax-resist methods.
   (b) Knife-cut stencils, made by cutting around the stencil image with a sharp stencil knife, usually by tracing this through a special laminate paper or film coating.
2. (a) Indirect photostencils, made by contacting an opaque positive image to a light-sensitive stencil film which is transferred to the screen mesh after processing.
   (b) Direct emulsion photostencils, made by coating the screen with a light-sensitive liquid emulsion which is exposed in direct contact with an opaque positive image, the stencil being formed directly in the screen mesh.
   (c) Direct/indirect photostencils, a combination of methods 2(a) and (b), wherein the stencil is made by bonding a film coating to the underside of the screen with a light-sensitive liquid emulsion, and exposing it in direct contact with an opaque positive image.
   (d) Capillary direct film photostencils, made by mounting a light-sensitive film coating on to the screen and exposing it in direct contact with an opaque positive image.

Since autographic stencil methods are used mainly in relatively specialized areas of the screen printing industry they are treated separately, in Chapter 13 (The art and craft of screen printing). The present chapter concentrates on the major photomechanical stencil systems, which are used across all areas and sectors of the industry.

Photomechanical stencil making

The most widely used stencils in modern screen printing are those that are produced by photomechanical methods. Whenever an image is too small or too intricate for knife-cut or autographic stencil making, or is required for repeat production, a photographic stencil will be used. There are four different photostencil systems. Each has its own distinctive advantages and limitations. They have been divided into two groups, and the differences in composition, processing and application will be highlighted.

Indirect films	*Direct emulsion*	*Direct/indirect*	*Capillary direct*
Gelatine-based films (oxidized post-exposure) – high definition line and half-tone, 4000/5000 runs (not water resistant)	PVAOH/PVAC emulsions and photopolymers which vary in density, light sensitivity and solvent/water resistance. Exposed direct on the screen, provide good definition and superior durability. Long-run work	PVAOH/PVAC precision film coating, bonded to the screen with a sensitized emulsion – used for high definition, fine line work in industrial and electronics applications, 10 000+ runs (not recommended for water-based inks)	PVAOH/PVAC presensitized precision coated films, range of thicknesses to suit application – high definition, fine line and half-tone work, 10 000+ runs (water and solvent resistant films)
PVAOH-based films (no post-exposure hardening), cold water development – general graphic work, 10 000+ runs (not water resistant)			

Indirect photostencil film (gelatine)

The first photographic stencil films were developed from the gelatine coatings used in photogravure surface preparation – the so-called 'carbon tissue' papers. These comprised a pigmented gelatine coating on a paper base. The process of making a stencil was complex and very messy; the user had to sensitize the gelatine in potassium dichromate and then expose the material to ultraviolet (UV) light while it was still wet – hence its name, 'wet process'.

Today presensitized films are used which are much simpler and safer to use. Dichromate, now being considered a health hazard, is banned in most EU countries and, though it is still used to a limited degree in Britain, recent legislation on the use of substances harmful to heath and regulations on environmental pollution discourage its use.

Modern gelatine based films, like Autotype's famous Five Star Film or

Ulano's Super Prep, are composed of a precision coating of pigmented high grade gelatine, carried on a 50 micron (0.05 mm/0.002 in) polyester film base. The stencil film is sensitized with ferric salts by the manufacturers and is supplied ready for use.

The film is sensitive to UV radiation between 350 and 400 nm (nanometres) and should be handled in subdued light; yellow or orange safe lights are recommended. When exposed to a suitable UV light source the gelatine will oxidize in the presence of an oxidizing chemical (hydrogen peroxide) to form a flexible, insoluble film.

To make a stencil, the film is simply exposed to UV light whilst in contact with an opaque facsimile (a positive image) of the design that is to be reproduced. Wherever the UV light reaches the stencil film it renders it insoluble in warm water, leaving the image areas to dissolve away when the film is washed after the hardening (oxidizing) process.

The basic procedure now follows in more detail, but it should be understood that this is a generalized guide. In practice it is always necessary to follow the manufacturer's product instructions, since each film will have its own exposure and processing specifications.

MAKING AN INDIRECT PHOTOSTENCIL

Preparing the screen

The screen must be correctly pretreated and degreased before the stencil is made. It is advisable to rinse the screen with cold water immediately before mounting the stencil.

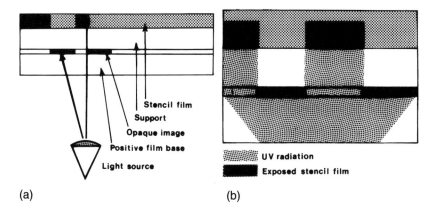

Stencil film
Support
Opaque image
Positive film base
Light source

UV radiation
Exposed stencil film

(a)   (b)

Fig. 22   (a) Sectional view of the exposure of an indirect photostencil. (b) The film coating is exposed approximately two-thirds through the complete coating thickness.

Cutting the film

The stencil should be cut to the required size, allowing a 50 mm border beyond the perimeter of the positive image for handling the film.

Exposing the film

The stencil film is placed in a printing-down or contact frame, in contact with the positive image. The image surface must be in contact with the polyester film support – indirect stencils are always exposed through the support.

During the exposure the UV light which passes through the non-image areas of the positive will penetrate the pigmented coating, its effect gradually decreasing as it is quenched by the pigment. The exposure used will be determined by the parameters of the film and the nature of the image. In all instances the optimum exposure will leave approximately one third of the film coating (the upper third) unexposed. This unexposed layer dissolves away when the stencil is developed, leaving a top layer of partially exposed, semi-soluble coating to act as an adhesive when the stencil is mounted on to the underside of the screen. This top layer is called the 'soft top', and its condition is critical to stencil press-life.

Hardening the film

After exposure gelatine films must be processed in an oxidizing solution of hydrogen peroxide (H_2O_2). The manufacturers recommend that their own peroxide preparations are used as they are more stable and reliable than the peroxide that is available from industrial chemical suppliers.

The strength of the solution is determined by the film type; some gelatine films are oxidized in a 1.2% solution, while others require 3%. The following formula can be used for making up solutions of H_2O_2, which is commercially available in the following concentrations:

100 volumes or 30%
40 volumes or 12%
20 volumes or 6%

Formula for calculating H_2O_2 solution strength:

$$(x - y)/y = \text{ratio of water to } H_2O_2$$

(where x = strength of H_2O_2 expressed as a percentage, and y = strength of desired oxidizing solution expressed as a percentage).

Example:

To find the ratio of water to H_2O_2 required to make up a 1.5% solution, using 12% H_2O_2.

$$(12 - 1.5)/1.5 = 10.5/1.5 = 7$$

therefore the ratio required would be 7 parts H_2O to 1 part H_2O_2 at 12% or 40 volumes strength.

It is important to stress here that hydrogen peroxide is an unstable chemical. It will deteriorate when exposed to the air. If exposed to light, especially UV light, it will deteriorate rapidly. A hydrogen peroxide solution will gradually become exhausted as exposed film is passed through it. As a rough guide, 1 litre of fresh solution will treat about 1 m^2 of film. If the solution is stored it should be kept in a dark bottle at below 20°C – if the temperature rises above 21°C deterioration is accelerated; if the temperature falls below 16°C the oxidizing process will slow down. Manufacturers recommend that a fresh solution of hydrogen peroxide should be made up daily. Gelatine films are usually oxidized for between 1 and 2 minutes, depending on the type of film.

Developing the stencil

The film is developed by washing it with warm water. The water temperature should be 40–50°C; if it is hotter it will damage the film, causing a loss of the 'soft top'; if cooler the gelatine will not dissolve in the unexposed image areas.

The whole surface of the stencil is gently sprayed with warm water until the image areas appear clear. When the stencil is fully washed it should appear even in colour and have sharply defined image openings. Care should be taken to ensure that the stencil is evenly washed, as undissolved gelatine can spread into the stencil openings, causing them to 'scum up'.

Chilling the stencil

After the stencil has been developed it must be chilled with cold water. This stabilizes the gelatine, preventing it from dissolving any further, and removes any scumming that may have occurred.

Mounting the stencil

The stencil is mounted in the conventional indirect manner, using a raised mounting pad to provide good stencil/screen contact. The stencil will adhere to the wet screen mesh on contact, since the structure of the screen provides very good physical attraction for the wet, soft gelatine film.

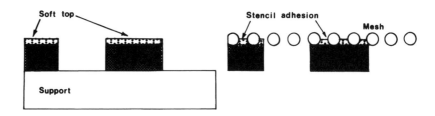

Fig. 23 Sectional view showing the adhesion of an indirect photostencil to the underside of the screen.

However, to ensure maximum contact between the stencil and the mesh filaments, the upper suface of the screen is blotted with newsprint and a roller. As the absorbent newsprint is pressed firmly into contact with the screen, the wet gelatine is drawn up through the mesh.

Drying the stencil

The stencil should be allowed to dry naturally in an ambient temperature of 20°C. A cold fan can be used to dry the stencil from the inside (squeegee side) of the screen. If warm air is used the temperature should not exceed 30°C, as this will cause excessive shrinking in the gelatine film. This results in a fault known as 'edge curl', where the stencil image profile peels back from the screen, causing loss of edge definition in the resulting print.

Peeling the support

When the stencil is completely dry the polyester support can be peeled away, leaving the stencil attached to the underside of the screen. The support should peel away quite freely. If it fails to do so, or resists peeling, then the stencil is not completely dry and should be left for a further period. If the stencil is dry and the support fails to release cleanly, this would indicate that there is an adhesion fault – either the screen has not been correctly prepared (see Chapter 3, Screen pretreatment and Degreasing a screen) or the stencil has been overexposed or overwashed in development and has lost its precious adhesive 'soft top'.

Stencil removal

One of the delights of using indirect stencils is that they are so easy to remove! After all ink and solvent residue has been removed from the screen the stencil should be degreased. The bulk of the stencil film can be removed by scrubbing lightly with warm water (50°C). The stencil should break up after a short reaction time (2–3 minutes). The gelatine residue that remains trapped in the screen can be quickly removed with a weak solution of sodium hypochlorite (4%) or a proprietary stencil remover like Autotype's Gelatine Stripper, Gibbon Marler's Stensolve Indirect or Ulano No 15 Gelatine Decoater. Should any stencil remain in the screen after this treatment, it is likely to be trapped by ink residue. In this case the screen must be treated with an appropriate solvent before it is treated again with stencil remover. There are some excellent low hazard, water miscible products on the market which can be combined with non-alkaline based de-hazing chemicals to remove ink residues and stains all in one go. Serisolve from Sericol Ltd, Pregan C 444M from Kissel & Wolf GmbH and the screen cleaning systems from CPS Graphics are all good examples of companies working to develop products which contribute to improving environmental performance. The use of a high pressure water lance will facilitate the rapid removal of indirect stencils, making the whole process more efficient.

Health and Safety Note:

Always ensure that chemicals and solvents are rinsed away from the screen before applying high pressure water to the screen. Failure to rinse away potentially hazardous solvents and chemicals will result in their atomization as soon as the high pressure water hits the screen. Therefore always rinse the whole screen and frame thoroughly with low pressure water before applying the high pressure wash. Ensure also that the ventilation/extraction system is drawing any water mist away from you. Whenever solvents and decoating chemicals are used, the manufacturer's safety data sheets must be consulted and the products used in accordance with the recommended safety precautions. Wearing protective gloves, visor and apron are standard requirements. It is also important to ensure conformance with the regulations on water pollution, especially in respect of preventing hazardous solvents and chemicals from entering the drains.

INDIRECT PHOTOPOLYMER FILMS

During the early 1970s Autotype introduced a new indirect photostencil film with a synthetic photopolymer coating. The new film was simpler to use, since it formed an insoluble stencil film when exposed to UV light, and did not require hardening before it could be developed.

The film also had a very wide exposure latitude. Exposure times could be varied without adversely affecting the adhesion of the stencil. The makers claimed that the film would produce stencils with a press life in excess of 10 000 copies – more than twice that of the traditional gelatine stencil.

Although the photopolymer films now available, like Autotype's Novastar and Ulano's Ulanolux Up-3, do provide very tough, solvent-resistant stencils, they require the same careful handling and processing as the gelatine products. The basic procedure for making a stencil with these synthetic polymer films is the same as outlined above. The differences are:

- The film is not oxidized after exposure.
- The stencil may be developed in cold or warm water (30°C).
- The stencil can be dried with warm air, not exceeding 40°C.
- The stencil is removed with a sodium metaperiodate decoating agent such as Stensolve from Gibbon Marler, Pregasol from Kissel & Wolf or Seristrip from Sericol.

All major suppliers market a range of products suitable for different stencil systems and reclaiming methods, manual or automated.

TROUBLESHOOTING

A number of common problems can occur with indirect stencils; in 99% of cases they are user-related.

Adhesion failure is usually caused by:

- inadequate screen mesh preparation;
- loss of 'soft top', due to overexposure or overwashing during stencil development – watch the water temperature.

Pinholes are tiny holes which appear in the stencil either during development or, more maddeningly, during the first wash-up on the press. They are most often caused by:

- specks of dust, grit or debris on the clear non-image areas of the positive, or on the contact frame;
- insufficient oxidizing of the gelatine film during post-exposure hardening, caused often by a failure to replenish the hardener frequently enough – remember that in warm weather the exhaustion rate is more rapid;
- the stencil film or screen has been contaminated by reclaiming or degreasing chemicals – keep the processes and associated chemicals away from one another in separate areas and ensure that screens are rinsed thoroughly, including the frame, before they are re-used.

A thin stencil usually results from underexposure, creating pinholes and early stencil breakdown. Stencil remakes cost the company money, and can result in the loss of a client. Check the system and try to build in some control mechanisms, like using a light integrator to control exposure and a reliable water temperature and spray-pressure control to increase consistency in processing.

Edge curl, as noted earlier, is usually the result of accelerated drying. It could also indicate that the stencil film has been stored in unsafe conditions; exposure to the air, especially warm air, will cause the film to dry out. Indirect stencil film should be stored in the light-safe packaging in which it is supplied in cool, light-safe conditions (55–65% relative humidity (RH); 15–20°C). In such conditions these materials may be stored for 18–36 months, depending on film type – specific data is available from suppliers.

Early stencil breakdown is usually the result of poor stencil adhesion. It may also be caused by overstressing the stencil film and breaking the very delicate film-to-screen mesh bonds. This is most commonly caused by:

- excessive squeegee or flo-coater pressure and high off-contact distances;
- damaging the stencil during cleaning; especially when aggressive ketonic solvents are used, which remove the plasticizers in the gelatine films and make them brittle.

An indirect stencil should never be cleaned from the underside; cleaning should always be carried out from the upper side of the screen, using a newspaper pad beneath the stencil. The screen should be swabbed gently with solvent. Rubbing aggressively at the screen should be avoided, as this will break down the stencil/mesh bonding.

Scumming occurs when the stencil film coating flows into the open areas of the stencil after it has been developed. It forms a thin film which will effectively block the screen and cause print failure. In most cases this film can be removed with a strong solvent like screen wash. The fault can always be prevented by washing the stencil thoroughly during development and then chilling it with cold water before transferring it to the screen. Some stencil makers advocate the use of a damp wash-leather to blot the stencil after it has been mounted on the screen.

Veiling is similar to scumming but the layer of stencil emulsion which fills the stencil opening is thicker and tapers from the stencil edges. It cannot ordinarily be removed without causing damage to the stencil. The most common causes for the fault are:

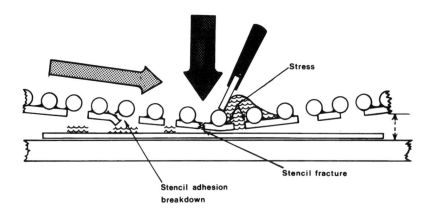

Fig. 24 The effects of excessive squeegee pressure and high off-contact distance.

- film fogging due to poor storage or use in unsafe light conditions;
- light undercutting the positive image during exposure, due to poor contact between the positive and the stencil film.

QUALITY CONTROL

Indirect photostencil films are fairly user friendly products, having considerable latitude in terms of exposure and processing. Most problems occur because the user has failed to follow the manufacturer's instructions, or something has gone wrong with the exposure or processing. The problems can usually be traced back to the cause very quickly by carrying out a simple quality check using a test positive of the type provided by most stencil and mesh suppliers.

When checking out the system think about building in some controls, such as using a light integrator. These devices measure the amount of light the film is receiving on each exposure and vary the exposure time as the UV lamp ages and its actinic output declines.

Invest in a stencil development unit with an illuminated back panel, so that more careful observation of the developing stencil may be made.

Consider investing in processing controls, such as water temperature and spray-pressure controls. This will help to provide consistency in stencil development. Find ways to clean up the working environment, by placing tack mats at entry points to prevent dust and grit from entering the stencil production area. Ensure that routine cleaning takes place, especially in critical areas like the print-down frame. Spotting-out a screen takes time and costs money. Cutting down on pin holes can save an extra job!

Some years ago I was shown around the stencil making area of a large and highly respected graphic and display printers. They proudly told me about the change they had made in moving from indirect film to direct stencil emulsion. 'Saved us £30 000 a year in film costs,' the technical director boasted. I was impressed until I saw four operatives scraping screen filler over the entire area of the newly developed screens. 'Why are you doing that?' I asked. 'Pin holes!' the man said. 'Easier to do it like this, en't it? Saves time.' How much more time and money they might have saved by cleaning up their act with a little good housekeeping discipline!

AUTOMATIC PROCESSING AND DEVELOPMENT

Quality control in the processing and development of indirect photostencil films has of course been greatly simplified by the introduction of

Fig. 25 The Svecia Automatic Stencil Processor SP. (Courtesy of Svecia Silksreen Maskiner AB.)

automation into the stencil making process. Machines like the Svecia Automatic Stencil Processor SP can be programmed to carry out the entire post-exposure procedure to very precise operational parameters, ensuring repeatability every time.

The exposed film is clipped emulsion side up on to an illuminated back panel. The machine is then programmed with the appropriate data and set in motion. If the film is a gelatine-based product it is first sprayed with a recirculated hardening (oxidizing) solution. It is then washed with water at a controlled temperature for a predetermined period. When the development is terminated the film is automatically chilled with cold water. The advantages of such automation are in the perfectly consistent results that can be guaranteed, and in the considerable labour savings that can be made through such automation.

It is interesting to note that, whilst some printers will not think twice about investing £150 000–£200 000 in a new printing machine, investment in the area most crucial to the whole production line and the quality of the final print is often balked at. This somewhat myopic view is often taken because the productive value of investment in stencil production is not so manifestly apparent as it is in a new printing machine. Yet if we stop to think of the costs of down-time resulting from stencil breakdowns we begin to see the sense in taking the more strategic view.

Direct emulsion photostencils

Direct stencils are much more durable than indirect stencils. They are strong enough to withstand the physical stressing and abrasion that occurs in long-run machine production. There is a wide range of emulsions available; some are designed to provide high resolution for fine line and half-tone work, whilst others exhibit exceptional solvent or water resistance for textile printing.

The main reason for the superior press-life of the direct stencil lies in the method by which it is made. The stencil is formed 'directly' in the screen by the photopolymerization of a UV-sensitive stencil coating, applied to the screen mesh prior to exposure. A closer consideration of the stencil making process will help to provide a clearer insight as to the relative advantages of the direct emulsion stencil system.

MAKING A DIRECT EMULSION STENCIL

Direct stencil emulsions are made from synthetic polymers such as polyvinyl alcohol (PVAOH) and polyvinyl acetate (PVAC). They consist of a very fine dispersion of resinous solids in water. When sensitized with a chromate or diazo sensitizer, they have the property of forming a tough flexible film if exposed to a suitable actinic light source, such as UV. The procedure for making a direct emulsion stencil is as follows.

Sensitizing the emulsion

Most direct emulsions are now sensitized with diazo compounds; dichromate is used less and less since it has been recognized as an unacceptable pollutant and can also present a potential health hazard to those who handle it. When mixing a sensitizer with the emulsion, adhere to the following guidelines.

- Always wear protective gloves and avoid any skin contact with the sensitizer. If accidental contact occurs, wash the area thoroughly in running water.
- Always follow the manufacturer's instructions very carefully.
- Diazo sensitizer is usually supplied in a measured quantity and must be mixed with distilled water before it is mixed into the emulsion. The diazo is usually in a powder or a concentrated viscous liquid state and must be mixed very thoroughly to ensure that none is left in the mixing container.
- The sensitizer must be stirred into the emulsion with a plastic or glass rod (the wooden spatulas supplied with some emulsions can introduce splinters into the emulsion).
- Some emulsions are also supplied with a dye which can be mixed into the emulsion as required.
- The sensitized emulsion must be stirred very thoroughly and allowed to stand for 30 minutes. It is then stirred again and allowed to stand for at least one hour before it is used. When the emulsion is stirred, air is introduced into it and this must be allowed to escape before coating takes place. If the emulsion is not mixed correctly the stencil coating may exhibit unevenness and pinholing.
- Dichromate sensitized emulsions must be used within 48 hours; diazo sensitized emulsions may be stored for up to three months in a cool environment, according to the manufacturer's instructions.

Preparing the screen

The screen mesh must be correctly pretreated and degreased before coating. The screen must also be completely dry and free from dust or foreign particle contamination.

Coating the screen

It is important to apply an even coating of emulsion, filling the screen mesh from both sides. The emulsion is applied with a special coating trough, the fore edge of which is very slightly convex to allow for the ballooning of the screen during the coating process. When using the more viscous emulsions it is common practice to apply multiple coatings 'wet-in-wet'. The first coating is applied to the underside (substrate side) of the screen. This is followed by two or more coatings applied on the upper (squeegee) side of the screen. The aim is to fill the mesh structure and to force the excess emulsion through to the underside of the screen, producing a very flat bottom surface to the stencil coating.

Drying the coating

After it has been coated the screen should be dried in a horizontal position (squeegee side up), allowing the emulsion to flow down through the screen mesh to enhance the coating on the underside of the screen. It is best to dry the screens in a drying cabinet. This will prevent dust contamination and provides a light-safe environment. Drying can be accelerated by raising the temperature to 30–35°C. Where fan-assisted drying is used it is best to filter the air to prevent dust contamination.

It is also worth investing in humidity controls in the dryer to ensure that the screen coatings are drying completely. In humid conditions and where production demands a fast turnover, it is possible that humidity levels inside the dryer may build up and the coated screens may not dry completely. If this happens then the photosensitivity (speed) of the emulsion coating will fall and underexposure will almost certainly result. The relative humidity for direct stencils should be 35–40%. Set the humidity control to 35% RH. When the screen goes into the dryer this will rise to 50% and fall again to 35% when the screen is dry. Monitoring the RH in the screen dryer will help to ensure that screens are completely dry before exposure. Where coated screens are stored before exposure, ensure that the RH is controlled at 40%. It is also important to monitor the RH in the exposure area as coated screens, especially capillary direct screens, are very hygroscopic (they soak up moisture in the air) and damp screens underexpose.

Exposing the screen

When the emulsion coating is dry the positive image is taped in position on the underside of the screen – this can be done using a pre-register table to position the work accurately on the screen, thus saving set-up time in make-ready.

The positive is placed on the table, aligning the set-up targets with the format grid. Small tabs of double-sided adhesive tape are strategically position at three points on the positive. The screen is then lowered into register on the table and the positive pressed into contact with the screen at the adhesive tape points. Using a pre-register system allows for quick and accurate registration of each image on the screen, especially useful in multicolour printing.

With the positive securely attached in position, the screen is placed into a large format printing-down frame, where it is exposed to a suitable UV

(a)

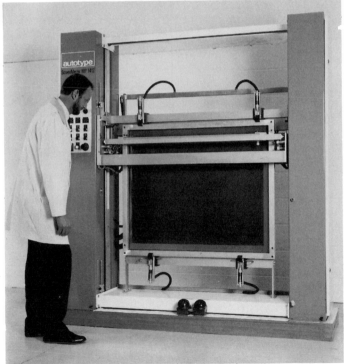

(b)

Fig. 26 Coating a screen with direct emulsion.
(a) Coating by hand. (Courtesy of Schweiz Seidengazfabrik AG Thal.)
(b) Automated screen coating. (Courtesy Autotype International Ltd.)

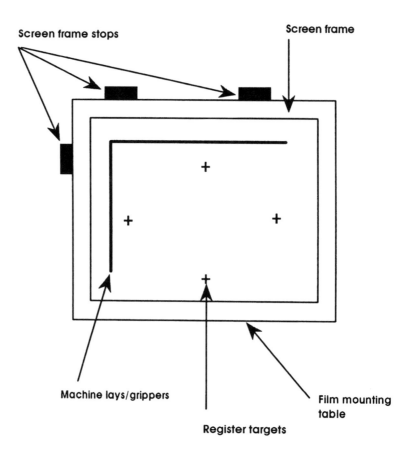

Fig. 27 Pre-registration table.

light source. The exposure time will be determined by a number of variable factors and must be calculated according to working conditions and the particular requirements of the work in hand. The exposure must be sufficient to ensure that the emulsion is completely light hardened (polymerized) right through, from the bottom of the screen to the top. If the upper layers of the emulsion coating are underexposed then the stencil coating will not be bonded into the screen mesh and will break down during development or, worse still, on the first wash-up on the press. If a stencil failure happens, run a quality check.

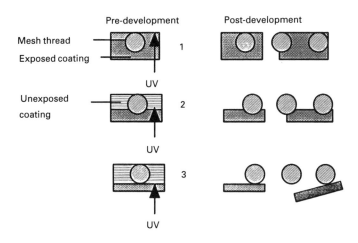

Pre-development   Post-development

Mesh thread

Exposed coating

1

UV

Unexposed
coating

2

UV

3

UV

Fig. 28 Effects of underexposure in direct stencil making.
1. Coating fully exposed, provides complete mesh bonding, excellent edge definition.
2. Underexposed coating produces weak mesh bonding and poor edge definition.
3. Excessive underexposure causes the coating to collapse away from the mesh.

Developing the stencil

The stencil is developed by washing the exposed screen with a cold water spray (medium fast, say 6–7 setting). Warm water can be used (15–40°C) to speed up the process. When the stencil areas begin to open up the water spray-pressure can be turned up to clear away any remaining emulsion. It is important to wash the screen thoroughly, all over and from both sides, to ensure that any unexposed emulsion is removed. It is also good practice to blot off or vacuum off surface water after washing, as this ensures that no waterborne emulsion residue is present on the screen before drying. If screens are not washed thoroughly, a film of emulsion can remain trapped at the edges of the frame, flowing down the screen, as it is transported to the dryer and causing 'scum' in the image areas of the screen. 'Scumming' in a direct stencil is very difficult to treat, careful application of the high-pressure water lance might remove it, but at the risk of damaging the image profiles. Avoidance is far better than remedy.

Drying the stencil

Direct stencils can be dried with warm air (40°C); to speed up the process. Some stencil systems may require post-exposure hardening by re-exposing the dry screen to UV; this is of course necessary where stencil emulsion is used for retouching. It may be more efficient to use a water-resistant filler for retouching, as this means that the screen making area is more productively utilized. Alternatively, a second exposure unit with fluorescent UV tubes could be used, providing for post-curing and retouching.

Stencil removal

Direct stencils can be difficult to remove if the wrong procedure is used. Suppliers give product-specific user instructions. However, the following procedure could form the basis for good practice.

1. Thoroughly clean the screen with an appropriate solvent (preferably a low hazard, eco-friendly type).
2. Apply a degreasing agent to both sides of the screen – gel-type agents are good, since they stay put whilst the job is done (see Chapter 3, Degreasing a screen).
3. Treat the screen with a proprietary decoating agent – Stensolve, Pregasol P, Seristrip and Autostrip are all equally good; again it is worth using a gel type for reasons stated above. Some suppliers sell decoating chemicals in powder form to be mixed up by the user. Preference depends very largely on:
   – emulsion type(s) used and ease of removal;
   – size and turnover of screens;
   – removal technology (manual, semi or fully automated).
4. The decoating agent must be left on the screen for the prescribed reaction time, in accordance with user instructions (for decoating techniques, see Screen reclamation later in this chapter).
5. Rinse the screen with low-pressure water to remove the decoating chemicals.
6. Treat the screen with a high-pressure water lance to remove any remaining stencil residue.
7. Where stencil/ink 'ghost' residue remains (and this can be common), proprietary 'ghost' removal preparations can be used. 'Ghosting' or 'ghost images' are caused by a build-up of ink and stencil residue which remains on the screen mesh threads after cleaning and reclaiming. The build-up usually occurs on the inner surfaces of the threads. The effect is to reduce the mesh openings. This can produce a reduced ink deposit, made visible in the print as a secondary ghost-like image.

Health and Safety Note:

See earlier note on using screen reclaiming solvents and chemicals. Always consult the product saftey data sheets and use products strictly in accordance with the manufacturer's instructions. Always ensure that the working environment is well ventilated; avoid inhalation of solvent vapours and any atomized chemicals. Wear a protective visor, gloves and apron and if necessary a vapour mask.

TROUBLESHOOTING

Early stencil breakdown is usually caused by underexposing the stencil (see Chapter 5, Exposure calculation). Underexposure will occur if the emulsion coating is not dried completely before the screen is exposed. Direct stencil emulsions are hygroscopic and will take on moisture from the atmosphere. As their photosensitivity is impaired by the moisture that is present in the coating it is important to ensure that they are completely dry before they are exposed, and that the humidity in the photostencil-making room is controlled. Stencil breakdown is also caused by inadequate screen mesh preparation. It may also be that the UV light source is ageing; a light-integrator will allow for the fall-off in actinic intensity by automatically increasing exposure times. The light-integrator should also be checked periodically to ensure that it is functioning effectively.

Pinholes may be caused by the following:

- Underexposure – quality check.
- Inadequate screen preparation – review procedures.
- Inadequate dilution of the sensitizer – check user instructions.
- Air bubbles transferred from the emulsion into the stencil coating – leave newly mixed emulsion to settle.
- Dust or foreign particles trapped in the coating or in the screen – clean up the environment and process procedures.
- Dust or marks on the positive or contact glass – clean up the environment and process procedures.
- Inadequate mesh filling (especially prevalent with very low mesh count screens, which must be multicoated with intermittent drying between coatings) – change your coating blade to a round edged blade, use a higher density emulsion and check the application techniques with some test coatings and exposures.

Sawtoothing is a term used to describe the jagged edges which are sometimes produced in prints that are made from direct stencils. The 'sawtooth edge' results from the concave drying of the stencil after it has been developed. As the stencil emulsion dries it shrinks into the structure of the screen mesh, shrinking most where it crosses the mesh openings. The poor mesh bridging characteristics of low viscosity emulsions increase the effect, giving a ragged appearance to type matter and a heavy, 'flooded' look to half-tones. The effect can be avoided by using:

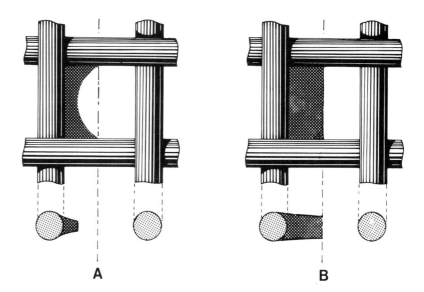

Fig. 29 Concave drying. (Courtesy of Zurich Bolting Cloth Mfg Co. Ltd.)
(a) Poor mesh bridging.
(b) Improved mesh bridging.

- a finer screen mesh (a higher count);
- a high viscosity emulsion with improved mesh-bridging;
- multiple coatings of emulsion to build up the stencil layer on the underside of the screen.

DIRECT EMULSION COATING MACHINES

Coating direct emulsion on to a screen is a skilled operation which requires a considerable amount of practice to perfect. One of the greatest difficulties in the operation is the control of coating thickness. Coatings can vary from one screen to another, and no two operators will coat a screen in quite the same way.

To meet the demands of more exacting quality control, especially in four colour process printing, direct emulsion coating machines have been devised. These machines will apply emulsion to both sides of the screen simultaneously, allowing for perfect mesh filling. The number of coatings applied to each side (wet-in-wet) can be independently programmed for up to a maximum of nine coatings. When the machine has been programmed the screen coating can be repeated exactly, any number of times. This is a considerable advantage in the production of work that requires precise control of ink film deposit.

DEVELOPMENTS IN DIRECT EMULSIONS

In recent years there have been a number of developments in direct emulsion formulation. Chemist have been working to develop emulsions which provide improved performance, in line with the requirements of a fast moving industry, where demands are changing all the time. Two recent developments are dual-cure emulsions, designed for use with water/solvent ink systems, and high speed polymer emulsions for use with projection and laser imaging systems.

Dual-cure direct emulsion systems

Modern high density emulsions formulated on PVAOH/PVAC (polyvinyl alcohol/polyvinyl acetate) chemistry provide high quality, high definition stencils. They have the capability of line resolutions down to 50 microns (0.002 in), producing very acute edge definition. Much of the quality in terms of edge definition comes from the addition of the polyvinyl acetate latex filler which improves water resistance and reduces the swelling and shrinking properties of the polyvinyl alcohol colloid. However, the problem with PVAC is that it has low solvent resistance. This has required the manufacturers to produce two types of emulsion: one with a PVAOH/PVAC ratio of 1:3 for solvent-based inks, and another with a 1:6 ratio for water-based inks.

With the recent trend in the development of water/solvent ink systems, the use of PVAOH/PVAC becomes a problem, since neither of the formulations produces an emulsion which is resistant to both solvent and water. The solvent/water mix in these inks attacks the stencil emulsion and breaks down the polymer. In response the manufacturers have invested much research and development time into finding new organic particulate fillers with good solvent resistance which might be used as a replacement for PVAC.

The system the chemists have come up with involves a two-phase process of photopolymerization (light-hardening and cross-linking of the emulsion particles). The water-phase PVAOH cross-links with itself, under the action of the diazo sensitizer, while the organic latex filler also hardens under the influence of ultraviolet light in the presence of a secondary compound, hence the term 'dual cure'.

The result is an emulsion with a high solids content (45–50%), high resolution and edge definition and superior water/solvent resistance. This has been achieved largely by the careful matching of the emulsion components: a medium to high molecular weight PVAOH solution, a liquid plasticizer, and a new organic latex filler which has all the right properties (a particle size of 4–8 microns, transparency to UV, and high solvent resistance).

Dual-cure emulsions have also been used in formulating new capillary direct films and these, too, have found application with the new water-based and water/solvent ink systems.

Photopolymer emulsions

Photopolymer emulsions based upon SBQ (soluble pyridine-based quaternary compound) and STQ (soluble tuiozole quarternary compound) have been developed to provide emulsions with the faster photographic speeds required for projection and direct-to-screen imaging.

The increased photosensitivity is provided by the unique way in which the photopolymerization process takes place during exposure to UV light. In a conventional emulsion the diazo compound reacts when exposed to UV radiation and causes the PVAOH/PVAC monomers to cross-link, forming polymer chains which give the coating its water/solvent resistance. The unexposed, non-image areas of the coating remain in their monomeric state and will readily dissolve when developed with water. In order to expose the emulsion coating right through, each monomer has to be cross-linked with its neighbours to form a complete network. This process of cross-linking takes time. The thicker the coating, the longer it takes.

Of course, the process can be speeded up to some extent by increasing the levels of UV radiation – by switching the metal halogen lamp from 2 to 6 kW, for instance, or reducing the lamp-to-screen distance. However, these are a very limited options which in some cases are simply not practical. This is the case with the recently developed projection and laser imaging systems.

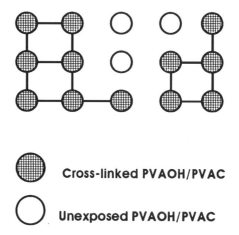

Cross-linked PVAOH/PVAC

Unexposed PVAOH/PVAC

Fig. 30 Polymerization of PVAOH/PVAC emulsion. On exposure to ultraviolet light the emulsion molecules chemically cross-link with one another to form a strong, plastic film.

Projection imaging has been used in offset-litho for several years. It is mainly used for large format work where the image can be projected on to the printing surface (plate) from a small original, using a specially designed camera which can produce image enlargements of 4–12× magnification.

The problem with projection imaging on screen is that the screen coating is 3–4 times as thick as the litho plate coating. The screen coating must also be hardened through at least 60% of the mesh section in order to obtain sufficient emulsion-to-mesh bonding. The only way to achieve this is to use more intense UV sources and to increase the light sensitivity of the stencil emulsion.

The new projection cameras for screen making utilize special micro-wave UV lamps, which operate at 2 kW and produce an intensely focused point source. To expose the screen coating to a sufficient depth the emulsion has to have a photographic speed 4–5 times faster than a conventional diazo or dual-cure emulsion. In comparison, SBQ and STQ emulsions have speeds of between 15 and 30 seconds, which gives a projection exposure range of 60–240 seconds for 10–12× enlargements.

The increased photographic speed is achieved by the novel way in which polymerization is promoted within the emulsion system. The chemical process is complex, involving a number of stages with associated reactions taking place which facilitate the increase in speed. Essentially the photosensitive SBQ or STQ polymer consists of a partially cross-linked chain of light-sensitive monomers, chemically linked to the PVAOH system. On exposure the already partially linked polymer chains cross-link, rapidly completing the polymeric network.

Unlike diazo sensitized emulsions, the hardening process of polymerization in dual-cure emulsions continues after exposure has taken

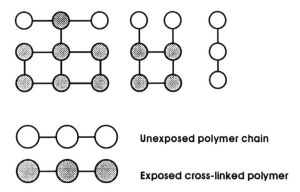

Fig. 31 Polymerization of preformed (SBQ/STQ) polymer chains, linking up rapidly to form a complete cross-linked structure on exposure to ultraviolet light.

place, which means that screens can be post-hardened after exposure to improve their durability.

As with most things, photopolymers do have limitations:

- They rely very much on controlled emulsion thickness.
- They are not recommended for water-based inks.
- When used in conventional contact printing, exposure latitudes are very narrow and difficult to control.
- They must always be used with dyed mesh, since white mesh will cause a halation effect during projection as the UV light is reflected within the mesh during exposure.
- Unless they are post-hardened or chemically treated, screens made by projection and laser direct imaging do not yet have the durability of conventional contact-printed direct emulsions.

Benefits of projection and direct-to-screen laser imaging

The above having been said, there are obviously considerable advantages to be gained from this new technology. The various functional principles of the available systems will be compared in Chapter 5. Here are some of the benefits of the new technology compared with conventional contact methods:

Conventional contact exposure

- Camera or scanned separations.
- Enlargement to SS positive films.
- Manual positioning films on screens.
- Exposing in a large contact frame.

Projection imaging

- Small (A3 maximum) positives.
- Preset programmed positioning of separations on screen.
- Automated exposure system from screen cassette.

Direct-to-screen laser imaging

- No films required.
- Image exposed directly on to screen from digital data.
- Image can be enlarged, reduced and electronically manipulated prior to screen making.
- Whole batches of jobs can be filed, accessed and edited electronically.
- No dust to contaminate films, no film work at all.

Diazo–photopolymer combination systems

Other novel emulsions have been recently produced which combined the benefits of both diazo and photopolymer systems. They produce fast emulsions with good resistance to water-based inks and improved durability when used with conventional contact printing methods.

The direct stencil has come a long way in the last few years. Clearly its development will continue as the demands of the product, the market and the environment continue to change. Each system has its own particular advantages and limitations. In the end choice will be dictated by the application and by the personal preference of the user.

Direct/indirect photostencils

Stencil thickness control is an important requirement in the production of printed circuits. In response to demands from this section of the industry the stencil manufacturers developed the direct/indirect stencil system.

As its name implies, the system is a combination of the direct and the indirect photostencil methods. The manufacturers have claimed that it provides the best of both methods. The advantages of the direct/indirect stencil may be summarized as follows:

- The stencil is made from a precision polymer coating which will provide a guaranteed stencil thickness.
- The stencil has a very smooth and flat underside thus eliminating the lateral image spread which can occur at the stencil/stock interface due to the effects of concave drying (see Direct emulsion photostencils: Sawtoothing).
- As the stencil is formed from a film coating which is bonded to the screen with sensitized emulsion the mesh openings are bridged completely, eliminating any tendency towards the 'sawtooth effect'.
- The physical bonding of the polymer film with the screen mesh gives the stencil a durability approaching that of a direct emulsion stencil.
- Direct/indirect stencils have excellent resistance to aggressive solvents and to abrasive inks such as those used in ceramic and glassware decoration.
- The film is less moisture sensitive than capillary direct films and therefore provides a useful alternative in climates where high levels of humidity are experienced.

MAKING A DIRECT/INDIRECT PHOTOSTENCIL

There are a number of products available and most of them may be sensitized with dichromate or diazo sensitizers, the former now being phased out in most countries. The system consists of a precision polymer coating (20 microns in the case of Autotype's Autoline H.D.) carried on a 0.076 mm (0.003 in) polyester film base; some materials are supplied on a matt film base which gives a matted finish to the underside of the stencil and helps to minimize the effects of static electricity. The film is supplied with a polymer emulsion which is used to bond the stencil film to the screen mesh whilst also making it sensitive to light. The basic procedure that is used in making a direct/indirect photostencil is as follows.

Sensitizing the emulsion

The sensitizer should be mixed very thoroughly into the emulsion, especially in the case of dichromate. The emulsion should then be left to stand for at least 30 minutes, remixed and allowed to stand for one hour before it is used. Dichromated emulsion should be used within 48 hours as its photosensitivity is adversely affected by storage.

Preparing the screen

The screen must be correctly pretreated and degreased before the stencil film is mounted on to it. Dust is a serious problem. Therefore every attempt must be made to keep the process area as clean and dust free as possible. The screen should be carefully examined and checked for dust contamination before the film is mounted. It is good practice to wipe the film coating with an anti-static cloth before mounting it.

Cutting the film

The film should be cut slightly larger than the dimensions of the positive image (including register targets and other references). A 50 mm border should be sufficient.

Mounting the film

The film is placed emulsion side up on a raised mounting platform; this should have a very smooth, flat surface (either plate glass or plastic laminate is suitable). The screen is then positioned with its underside in contact with the polymer film. The upper side of the screen is then masked at each end to allow for a clean application of the bonding emulsion. This is applied at one end of the screen and then forced through the mesh in one stroke, using a printing squeegee with a rounded, medium soft blade.

As the sensitized bonding emulsion reaches the film it is immediately absorbed and the softened surface of the film is drawn into the screen mesh. The polymer film is hygroscopic and quickly absorbs the sensitizer. All operations involving light-sensitive materials must, of course, be

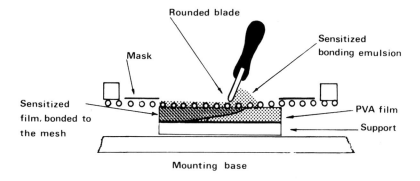

Fig. 32 Mounting the film.

carried out in safe light conditions; yellow filtered or tungsten lighting is suitable.

Drying the film

The masking material is removed from the upper side of the screen and the coating is dried with warm air. Dichromate sensitized coatings should be dried with cold air and used within a short period, as they are subject to 'dark-hardening'. (The coating will polymerize without the influence of light. Heat will also cause this to occur.)

Peeling the film base

When the stencil film is completely dry the film base can be peeled away. It should separate quite freely; any resistance will indicate that the stencil film is not completely dry and that the drying process should continue.

Exposure

Exposure must be ascertained from the manufacturer's product data sheet. It is advisable to conduct tests to assess local conditions (see Chapter 5, Exposure calculation). The positive image is taped to the underside of the film coating (emulsion to emulsion). The screen is then placed in the exposure frame and exposed in the conventional manner.

Development

The stencil is developed in the conventional manner. When the stencil begins to open up a strong spray should be used to ensure that all surplus emulsion has been removed from the screen.

Filling and drying

The open areas of the screen surrounding the film coating are filled with a suitable screen filler. In some cases, where standard print formats are established, the non-printing areas around the perimeter of the screen are permanently blocked and sealed when the screen is tensioned; this saves time and materials in screen preparation.

Stencil removal

Stencils are removed in exactly the same way as direct emulsion stencils (see Direct emulsion photostencils: Stencil removal).

TROUBLESHOOTING

Early stencil breakdown is usually caused by errors in procedure, such as:

- inadequate mesh preparation;
- underexposure;
- inadequate screen preparation;
- dust or grit trapped between mesh and film.

Capillary direct film photostencils

Capillary direct stencil systems are widely used throughout the industry. They were a logical development of the direct/indirect method, employing the same principle of capillarity that is used in the adhesion of water-soluble knife-cut stencil film. The material consists of a precision coated photopolymer film on a 75 micron high stability polyester base. A range of film thicknesses are available, from 18 to 80 microns; the choice of film will be determined by ink type/film thickness requirements.

The Capillex Range of capillary films is made for use with conventional solvent-based and UV ink systems. For solvent and water-based ink systems the XR Range is recommended.

Other suppliers include the Ulano Group of Companies who produce the CDF™ range of films, Follex Ltd with their range of Follex films and Chromaline with their range of Magnacure products. Specific guidance on film selection can be obtained from the suppliers; in the UK they are Sericol Ltd, Coates Screen, George Hall Sales, Follex Ltd and John T. Keep & Sons Ltd. These are just some of the major suppliers to the industry. Suppliers of alternative products and services can be found in the Suppliers section at the end of the book.

Autotype International Ltd: Capillex Range grade selection

Mesh (cm)	40	80	120	160
Mesh (in)	100	200	300	400
Capillex 18			//////////////////// ////////////////////	
Capillex 25			///// /////////////////////	
Capillex 35		/////// //////////////////////////		
Capillex 50	//////////////////// /////////////			

MAKING A CAPILLARY DIRECT PHOTOSTENCIL

A number of different methods may be used to mount a capillary direct film on to a screen. The two methods described are recommended by Autotype for use with their Capillex films.

Preparing the screen

The screen must be correctly pretreated and degreased before the film is mounted on to it. It is best to degrease and rinse the screen just prior to mounting the film, as this prevents any atmospheric contamination of the mesh. The use of a proprietary wetting agent like Universal Mesh Prep or Ulano No. 25 CDF Prep is recommended as it promotes water retention in the mesh and improves the penetration of the film coating into the mesh.

Cutting the film

The film should be handled in safe lighting conditions; yellow filter or tungsten illumination. The film is cut slightly larger than the overall dimensions of the positive image: a 50 mm border should be sufficient.

Mounting the film: small format stencils

Small format stencils can be made by mounting the film on to the screen with a fine water spray (the kind used for indoor plants). The cut film is placed emulsion side up on a raised mounting platform, and the underside of the screen is brought into contact with the film. Using the fine mist water spray the film is wetted through the screen; it will darken in appearance as it makes contact with the wet mesh. The excess moisture is then drawn across the screen with a single stroke of a printing squeegee.

Mounting the film: large format stencils

Large format stencils are made by mounting the cut film directly on to a wet screen. The film is rolled emulsion side out round the clear plastic tube, supplied with the roll of film, leaving approximately 2.5 cm (1 in) of film unrolled. The screen is placed in a vertical position and it is sprayed with water to provide an even coating over the entire screen. The leading edge of the film is contacted to the top of the screen and the film is simply unrolled on to the mesh in a smooth downward movement. Excess moisture is then removed from the inside of the screen with a glass-cleaning squeegee. Care must be taken not to overwet the screen and cause rivulets of water, as these can affect the thickness of the stencil. Any excess water should also be wiped from the edges of the frame before the screen is moved.

Drying the film

The film can be dried with warm air, at a maximum temperature of 40°C. The film should be thoroughly dry before it is exposed, as incomplete drying can lead to underexposure, and cause stencil collapse during development.

Peeling the film base

When the film is completely dry the polyester base can be stripped away. It is good practice to continue drying the film for a further 5 minutes after the base has been peeled, as this ensures that the film has been dried right through.

Exposure

The screen is exposed in the conventional direct manner, the positive image being taped on to the screen, emulsion to emulsion. Exposure times will vary according to the type of film being used and the conditions under which it is exposed. In any event, the manufacturer's product data sheets must be consulted before any tests can be made. The film must be completely exposed right through its thickness; as with all direct stencils, underexposure will cause early stencil breakdown, usually at the development stage.

Development

The stencil is developed by washing out with cold water. It should be thoroughly washed from both sides, using the same method as for direct/indirect stencils. When development is complete the screen should

(a)

(b)

Fig. 33 (a) Rolling the film on to the screen.
          (b) Removing the excess water.

be blotted with absorbent paper (newsprint) or vacuum dried to remove
any excess water.

Drying

The screen may be dried with warm air at a maximum temperature of
40°C.

Stencil removal

Capillary direct stencils are removed in exactly the same way as direct
emulsion stencils.

TROUBLESHOOTING

Early stencil breakdown is usually caused by underexposure, often as a result of inadequate drying of the film before it is exposed. It may also be caused by inadequate screen preparation.

Pinholes are most often caused by dust or dirt on the clear areas of the positive or on the contact glass. They may also be a sign of screen contamination or underexposure.

Blocked stencil openings may be caused by 'light undercutting' the positive image during exposure. This can result from poor contact between the positive image and the stencil film, or by 'light scatter' (reflection of UV light within the mesh structure) where white screen mesh is used. Coloured mesh is recommended.

Uneven stencil thickness may be caused by excessive wetting of the screen during the film mounting procedure. Any surplus water which remains at the edges of the screen frame should be removed by blotting or wiping the screen with absorbent tissue.

Screen reclamation   The cleaning and reclaiming of screens is the least attractive and yet one of the most important aspects of screen process printing. Ineffective cleaning and reclaiming will lead to expensive stencil remakes. The improper use of aggressive cleaning and reclaiming chemicals can also cause damage to the screen mesh and result in additional costs in screen replacement. The increasingly restrictive health and safety and environmental regulations which now apply make it all the more vital that the processes and procedures used in screen cleaning and reclamation conform to the requirements of the law.

MANUAL CLEANING AND RECLAIMING

In the small to medium size company, with a turnover of 10–20 screens per day, it is likely that manual screen cleaning and reclaiming methods will be adopted. Screens are placed inside a cleaning booth and treated with screen wash to remove residual ink which remains after printing. The booth should provide a facility to clean and recycle the screen wash through a filtration unit. This separates out the ink solids, compounding them for safe disposal. The booth should also provide an extraction facility, which draws solvent vapours away from the operator, thus preventing any inhalation. Effective ventilation of the screen cleaning area is extremely important (see the Heath and Safety Note below, also Chapter 10).

Screen reclaiming is carried out in a second booth, using appropriate stencil decoating chemicals and a high-pressure water lance. Considerable efficiency gains can be obtained in this process by using a decoating tank. This allows coated screens to be immersed in the decoating chemicals for a short period, prior to treatment with the high-pressure water lance. The tank-decoating treatment reduces wastage of costly decoating chemicals, since they are retained within the tank; it also facilitates a more rapid breakdown of stencil coatings, thus saving operator time.

Health and Safety Note:

It is important to stress that manual screen cleaning and reclamation are activities which involve the use of potentially hazardous chemicals and equipment. It is essential that operators are made aware of the potential health hazards associated with these processes; that they are properly trained in the safe use of chemicals and equipment; and that adequate precautions are taken to protect them against any hazards which the processes may present. Safe practice will almost certainly involve: the use of adequate ventilation to prevent accidental inhalation of solvent vapours and atomized chemicals; and the wearing of protective visor, gloves, apron and, when using a high-pressure water lance, ear protection.

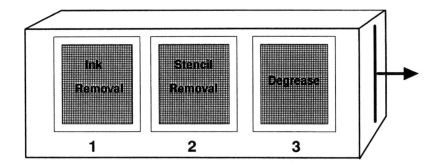

Fig. 34 Automated screen cleaning and reclaiming.
1. At this point ink is removed with recycling solvents – ink solids are filtered and compounded for safe disposal.
2. Stencil coatings are removed with recycling chemicals and high-pressure water jets; harmful waste is filtered and collected for safe disposal.
3. The screen is chemically cleaned and delivered to the drying rack ready for re-use.

AUTOMATED SCREEN CLEANING AND RECLAMATION

In the larger company, with a turnover of 50+ screens per day (especially where these are large format screens), automatic screen cleaning and reclamation equipment may be employed. Here the cleaning and reclaiming process is fully automated within an enclosed ink and emulsion removal unit. The machines are designed to carry out the two processes independently, to pre-programmed specifications. They facilitate the recycling of chemicals, water filtration and the collection of solid waste products for safe disposal. The containment and automation of what are unpleasant and potentially hazardous processes is in line with current health and safety and environmental legislation, where the controlled use of solvents and chemicals has become an important focus of attention.

Quality assurance 5

Quality assurance in any printing process begins with the origination of the image that is to be reproduced. The designer and layout artist must consider the technical requirements of the processes for which they are producing artwork. In screen process printing there are certain technical limitations which must be taken into account in origination if the work is to be successfully and economically produced.

The following guidelines are set out as general principles which apply to the origination of artwork for graphic arts printing. They are not intended as the last word on what can or cannot be screen printed; nor are they by any means all that the designer or graphic artist should know about the technical requirements of origination for the process. If in doubt, always consult the printers.

REGISTRATION TOLERANCES

'Registration' or 'register' are terms commonly used in printing when referring to the printing of two of more colours in close proximity. In order to achieve any degree of accuracy in registration there must be a high degree of dimensional stability in the image reproduction system. In most printing processes the image is reproduced from a relatively stable image carrier (plate or cylinder) but in screen printing the screen supporting the image-forming stencil is not dimensionally stable; indeed, in order for the print to be made the screen and stencil must flex.

Because of this inherent instability, some dimensional change in the printed image is likely to take place. This means that very close registration tolerances between adjacent printings are often difficult to achieve. So-called 'butt register', where one colour fits exactly next to another without any overlap, is to be avoided. In most circumstances the colours can be very slightly overlapped, referred to variously as 'trapping', 'catch-on' or 'grip'. This allows for any dimensional change that may occur during printing and minimizes its visible effects.

Difficulties can arise when two translucent colours are to be printed in exact register. Here any overlap must be kept to an absolute minimum since it will be clearly visible. Again, such colour combinations are best

Fig. 35 Colours are 'underdrawn' beneath the 'key line' to allow for 'grip'.

avoided at the design stage, where a simple adjustment to the design can often prevent considerable technical and cost problems in production.

TYPE FACES AND POINT SIZES

Some typefaces are more suitable for screen printing than others. This is especially true when it comes to the reproduction of type matter in small point sizes, down to 6 pt.

The difficulties are due to the interference caused by the screen mesh closures. If we consider that 30–60% of the screen will not allow ink to pass through it, then it is quite evident that the very finely drawn parts of certain type faces will lose weight or even fail to print, since they will be blocked by the mesh.

Typefaces like the one in Fig. 36 which have very finely drawn thin strokes and unbracketed serifs are not really suitable for screen printing. The lineal type faces, which have no serifs and are uniform and open in their design, are the most suitable for screen printing. Slab-serif typefaces are also very suitable. If a typeface with a contrasting stroke weight is required, those which have bracketed serifs, like the Humanist, Garalde or Transitional classes of typeface, are the best choice. The minimum

The famous Eros fountain in Piccadilly Circus was set up as a memorial to the 3rd Earl of Shaftesbury who did so much for the poor of London, but few who see it realise that the arrowhead or 'shaft' in Eros's bow stands for Shaftesbury, the town of the arrowhead whence his family took their title. The arrowhead is that wedge of sandstone rock which juts out some 400 feet above the Blackmoor Vale giving views over the countryside which are some of the most beautiful in England.

The famous Eros fountain in Piccadilly Circus was set up as a memorial to the 3rd Earl of Shaftesbury who did so much for the poor of London, but few who see it realise that the arrowhead or 'shaft' in Eros's bow stands for Shaftesbury, the town of the arrowhead whence his family took their title. The arrowhead is that wedge of sandstone rock which juts out some 400 feet above the Blackmoor Vale giving views over the countryside which are some of the most beautiful in England

Fig. 36 Parts of certain letterforms are blocked by the screen mesh.
(a) Original.
(b) Screen printed reproduction.

(a)   (b)

Fig. 37 (a) A slab serif face.
(b) A face which has finely drawn serifs and extreme contrast between thin and thick strokes. As a general rule, it is advisable to avoid typefaces which have serifs in point sizes below 8 pt.

point size should be 6 pt with linear work limited to a minimum line width of 100 microns for solvent-based inks and 50 microns for UV-cured inks.

HALF-TONE REQUIREMENTS

Continuous tone images that are produced in photographs can be reproduced in print by simulating the continuity of tone from white to black with dots of varying sizes. This method of reproducing continuous tone is commonly known as half-tone.

As can be seen from the grey scale (Fig. 38) the highlight (closest to white) areas of the image are simulated by very small dots that cover only 5% of the printed surface. In the middle tones, the dots form a regular chequer-board pattern and cover 50% of the surface. The shadow areas are simulated by very large dots which join up to cover 95% of the printed surface. In screen printing the tonal scale or 'screen range' is generally accepted to be limited to 15% in the highlight and 85% in the shadow (see Chapter 2, Mesh selection).

It is possible to reproduce the full range of tones, from 5% to 95%, but only on screen rulings of 28 lines/cm. The reason for this is that the size of the smallest dots in the shadow and highlight areas at either end of the tonal scale have to be big enough to create sufficiently large mesh openings to allow free ink passage or, in the case of the small shadow dots, to find sufficient mesh threads for support.

If we consider that the thinnest mesh threads have a diameter of 27–30

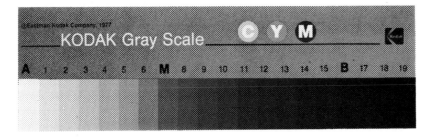

Fig. 38 A half-tone grey scale.

microns, the smallest half-tone dot we can reproduce must be three times as large, i.e. 81–90 microns. This would allow sufficient mesh/stencil opening to reproduce the highlight dot, and enough shadow dot area to ensure that the dot finds sufficient mesh thread support. Using these basic principles we can see from the table below that it is possible to reproduce the full 5%–95% tonal scale for half-tone line counts up to 28 lines/cm. When we get to line counts above this we see that the highlight and shadow dots become too small to print and the tonal scale is reduced in range to 10–90%. At 48 lines/cm the scale is further reduced to 15%–85%, at 54 lines/cm the range reduces to 20%–80%, and at 60 lines/cm the tonal range is 30%–70%, which would produce a very 'flat' looking image with insufficient contrast.

Screen printable tonal range

L/cm	5%	10%	15%	20%	30%	70%	80%	85%	90%	95%
12	210	296	364	420	516	516	420	364	296	210
16	158	223	273	315	386	386	315	273	223	158
20	126	178	218	252	309	309	252	218	178	126
22	114	162	198	229	280	280	229	198	162	114
25	101	142	175	202	247	247	202	175	142	101
28	90	127	156	180	220	220	180	156	127	90
30	84	119	145	168	206	206	168	145	119	84
32	79	111	136	157	193	193	157	136	111	79
34	74	105	128	148	182	182	148	128	105	74
40	63	89	109	126	154	154	126	109	89	63
48	52	74	90	105	128	128	105	90	74	52
54	46	66	81	93	114	114	93	81	66	46
60	42	59	72	84	103	103	84	72	59	42

MOIRÉ

As is apparent from the above considerations, screen printing is not entirely suited to the requirements of half-tone printing. The main difficulty is caused by the presence of the screen mesh threads, which can cause interference patterns by conflicting with the regular pattern of the half-tone dots. As indicated above, in the highlight areas the mesh closures can partially block the very small stencil apertures and in extreme cases they may become completely blocked, producing a strong linear pattern in the print. The patterns produced by this effect often resemble the patterns found in watered silk, and it is from this that they derive the name 'moiré'.

The moiré effect produced by screen mesh/half-tone interference is most noticeable in monochrome work; in three and four colour work the effect is considerably less apparent. It can be minimized in a number of ways:

Fig. 39 Moiré effect.

- By using a photostencil system that provides good mesh bridging. Direct emulsion stencils tend to increase the effect; for this reason indirect, direct/indirect and capillary direct film stencils are to be preferred.
- Using a fine screen mesh can greatly minimize the effect. The mesh count should not be in an exact mathematical ratio to the half-tone screen: i.e. it is better that it be 4.25 times finer than the half-tone than exactly 4 times finer.
- Recent research has indicated that the best angles to use for single colour half-work are between 15° and 35°. For four colour half-tone work the screen separations should be made at:
  - Black 7°
  - Magenta 37°
  - Cyan 67°
  - Yellow 97°

STOCHASTIC SCREENING

Recently developed 'stochastic' or frequency modulated screening technology promises to provide a solution to the moire problem. Since the stochastic screen consists of a random pattern of dots rather than the regular grid pattern of conventional half-tone screening, little or no interference pattern is created. Furthermore, stochastic screening produces smoother tonal gradations and this prevents the occurrence of a fault known as 'tone jump', created where the mid-tone dots join up at the horizontal and vertical axes, causing a perceptible sudden tone shift. Using an elliptical dot shape can also help to prevent this fault.

A number of companies are developing stochastic screening systems. Essentially, two systems are available, although different software/ scanner manufacturers place slightly different interpretations on them. First-generation stochastic screening provides screen dots of equal size, with tone variations achieved by varying the spacing of the dots, whereas second generation screening provides dots which vary in size and spacing. Second-generation screening produces smoother tonal gradations and has a less 'grainy' appearance. However, the very fine highlight dots produced create problems for screen printing reproduction, and so it seems likely that first generation stochastic screening is the more easily adopted form for screen printing applications.

Companies who are currently engaged in developing stochastic screening software and scanning systems include:

Adobe – Brilliant Screens
Agfa – CristalRastar
Linotype-Hell – Dispersed Screening
R.R. Donelly – Accu-tone
ScanCorp – Opal Screening
Scitex – Full Tone.

With such a wide range of developmental interest in this new prepress technology, it is very likely that we shall see a range of screening programmes developed with specific application for the graphics and textile areas of the industry. The T-shirt and garment printer will probably be the first to grasp the benefits which accrue from reductions in moiré. The rather grainy appearance of the stochastic screen may limit its application in graphic printing. Extending the range of visual effects which can be rendered in four colour printing may encourage its wider use. In the final analysis this will be determined as much by the dictates of design and fashion as by the technical benefits it creates for the printer.

Four colour process printing

The cover of this book has a colour photograph printed on it. When we look at it, we see a fairly faithful reproduction of the original colour transparency. Look at it again more closely, preferably under 10× magnification, and you will see that what looks like simultaneity of tone and hue is in fact a pattern of tiny coloured dots – Yellow, Magenta, Cyan (YMC). These are the three pigment primaries used in four colour process printing. You will also see a black dot (K), the fourth printer which provides the grey tones in each of the hues. The overall effect is produced by an optical illusion: the naked eye, being unable to focus the tiny dots, mixes the colours and we receive the sensation of simultaneous colour tone.

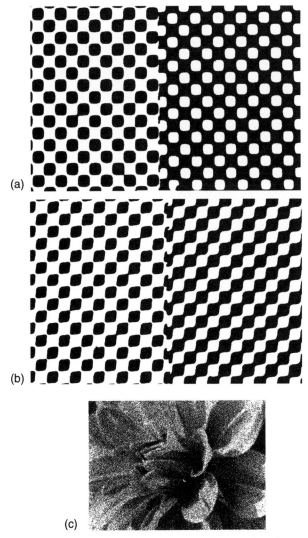

(a)

(b)

(c)

Fig. 40 (a) In conventional half-tone the mid-tone dots join up to form a chequer-board pattern, and this can produce a noticeable 'tone jump'.
(b) With an elliptical dot screen the dots join in two stages, first in the long axis and then across the short, thus producing a smoother tonal transition.
(c) Grained screen has a softer, less mechanical tonal effect.
(Courtesy of Schweiz Seidengazfabrik AG Thal.)

In spite of the many problems associated with half-tone printing there is currently a 10% growth in screen printed process colour work. Much of this growth results from continued improvements in screen mesh, stencil materials and inks. However, it is the developments in electronic scanning which have made the biggest contribution by providing the

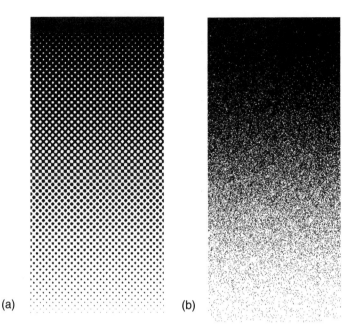

(a)   (b)

Fig. 41 An example of stochastic screening.
(a) Conventional screening vignette shows grey levels represented by equally spaced half-tone dots. The range of grey levels is limited by the resolution of the output recorder.
(b) CristalRaster vignette is made of microdots whose distribution varies according to tone value.

facility to match colour separation and screening parameters to the reproduction requirements of the printing process.

Most four colour process work is now scanned electronically, either from original transparencies or flat artwork. The scanner optically scans the original and translates the colour values for each hue and level of grey into digital format. The scanning process electronically analyses the image and separates it into the three primary colours (Yellow, Magenta, Cyan) and levels of grey. The scanner then produces film separations in each of these colours, together with a black separation which is used to enhance the shadow detail and increase the contrast of the printed image. When the four colour separations are printed and superimposed in register, the full polychromatic effect of the original image is reproduced.

It is only recently that the full potential of electronic image manipulation for screen process has been fully grasped. One of the first benefits to have an impact on screen printed process colour work is the adoption of what are variously called achromatic colour separation, undercolour removal (UCR) or grey component removal (GCR). Here, the scanner is programmed to reduce the dot size of the YMC pigment primaries and increase the black dot component so that the shadow areas of the image are produced entirely by the black printer. With GCR, the YMC components are reduced across the full tonal range and replaced by the black component. This renders all the grey areas of the image as well as the shadow detail.

These techniques produce images with increased sharpness. Printing colour only where colour is needed considerably reduces ink consumption. Furthermore, because the process colour inks are more expensive than process black there is an additional saving in the ink costs. In four colour process work for T-shirt and garment printing, the use of GCR provides for increased softness in the tactile quality of the print, and this is often valued by the designer and client.

It is also the practice in certain sectors of the industry, where colour process printing has presented ink-related problems, to print additional colour separations. The colour gamut produced by the conventional process colours can be enhanced by the addition of Orange and Violet, or alternatively Royal Violet and Warm Red screens to the conventional YMCK printers. This practice has also been adopted in the production of four colour process work for ceramic transfers, where the range of pigments available is limited. Of course, in scanning the orginal, allowances must be made for the extended gamut created by the use of additional colour separations.

Research into the dynamics of the printing process has taken giant steps forward in the last five years. Research already undertaken by the Screen Printing Association UK Ltd's project team to develop colour standards for screen process colour printing has provided a better understanding of the problems inherent in the system. What on the face of it looks like a simple process of ink transfer is in fact a highly complex dynamic, involving as many as 80 major variables. It is not uncommon to find that a particular production problem occurs as the result of the interaction of several different variables: ink viscosity, off-contact, squeegee angle/speed, etc. It is only by estabishing control across all the variables involved that optimum press efficiency and print quality are obtained.

Some of the major areas where control must be established are:

- screen mesh count/grade/bolt number
- screen tension
- stencil thickness
- ink rheology and viscosity
- ink drying and colour trapping
- screen off-contact
- squeegee and flo-coater design and function
- print release speed.

Screen mesh count/grade/bolt number

The screen mesh has an important influence on the quality of the printed image. The grade of mesh, the type of weave and the mesh count used will influence ink deposit thickness and print definition.

Inconsistency in ink deposit thickness and in print definition, screen to screen, will result in inconsistency in the colour reproduction of the print. As has been noted earlier, these factors vary between one manufacturer and another and even between one bolt of screen mesh and another. It is important, therefore, to standardize mesh selection and screen matching to ensure that the set of screens used for a job will provide consistent and predictable results.

Screen tension

The tension of the screen has an important influence on register and print definition (see Chapter 3, Measuring mesh tension with a meter). Screen tension has a direct influence on off-contact adjustment, squeegee pressure and print-release. All of these variables can adversely affect ink film weight and print definition. When mesh tension falls below 16 newtons, the screen will fail to provide the required performance for consistent print quality. This is especially important in four colour process work where dot gain and image distortion will result. In four colour process garment printing, the recommendation is that screen tension should be maintained at 25 newtons and that the off-contact distance of the screen above the pallet should be 1–2 cm.

It is therefore essential that screens are tensioned correctly and that they are tension-matched in sets to ensure consistency screen to screen. The only way to ensure this is to use a tension meter and self-tensioning frames (see Chapter 3, Self-tensioning frames).

Stencil thickness

The thickness of the stencil will also influence ink deposit thickness. The type of stencil used will also influence the acuity of the half-tone dot reproduced. The characteristics of film-based stencils, especially capillary direct stencils, produce half-tone dots which are not subject to the influence of the screen mesh structure and have a more predictable and thus controllable thickness. Direct emulsion stencils, even when machine coated, can be subject to variation in coating thickness. In order to approach the quality of print definition provided by a film-based stencil the screen must be multicoated with intermittent drying between coatings; the number of coatings will depend on the mesh used and the density of the screen emulsion (see Chapter 4, Direct emulsion photostencils: Troubleshooting).

Ink rheology and viscosity

The viscosity and more importantly the rheology of the ink is an important aspect of control in process colour printing. In order to ensure consistency print to print, colour to colour and run to run, it is necessary to have control over the nature of the ink being printed. Research has shown that during printing several variables influence the levels of pigment transferred through the screen/stencil system on to the stock.

The first of these is related to the solvent in the ink which acts as a diluent, controlling the viscosity of the ink (its resistance to flow). Solvent-based inks are not supplied in a press-ready viscosity. They are usually thinned with a solvent additive by the user according to requirements. The addition of a thinner (accelerative, standard or retardant) has a dynamic influence on the printing characteristics of the ink. The viscosity of the ink will be lowered and it will flow more readily. The resistance it presents to the squeegee and flo-coater will be lower and the dynamic pressures created in the ink wave will change as a result.

The addition of a diluent will also lower the surface tension of the ink, increasing its surface wetting properties. This will increase the ink film release rate (the speed at which the ink will pass through the screen and release from the surface of the mesh). The addition of the diluent will increase the level of solvent/ink penetration into the stock and thus influence the appearance of the ink film.

The addition of a diluent will directly increase the non-pigment, non-solids content of the ink, thus reducing the levels of pigment and extender deposited on the stock. This will have a direct influence on the level of colour saturation provided by the ink film.

It can be seen from this that the addition of thinners to an ink has a complex and dynamic influence upon the nature of the ink transfer process, the ink film and thus the quality of colour it produces. Whenever thinners are added to the ink, this should be done in a controlled way, allowing for the variations in colour which may occur as a result.

Once on the press, the ink is subject to a number of variable influences. The main one is the influence of the sieving action produced by the squeegee and flo-coater blades forcing the ink back and forth across and through the screen. Two things happen here. Firstly the solvents in the ink (including the water in water-based inks) will evaporate rapidly as the ink is spread in a thin film over the surface of the screen. Thus during printing we have a continually changing percentage of solvent in the ink. This can be minimized by isolating the screen within a solvent retention hood.

The second problem is more difficult to resolve. As the ink is forced through the mesh openings the screen acts as a sieve, allowing the passage of the solvent/resin elements whilst trapping the pigment/extender solids. Thus during printing the ratio of liquids to solids is in a state of continuous change. This poses difficult problems in relation to colour balance control through a print run.

Imagine, for example, that we charge the screen with a given volume of ink and we print until all the ink is used up. As we print, the pigment solids in the ink are increasing in volumetric ratio to the solvent/resin content. It is clear that as production proceeds the colour values produced by the ink, with its increasing levels of pigment concentration, will change. The colour will gain in saturation.

Clearly, such variability is unacceptable. How are we to improve the situation? Research currently in progress aims to identify standard colour deviation parameters which can be quickly assessed during production. In simple terms, this may amount to the development of ink supply technology which ensures that acceptable levels of on-screen ink replenishment and replacement are maintained during production, thus ensuring consistency of pigment ratios throughout the print run. Until such technology becomes available, we must monitor and control as we have in the past by frequent ink replenishment and periodic ink replacement. The use of a control strip and densitometric measurement will help us to make more precise and objective judgements (see Exercising colour control).

Ink drying and colour trapping

The effectiveness of ink drying, or 'curing' in the case of UV inks, is particularly important in process colour work. If the ink film fails to dry or cure adequately then this can lead to 'set off' and 'blocking' in the stacker. Such problems are of course serious, but they do not impact directly on process colour control in production. However, if the ink fails to dry or cure sufficiently this could influence the way that subsequent colours are printed. An ink which is still partially wet will re-wet more readily and may prevent subsequent colours from printing cleanly. Where one colour partially overlaps another, in the mid tones, it may fail to trap (fully cover) the undercolour, thus causing a colour shift in favour of the first colour. For optimum results, 90% of the ink film should trap. In some cases this can fall as low as 65% on long print runs, causing an unacceptable variation in colour reproduction. This is a particular problem with UV inks where the first colour has been overcured, and has insufficient surface wetting and bonding characteristics. The tendency is for the hard surface of the ink to reject the subsequent colours.

Again, it is essential to be able to make objective assessments of colour values in printing, using a colour control strip of the type referred to later in this chapter, setting the dryer correctly during the proofing stage and monitoring the drying/curing levels during the production run.

Screen off-contact

The 'off-contact' or 'lift-off' adjustment will determine the ink/mesh release rate. In so doing it will influence the thickness of the ink deposit and the acuity of the print. It will also influence the dimensional stability of the printed image, since high off-contact distances will mean increased squeegee pressures, and this will lead directly to increased screen/stencil/print distortion. Wide variations in off-contact adjustment will result in poor register. The control of print register in colour process work is of critical importance and its effects can be clearly recognized as a loss of colour and image definition. Failure to control off-contact adjustment can also lead to differentiated screen/stencil/print distortion, screen to screen, which means that not only will one colour fail to fit with another, but also it will occur unevenly across the printed image. Such faults can be commonly observed in 'white-out' text on posters and point of sale work, where colours 'fringe' at the edges of the print.

The answer is to standardize on mesh tension and ink viscosity (especially tack values) and keep the off-contact or lift-off and squeegee pressure to a measured minimum, consistent screen to screen.

Squeegee and flo-coater design and function

The design and functional principles of the squeegee and flo-coater blade will be treated in more detail later in the text (see Chapter 8, The squeegee). Here it is sufficient to note that these two instruments have a primary influence over the ink transfer process. The basic squeegee control variables are: blade hardness, shape, angle of attack, pressure and speed. The flo-coater blade shape, angle of attack and speed are also variables which require control and standardization.

Print release speed

This factor has been touched upon above as it is of course determined (like much else in this process) by a number of other variable factors. One of the most important of these is the area of the contact surface, i.e. the ink/mesh/substrate contact area along the squeegee blade. Ideally the print should separate away directly behind the squeegee blade. The wider and more open the screen is, the more slowly this is likely to occur, simply because there is a greater volume of ink and thus a greater resistance to ink film splitting.

Variations in print release speed can take place across the print, not solely but perhaps most significantly in the squeegee direction. Variation can also take place throughout the print run, caused by changes in the viscosity and tack levels in the ink. Both variables will cause changes in colour balance, since poor print release influences ink film thickness and print definition. It is important, therefore, to control this aspect of the process and to recognize that such control is part of a complex dynamic, which can only be controlled through the systematic application of standardized procedures, and objective measurement and adjustment.

If we are to produce consistent results, print to print and run to run, we have to find a way of controlling these variables. Having a set of established and internationally recognized standards for the process is the only way we will ever get quality assurance in four colour printing to a level approaching that of the other major printing processes. The traditional view is: 'Why should we be trying to emulate offset-litho, etc?' The answer must be because, like Everest, it is there, and we know that we can do better – a lot better, in many ways. One way is to exercise greater control. This will only be achieved through a deeper, more scientifically analytical understanding of how the process works. Screen printing is still in its youth. There is still much about it that we do not yet fully understand.

Exercising colour control

Recent and continuing research carried out by the SPA Project Team has produced a set of draft ISO Standard Specifications for Four Colour Printing for use with UV-cured water-based inks and conventional solvent-based inks. It is hoped that the standards will become universally accepted by the industry, and to develop them further to cover other inks and substrates.

The standards comprise detailed specifications which aim at providing a set of process parameters. The parameters and values are chosen to provide a comprehensive control mechanism for all the processes involved in the production of four colour process printing. They include:

- half-tone film quality
- screen ruling
- screen angles
- dot shape references
- image size tolerances, i.e. dimensional stability of films
- maximum tone value sum
- grey balance statement
- stencil profile
- stencil resolution
- mesh colour
- mesh tension
- squeegee profile/durometer
- substrate – colour, finish and brightness
- viewing conditions for proofing
- CIELAB colour tolerances for primary process colours
- tone value limits on the print

- image positioning tolerance
- dot gain values.

The benefits which will accrue from this pioneering work will lead to a raising of the quality standards in the industry, cutting spoilage and waste, reducing costs and (perhaps most important of all) raising the profile of the process in the minds of the print buyers, who will come to regard the process with more confidence, seeing it on a par with the other major processes where quality management systems are well established.

TEST FORMES AND COLOUR CONTROL STRIPS

Using a test forme, colour control strips and densitometric measurement are all essential elements of a systematic approach to colour control. A number of formes and colour test strips are now available for use in screen printing. Colour formes consist of a set of film positives, of neutral tone and full colour subjects, together with target areas for stencil and print control. These devices allow the printer to establish colour differences which can occur in stencil production and on the press and to establish appropriate parameters for the control of consistent quality in four colour process printing.

Colour test strips or bars are printed at the edge of four colour process work to provide a standard measure of variables such as dot loss and dot gain, trapping, slurring and register. Used in conjunction with the densitometer they enable accurate measurements to be made as to colour and tone density shifts from the film separations to the print, and throughout the duration of the print run.

Although the development of thermal imaged films like the CalComp EcoGrafix film are having an impact, the majority of film work is still silver based. In fact recent research shows that some 98% of origination for screen printing ends up in silver-based film positive form for contact exposure to the screen or stencil film (see Stewart Partridge, *The Impact of Non-impact and Other Competitive Pressures*, SPA (UK) Ltd, 1994). These positives are made in a number of ways.

Contact positives

Process camera origination

This is still used in the production of line work from flat artwork, black-and-white original copy. Many printers use diffusion transfer film for reasons of simplicity in processing.

Scanned positives

Most colour work is now produced electronically and output as screened film positives.

Image setters

Some positives are produced from high end image setters linked to desktop scanning systems.

However the positives are produced, they must conform to certain essential screen and stencil making requirements:

- They must be in positive form, i.e. a facsimile of the image that is to be produced.
- The image must be 'SS' (same size as the required reproduction).
- The image must be 'right reading' with the emulsion on the upper side of the film.
- Film planning should be undertaken to provide one piece, single films where possible; overlapping films should be avoided.
- All necessary production data should be on the positive – register targets, colour control strips, trims marks etc.

Environmental controls   The following conditions should be maintained in stencil-making areas:

- The areas should be kept at a temperature of 15–20°C. All stencil materials are influenced by changes in temperature.
- The atmospheric humidity should be carefully controlled. Ideally it should be maintained at 40–50% RH. Changes in humidity can seriously affect the photosensitivity of stencil materials.
- The lighting should be non-actinic, i.e. it should not contain any ultraviolet or blue-violet wavelengths of light. Yellow fluorescent lighting is recommended.
- Dust is an enemy that must be repelled on every front. All exposure and processing areas should be kept scrupulously clean. If at all possible a double-door entrance to stencil-making areas should be used, thus preventing any direct draughts from entering the areas. Airborne dust is one of the major causes of stencil pinholing, which can so often result in expensive retouching or stencil remakes.

It is very difficult and costly to eliminate all dust, but a considerable reduction in the instances of pinholing can be achieved by insisting on basic clean working methods:

- Keep all work surfaces clean.
- Clean the contact frame glass before each exposure.
- Check and clean all positives and film before exposure.

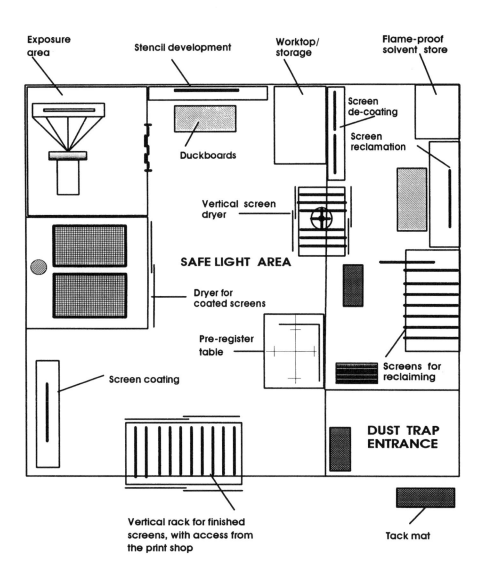

Fig. 42 Plan of screen processing facility.

- Rinse the underside of the screen prior to mounting indirect stencils.
- Mix emulsions with a plastic or glass mixing rod.
- Keep emulsion containers clean; dried emulsion at the lip of the container, or in the threaded lid, can so easily contaminate the emulsion and cause streaked coatings.
- Ensure that chemicals are stored correctly and that any spills are cleaned up immediately.
- Do not allow screen reclamation chemicals to come into contact with stencil materials. They should be used and stored in separate areas.

Exposure calculation   Each stencil material has its own sensitivity parameters and must be used according to the technical data supplied by the manufacturer. All stencil products are supplied with exposure guidelines, which form the basis for tests to be conducted under local conditions to ascertain the 'basic optimum exposure'.

Exposure guide: Autotype 'Five Star' Indirect Film (courtesy of Sericol Ltd)

Light source	Lamp/glass distance	Recommended exposure
1kW metal halide	120 cm (48 in)	8 minutes
2kW metal halide	120 cm (48 in)	4 minutes
5kW metal halide	120 cm (48 in)	2 minutes

When using a new material for the first time the light source is matched with the examples given in the above exposure guide, and a series of tests are carried out, matching local conditions with those in the guide. A simple way of conducting such a test is to make a stepped exposure.

CONDUCTING A STEPPED EXPOSURE TEST

A sample of the strip of stencil film, or a small coated screen, is placed in contact with a test positive – one that consists of fine line detail, small type matter and screen work, preferably of varying line counts. Special test positives and process colour formes can be purchased from suppliers. These contain very useful objective measures relating to loss and gain in line and tone.

To carry out a simple test strip exposure, a series of five separate exposures are made across the sample stencil film or screen coating, say in 50-second steps, giving a range of 50–250 seconds. The test is processed and carefully examined under magnification and with back illumination to assess resolution and thickness.

The thickness of the stencil will be indicated by its colour density,

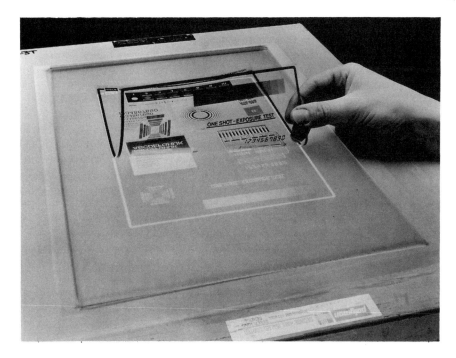

Fig. 43 Exposure test forme. (Courtesy of Coates Screen.)

which should increase with exposure time. Indirect films can be dried and their thickness measured with a micrometer: optimum thickness is 8–10 microns. Direct stencils will exhibit a colour change after exposure due to the bleaching out of the sensitizer, indicating that the coating has been exposed right through. At the point where the colour change stops, the coating is fully exposed. Any further exposure would simply reduce the stencil resolution by light undercutting the image (see Light geometry and light undercutting, below).

To assess the material fully the test should be printed. It is difficult to ascertain the precise print characteristics of a stencil simply by looking at it under magnification.

AUTOTYPE EXPOSURE CALCULATOR

The Autotype Exposure Calculator is an exposure test forme which allows five separate exposures to be made in one step. It contains five columns of type, each with a definition target above it. The first column is on a clear base and is given an exposure factor of 1.0. Behind each of the other four columns there is a neutral density filter which reduces the amount of light that reaches the test sample by factors of 0.7, 0.5, 0.3 or

0.25. Using the calculator it is therefore possible to ascertain five different exposure values with a single exposure.

To use the calculator:

1. First estimate the correct exposure time. Double this value to provide the exposure latitude required by the parameters of the calculator.
2. The sample stencil film or screen coating is then exposed in contact with the calculator and is processed and developed in the normal way.
3. Examine the developed stencil for optimum detail fidelity. If the estimated exposure is correct, the column below factor 0.5 should exhibit the best results. The actual exposure (double the estimated exposure) is multiplied by the factor at the top of the chosen column.

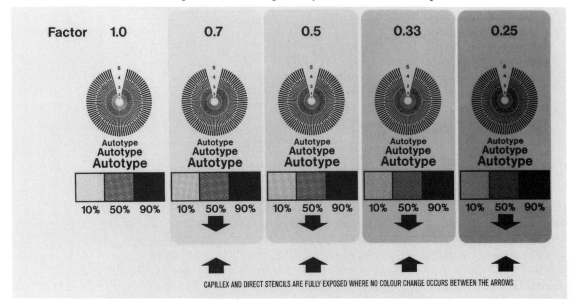

Fig. 44 The Autotype exposure calculator. (Courtesy of Autotype International Ltd.)

For example:

- If the exposure time is estimated as 4 minutes, the test sample is exposed to the calculator for 8 minutes.
- If the central column indicates the best results, the actual exposure of 8 minutes is multiplied by 0.5, giving an optimum exposure time of 4 minutes.
- If the column below factor 1.0 looks to be the best, the actual exposure time must be doubled to 16 minutes and the material re-tested.
- If on the other hand the factor 0.25 is the best, the actual exposure

is halved to 4 minutes and a second test made. As with the stepped exposure test, the final proof is in the print.

When stencils or screens are made using a free-standing lamp and printing-down frame, it may be necessary to change the lamp-to-contact-frame distance. In this case a few simple calculations are made to ensure that the optimum exposure is maintained. The first of these is the establishment of the minimum safe light distance (MSLD) to ensure evenness of illumination.

EVENNESS OF ILLUMINATION

When using free-standing equipment it is important to ensure that the stencil/screen is evenly illuminated during exposure. If the lamp is positioned too close to the contact frame it might produce a 'hot spot' in the centre of the stencil/screen and 'fall off' with the decreasing intensity of illumination at the edges. To ensure that there is evenness of illumination, the diagonal of the photostencil material is measured and the lamp distance is set at 1.5 times this dimension.

INVERSE SQUARE LAW

If the lamp distance is changed, a new exposure time must be established. The new exposure can be calculated by applying the inverse square law, which states that the intensity of illumination decreases in inverse proportion to the square of the distance. So if the lamp distance is doubled, the photostencil material will receive four times less light, therefore the exposure time must be increased four times to maintain the basic optimum exposure. If the distance is halved, the exposure time must be reduced to one quarter. The following formula is used to apply the inverse square law in practice.

$$NET = OET \times ND^2/OD^2$$

where NET = new exposure time; OET = original exposure time (basic optimum exposure time); ND = new distance; OD = original distance.

For example: if the basic optimum exposure time is 4 minutes at a lamp distance of 1 m (40 in) and the distance is increased to 1.5 m (60 in), the new exposure time would be calculated as follows.

OET = 4 minutes
ND = 1.5 m
OD = 1.0 m

$$NET = 4 \times 1.5^2/1.0^2 = 4 \times 2.25 = 9 \text{ minutes.}$$

LIGHT INTEGRATORS

Light integrators are used to measure the amount of light that is received by the photostencil material. They consist of a light sensor, usually placed on the contact frame, and a measuring device. The sensor receives the light from the exposure lamp and transmits it to the integrator, which can be set so that it will terminate the stencil exposure when the required level of illumination (usually measured in units of light) has been reached. The advantage of such a device is that once the optimum exposure has been established the integrator will automatically adjust the exposure time when the lamp distance is altered. Furthermore, the integrator will compensate for the gradual loss in output as the UV lamp ages and loses actinic intensity.

Light sources and contacting equipment

All photostencil materials are sensitive to the wavelengths of light that occur in the narrow band on the electromagnetic spectrum between 340 and 440 nm; that is, the region between the invisible ultraviolet and the visible blue-violet wavelengths. This radiation is present in the light from the sun, but it can also be produced artificially by electrical discharge.

The light sources that are used in photostencil making are gas discharge lamps. They operate by generating the required wavelengths of actinic light from a discharge of high voltage electricity in the presence of a gas. The most widely used lamps are the high pressure reflux (HPR) mercury vapour lamp and the metal halide lamp; other lamps such as pulsed xenon and blue fluorescent tubes are rarely used. Fluorescent UV units are popular in the USA and may be used for post-hardening polymer emulsions.

THE HIGH PRESSURE MERCURY VAPOUR LAMP

The HPR lamp consists of a glass envelope with a built-in reflector. It contains mercury which is vaporized and ionized when the lamp is switched on. The lamp produces a discontinuous line emission with peaks in the ultraviolet and blue-violet regions. However, the output of the lamp is relatively low, making it suitable only for small format stencils. If larger work is undertaken a number of lamps must be used; this unfortunately produces poor light geometry, causing image undercutting.

HPR lamps have a normal running life of about 1000–1500 hours, after which their spectral output in the UV region tends to fall off. When the lamps have been switched off the mercury has to condense before they will relight. They are usually found in 'fixed distance' contact frame units, the lamps being an integral part of the contact unit.

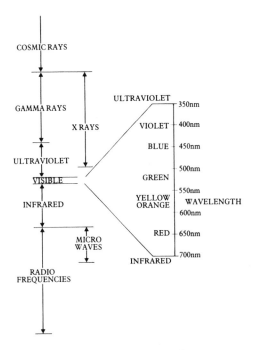

Fig. 45   The electromagnetic spectrum. (Courtesy of Autotype International Ltd.)

THE METAL HALIDE LAMP

This is the most widely used light source in the printing industry for photomechanical operations. It is a development of the mercury lamp and consists of a quartz envelope containing mercury with the addition of metal halide. When the lamp is switched on the surge of high voltage electricity causes the mercury to vaporize, and the metal halide additives serve to intensify the radiation in the actinic wavelengths. This lamp has several advantages over other light sources:

- The lamp has a very high output – 5 kW lamps are available for large format work.
- The lamp provides a single point source, causing very little under-cutting.
- Most lamps are designed to restart almost instantly and are therefore switched on and off for each exposure; earlier lamps were shuttered and ran continuously on half power between exposures. The average life of a metal halide lamp is 1000 hours.

Health and Safety Note:

The ultraviolet emissions from exposure lamps can cause serious damage to the retina. On no account should they be looked into when they are switched on. To prevent accidental exposure to their potentially hazardous UV emissions, it is good practice to have the lamps screened when they are in operation. Some units have automated UV screening which operates when the lamps are switched on.

Light geometry and light undercutting

When a photostencil is made by contact exposure an opaque image is copied by casting its shadow on to a photosensitive material. If the light rays that are used to cast this shadow are not parallel they will produce an ill-defined shadow of the positive image. This happens because some of the light rays spread around the edges of the image, causing what is commonly called 'light undercutting'.

The effect can be easily demonstrated by casting a shadow with an electric torch beam: the closer the torch is moved to the object, the softer and more diffuse the shadow becomes. This occurs because the relative size of the light source increases in relation to the object as the distance between the two decreases. The larger the surface of the light source, the more acute will be the angle of the incident rays to the surface of the object. If the light source is moved away from the object the shadows become more sharply defined and the angle of the incident rays less acute. This distance is called the minimum safe light distance (MSLD); it is the distance at which the light source will give the maximum amount of illumination with the minimum degree of undercut.

In general printing work the effect of light undercutting would go unnoticed, but in fine line and half-tone printing it can pose a serious problem. It is generally most apparent with indirect films. The typical 0.05 mm (0.002 in) film base which comes between the positive and the photosensitive coating causes the incident rays to refract, thus adversely affecting light geometry. The use of multiple point light sources has the same effect as increasing the surface area of the light source.

Light undercutting can also be caused by inadequate vacuum contact between the positive and the photostencil material. For this reason it is essential that the contacting equipment is correctly designed for photostencil work, especially if it involves the exposure of direct stencils. There are various designs available, but they can usefully be described under two headings:

- Self-contained exposure units.
- Free-standing printing down frames and light sources.

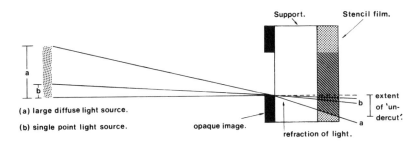

Fig. 46 Light undercutting.

SELF-CONTAINED CONTACT EXPOSURE UNITS

These consist of a vacuum contact frame with an in-built, fixed-distance, light source. Some models have the light source mounted above the contact frame; in others it is mounted beneath. Most units are fitted with 800–5000 W metal halide lamps. Originally designed for use with indirect photostencil films, they are now commonly used for direct stencil work. In order to accommodate large frames they must be fitted with a 'deep draw', flexible contact blanket, which should also permit the rapid release of vacuum pressure. Some units have integrated timers, linked to a shutter or to the lamp; others have light integrators which measure the amount of light received by the photostencil material.

The main advantage of this kind of equipment is that it saves space. Many of the models also contain safe-lamp illumination as well as fluorescent tubes, so that they may be used for retouching purposes as well as for stencil making.

FREE-STANDING CONTACT EXPOSURE FRAMES

These are designed for large format direct stencil work. They consist of a toughened plate contact glass with a deep frame contact blanket. The blanket must be made of a specially flexible rubber to allow for the deformation caused by the screen frame when the contact pressure is applied. Vacuum contact is provided by an electric vacuum pump which draws air out from between the glass and the blanket. Most frames are now fitted with a fabric-backed blanket which facilitates rapid contact and vacuum release.

The whole assembly is mounted on hinges so that it can be locked in the horizontal position for screen loading and then swung into the vertical position for exposing. These units are supported on heavy-duty castors so that they can be moved easily.

Developments in screen making technology

Recent developments in screen making technology have focused around three new systems, two of which involve computer imaging directly on to the coated screen, whilst the third provides a kind of half-way house between contact exposure and direct-to-screen.

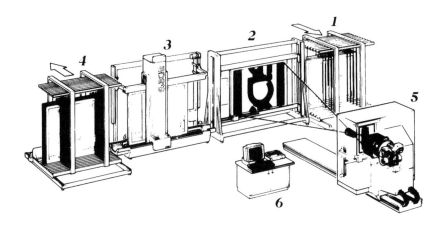

Fig. 47 Svecia direct projection screen making system. (Courtesy of Screen Process – Batiste Publications Ltd.)
1. Cassette for coated screens; 2. Screen projection carriage; 3. Screen development unit; 4. Screen drying unit; 5. Projection camera; 6. Computer control unit.

SCREEN-MAKING BY IMAGE PROJECTION

This relatively new method of screen making was alluded to earlier (see Chapter 4, Direct emulsion photostencils: Photopolymer emulsions). It has been developed for use in the production of large format vehicle livery, sign and display, and multisheet posters, and where the costs of silver-based film and chemistry form an important element in the costing of work and half-tone screen work does not exceed 20 lines/cm (50 lines/in).

The projection system allows large format screens to be exposed from a small original film positive (maximum A3). There are several systems available, ranging from basic fixed magnification units, currently costing around £70 000, to the larger computer-controlled systems with magnification of 4–12× and costing as much as £300 000. Special systems can be manufactured providing magnification of 20–30×.

The Svecia projection unit is a good example of the technology. It consists of a special camera with a highly sophisticated lens system, capable of sharply focusing the point light source, provided by a 2 kW microwave UV lamp. The lamp has no electrodes and has, it is claimed, an estimated life of up to 100 000 exposures. The system is fully automated and computer driven, with screens automatically loaded into position for exposure from a cassette where up to ten coated frames can be stored ready for projection. The computer allows the operator to programme all the job parameters for multisheet work. Once programmed the whole process of screen loading, image location, exposure, development and drying is undertaken automatically, leaving the operator to work on the next job.

There are clearly a number of advantages which can be claimed for direct projection. Here are some of the major benefits claimed by the manufacturers:

- The system saves expensive film and chemistry costs.
- Labour costs are considerably reduced with automation of screen handling, image planning and screen development.
- Space is saved, since the projection camera performs the function of the camera and contact frame.
- Film storage is also more economically managed, with positives stored in A3 files, instead of large format plan chests or film files.
- Variations in film processing which cause colour balance changes across multisheet work are eliminated, since the screens are made from one positive with computer-controlled exposure.
- Screen remakes can be effected quickly and accurately, since all the relevant data is stored by the computer and can be accessed with a single command.
- The size of image is no longer limited by the size of film. Svecia has manufactured a projection system and printing press to accommodate a print area of 2 × 4 m.

INKJET DIRECT-TO-SCREEN IMAGING

The ScreenJet system developed by Gerber Scientific Products utilizes the novel concept of printing an opaque positive image directly on to the emulsion-coated screen, using an inkjet printer. The printed image performs the function of a film positive, and once imaged the screen is simply exposed to a UV light source. There is no need for a contact frame, because the printed image is in perfect contact with the screen coating. The stencil is developed in the normal way and the printed positive image dissolves with the unexposed emulsion.

This allows an image to be directly imaged on to a screen from digital data. The system will accept PostScript files from Mac or PC. As this is the standard page description language adopted by the printing industry, the ScreenJet will be able to handle most text and graphic files. This means that artwork can be received in digital format on disk or via ISDN or a modem link. It can then be enlarged or reduced, manipulated, colour separated and proofed before the screens are made. The printer can therefore work more efficiently through more direct communication with the designer and/or the client.

Of course the system does have limitations. As yet line resolution is limited to 300 dpi. This is perfectly adequate for certain screen printing applications, such as garment and fashion piece goods. However, the quality of inkjet printing is improving all the time and therefore the market

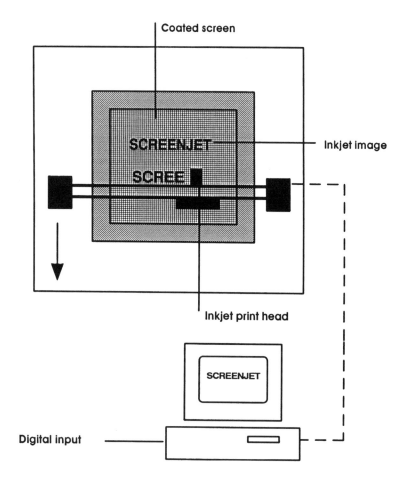

Fig. 48 ScreenJet direct-to-screen inkjet imaging system.

for the system may broaden in the future. The maximum format for the machine currently supplied is 66×960 cm (26×38 in). Gerber claims that output rates can reach 30–40 screens per hour, depending on the extent of solid areas of the image, which of course take longer to print.

DIRECT-TO-SCREEN LASER IMAGING

The concept of laser imaging in screen printing is not new. Lasers have been used to produce engraved rotary screens for textile printing for some years. Direct-to-plate systems in offset-litho have also been around for some time. However, the concept of direct imaging with a laser on to an emulsion coated screen is new.

Two systems are currently available: the Mesac In.sor 80 and the Mografo DISE 3. Both systems were developed for the textile industry, where large format volume screen making (commonly 6–12 colours per design) is required.

The DISE 3 system consists of a powerful 500 mW argon-ion laser which moves across the screen exposing the coating in bands of 370 mm wide. The precision optics and computer control ensures that each image band is exposed in perfect register. The system is produced with two levels of image resolution.

Like the ScreenJet, the Mografo system is PostScript compatible, accepting any Adobe .EPS or .PS file. It will operate within most of the standard design programme formats, such as Aldus FreeHand, Adobe Illustrator, Adobe PhotoShop and Quark Xpress, generated on either Mac or PC platforms. Links from the front end system to the DISE 3 RIP (raster image processer), which receives the incoming image data and converts it into the laser image, can be via Apple Talk, Ether Talk, TCP/IP networks or by Centronix parallel connection.

The main advantage of the direct-to-screen systems is that they are filmless. The DISE 3 system is capable of producing a maximum image size of 130 cm $\times$ 185 cm. Mografo claims that exposure times are typically 5–10 min/m^2. By contact exposure standards this is slow, but one has to consider the savings that are made in origination and screen/film handling. With direct to screen there are no films – only the screen, the computer and the image setter.

At present these systems are used mainly in the field of printed textiles,

Mografo DISE 3 image setter

System	Resolution	Screen ruling
A	40 mic., 635 dpi	20 lines/cm, 50lines/in
B	20 mic., 1270 dpi	40lines/cm, 100lines/in

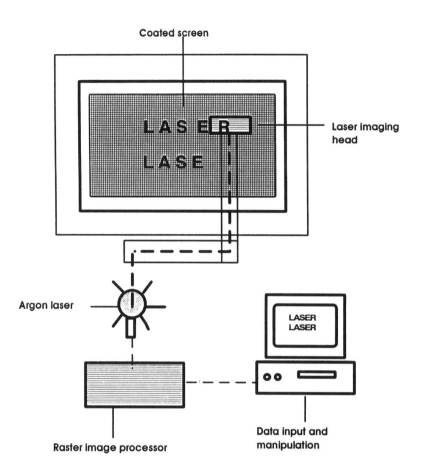

Coated screen

Laser imaging
head

Argon laser

LASER
LASER

Raster image processor

Data input and
manipulation

Fig. 49 The Mografo DISE 3 direct-to-screen laser imaging system.

where the turnover of screens is high and the print definition is less critical
than in other applications, such as graphics. One of the current limitations
with laser imaging is that the lasers used are simply not powerful enough
to expose the relatively thick emulsion coatings or capillary films used in
some of the more demanding applications, such as in PCB and membrane
switch printing and in CD printing.

However, developments in electronic imaging technology are moving
at what seems like an ever increasing pace, and it can be predicted that
by the end of the decade, with developments in emulsion chemistry, ink
systems and imaging technology, we shall see laser screen making on a

much broader scale. From the design management point of view, electronic imaging and communications are just so much more convenient than working in what has already become an antiquated and inefficient way. Recent research (Stewart Partridge, *The Impact of Non-impact and Other Competitive Pressures*, SPA (UK) Ltd) indicates that some 40% of graphic printers receive work in digital format.

Whilst this may not be entirely representative of the whole industry, it is a trend which may well be mirrored in many other sectors. In the printed textiles and industrial sectors (especially in electronics, where CAD has been widely used for several years) the proportion will be much higher. Of one thing we can be sure: electronic imaging is here to stay!

6 Printing machinery and equipment

Screen printing has developed a long way since its emergence as a commercial and industrial process in the 1950s. Even today it is still carried out in a craft context in some small companies, especially those producing small runs of specialist graphics and limited edition fine art printing. Many of those who now operate the latest fully automatic presses will have had at least some experience of hand-bench operation. It is therefore quite proper that this chapter should begin by looking at the hand printing table, the principles of which are embodied in many of the modern screen presses in use today.

Hand-bench printing equipment

The design of the hand-bench can vary considerably from one manufacturer to another. However, most will provide the following basic functional requirements:

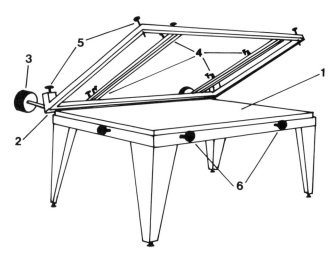

Fig. 50 Hand-bench printing table (see overleaf).

1. a flat printing base with a vacuum suction facility;
2. a hinge assembly;
3. a frame counterbalance system;
4. a frame clamping system;
5. front and rear 'off-contact' adjustment;
6. register adjustment.

Flat printing base

This is usually made in a rigid box construction. It must have a very flat and true surface, as any deformation will show in printing. The surface is usually a plastic laminate, although aluminium bases are sometimes used. The printing area will be drilled at 2–3 cm intervals to allow for the vacuum suction, which controls the stock during printing. The vacuum motor draws air from beneath the table. The printing bed is a box construction with a honeycomb inner structure which provides the necessary rigidity and strength whilst acting as an air baffle to give an even distribution of suction over the printing area. The vacuum is either operated by a foot pedal switch or is integrated with the hinge assembly and comes into operation as the screen frame is lowered for printing.

Hinge assembly

This must be of very robust construction, since any play at the point where the screen frame is hinged to the printing base will cause variation in print register.

Frame counterbalance

On most printing tables the counterbalance is provided by adjustable weights, situated at the rear of the table, in counterpoise to the screen frame. On some tables the hinge gear is countersprung to allow the screen frame to remain in the raised position.

Frame clamping system

Many tables are now fitted with rapid-action cantilever toggle clamps. Some tables have threaded toggle clamps. The advantages of these forms of frame clamping are that they are capable of accommodating various frame sections, and are very simple and quick to operate.

Off-contact adjustment

The distance between the underside of the screen and the printing surface is commonly known as the 'off-contact' or 'snap' distance. Its adjustment is critical to print quality control, since it influences the rate at which the print is released from the screen. It can also contribute to screen/stencil distortion, resulting in differential image distortion and intercolour misregister.

The adjustment is often positioned at the rear of the table, as an integral part of the hinge assembly. At the front of the table the height of the screen frame is usually adjusted at each corner.

Register adjustment

Most hand-bench printing tables are fitted with one of two types of register adjustment. Adjustment to the position of the print on the stock can be made by either moving the stock in relation to the screen or vice versa. The first method involves the movement of the printing base. Many tables are fitted with a 'floating bed' register adjustment, which allows the printing base to move in four directions: front to back and side to side. The second method involves moving the screen frame; this is usually effected by adjustments made to the hinge assembly which allows the whole screen carriage to move in four directions.

ONE-ARM SQUEEGEE BEAM ASSEMBLY

On large format printing tables (Quad Crown and larger) it is common to have a one-arm squeegee device fitted. This enables the operator to print very large areas literally single-handed.

The squeegee is fitted into a clamp that locks on to a laterally moving arm or beam. The arm runs on ball races along a steel bar at the rear of the table which is attached to the hinge gear at either end.

Adjustments can be made to the squeegee clamp so that the angle of attack can be set for both the printing stroke and the ink-return flo-coat. The squeegee arm is counterbalanced with a weight so that very little pressure is required to carry out even the widest printing stroke.

VERTICAL FRAME-LIFT TABLES

One of the disadvantages of the conventional hinged frame principle is that there is a tendency for the ink to flow to the rear of the screen every time the screen frame is raised. This problem has been overcome by the introduction of tables like the KPX Paraprint. Here the screen carriage is raised in a horizontal attitude by a cantilevered hinge assembly. The hinge gear is very robustly engineered and the positive frame location at the front of the table ensures the precise closure of the screen frame at each operation.

Such machines are particularly useful in the production of large format work, where large areas of solid colour are being put down. Because the frame remains in a horizontal position, the ink also remains in the printing plane. This makes for more efficient operation, since the operator can work with greater continuity. Rather than frequently interrupting the printing cycle to scrape ink from the rear of the screen, the only stoppage necessary is to add more ink when it is required. These tables are also useful for printing controlled blends where inks are mixed together in bands on the screen to create a smooth and delicate gradation or vignette of tone or colour.

Screen printing machines

One of the first fully mechanized screen printing machines was the McCormick machine, which appeared in 1948 (an example of this machine can be seen at the Science Museum, Exhibition Road, London). The early machines were very simple in design. By modern standards they appear slow, cumbersome and labour intensive.

The range of machinery now available, in both design and format, clearly reflects the growth and diversity of screen printing. Whilst it is impossible to describe all the various innovations in press design, most machines conform to one of the following design principles:

- Flat-bed hinged frame
- Flat-bed vertical lift
- Cylinder-bed presses
- Container printing machines
- Rotary screen
- Carousel machines.

FLAT-BED HINGED FRAME

This machine design is based upon the principle of the hand-bench. The early machines were hardly more than mechanized hand-benches. The screen opens and closes with a mechanism that is synchronized with a mechanically driven squeegee and flo-coater carriage.

On most machines the ink is returned to the preprint position by a metal scraper blade, technically referred to as a flo-coater, which is positioned directly behind the squeegee. The angle and the pressure of the squeegee and flo-coater can be adjusted to suit the exact inking requirements of the job. Once these two instruments have been set they will continue to give consistent inking throughout the run. Consistency is one of the primary advantages of machine printing; the other advantage is speed.

The printing cycle begins with the screen open so that the printing stock can be fed into the 'lay stops' – three fixed guides on the printing base which control the precise placement of the stock. The screen closes and the squeegee begins its printing stroke, forcing the ink through the screen and on to the stock beneath. At the end of the stroke the squeegee lifts and the flo-coater drops into contact with the screen. As the screen opens the flo-coater draws the ink back across the screen, ready for the next printing sequence. The printed stock is then delivered to the dryer and the whole cycle begins again.

Machines designed on this principle are mostly semi-automatic: the screen and squeegee action is mechanized, but the stock is manually manipulated. There are some ¾ automatic machines,which have delivery systems to transport the printed stock to the dryer, leaving the operator free to feed sheets into the lay stops. Some machines can also be fitted with automatic sheet-feeding devices, or in some cases they will print from reeled material, though web-fed presses are not common.

The speed of a semi-automatic machine is largely determined by the skill of the operator, but speeds of 300 copies per hour (cph) are not uncommon; with an automatic 'take-off' this can be increased to 1200 cph. A fully automatic machine operates at 2000 cph. Machines are available in a wide range of formats and sizes; they can be as small as the precision thick film circuit press with a print area of 390×510 mm (15×20 in) or as big as the monster machines with print areas of 2000×3000 mm (79×118 in).

FLAT-BED VERTICAL LIFT

Here the screen lifts vertically from the printing base and remains in the horizontal attitude throughout the printing cycle. This gives more efficient ink control and a faster printing cycle, since the screen lifts only some 3 mm to allow the feeding of the stock.

The most basic machine features a reciprocating printing base.This slides from beneath the screen to receive the stock, back again for printing and out again for print delivery. The ¾ automatic version has a stationary printing base. The stock is picked up by grippers from a pre-register table at the front of the machine. It is taken beneath the screen and held in position on the printing base during the printing sequence. After printing, it is transferred to a delivery belt at the rear of the machine, and thence to the dryer. The advantage of the pre-register system is that the speed of the machine is no longer limited by the speed of the operator, since the stock is fed into lay while the printing sequence is taking place. With the addition of an automatic feeder this machine can be very easily converted to fully automatic operation.

The maximum speed of the semi-automatic is in the region of 1000 cph; a ¾ automatic will reach 1700 cph; and the fully automatic, 2500 cph. These machines are made in a wide range of sizes and formats,

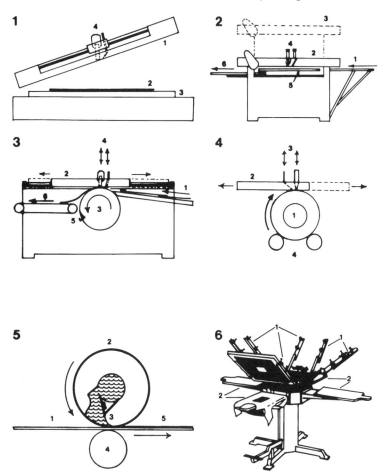

Fig. 51 Screen printing machinery.
1. Flat-bed hinged frame
   1.1 Screen frame carriage
   1.2 Printing stock
   1.3 Vacuum base
   1.4 Squeegee/flo-coater carriage
2. Flat-bed vertical lift
   2.1 Feed
   2.2 Screen frame carriage
   2.3 Screen frame carriage fully elevated
   2.4 Squeegee/flo-coater carriage
   2.5 Vacuum base
   2.6 Delivery
3. Cylinder-bed presses
   3.1 Feed
   3.2 Screen frame carriage
   3.3 Vacuum cylinder
   3.4 Squeegee/flo-coater assembly

   3.5 Gripper
   3.6 Delivery conveyer
4. Container printing machines
   4.1 Container
   4.2 Screen frame carriage
   4.3 Squeegee/flo-coater assembly
   4.4 Supporting rig
5. Rotary screen printing machines
   5.1 Web feed
   5.2 Rotating cylindrical screen
   5.3 Squeegee blade
   5.4 Web support cylinder
   5.5 Printed material
6. Carousel machines
   6.1 Rotational screen frame carriage
   6.2 Rotational printing platens.

with print areas as small as 400×600 mm ($15\frac{3}{4} \times 23\frac{5}{8}$ in) or as big as 2000×4000 mm ($79 \times 157\frac{1}{2}$ in).

CYLINDER-BED PRESSES

An entirely different concept in press design, the cylinder machine consists of a perforated vacuum printing drum which carries the stock beneath a reciprocating screen. The squeegee and flo-coater remain stationary.

The printing stock is fed by tapes into the pre-register position. The printing cylinder rotates to a position where its grippers open to accept the leading edge of the stock. The vacuum suction of the printing cylinder holds the stock in contact while it is printed. As the cylinder rotates under the screen, the screen moves through its print cycle, with the squeegee forcing the ink through on to the stock beneath. At the end of the print sequence the printed sheet is released by the grippers on to a delivery belt. The cylinder then returns to pick up the next sheet as the screen moves back to the preprint position.

Although the cylinder-bed press can be supplied as a ¾ automatic, it is generally configured with an automatic sheet feeder as part of a fully automated print line; in some situations it can be configured to form part of a multi-unit line of two or more in-line print units. A facility for automatic screen changing may also be fitted. The devices allows pin-registered screens to be loaded into a cassette screen carriage at the rear of the press. When the first two colours are complete, the screens are automatically removed and replaced by the new screens from the cassette. Because the screens are pre-registered with a pin-register device, colour changes can be effected with minimum adjustment. This can reduce down-time between colour changes to less than two minutes.

The latest machines can achieve speeds of 6000 cph, although an average speed of 3500 cph is more common in practice. The machines are limited to printing on stock which is flexible enough to conform to the printing cylinder – paper and board with a maximum weight of 600 g/m^2. There are machines which have a large curved printing 'sector' rather than a cylinder, and these are designed to cope with heavier and more rigid printing stock, e.g. paper and board up to 800 g/m^2. Cylinder-bed machines are available in sizes ranging from 550×750 mm (22×30 in) to 1200×1600 mm (48×64 in); and sector-bed machines in sizes from 400×600 mm (16×24 in) to 750×1050 mm (30×42 in).

CONTAINER PRINTING MACHINES

These machines are designed on the cylinder-bed principle. The curved surface of the printing cylinder is replaced by the curved surface of the container, which is supported from beneath on roller bearings. The printing action is exactly the same as on the cylinder press; the screen reciprocates over the rotating container while the stationary squeegee forces the ink through the screen. The machines are often integrated into the container-making and filling process, though some preprinted containers are still produced by specialist printers. The machines are made in a range of sizes to print the smallest perfume container or large oil drums. They are designed to accommodate adjustable container support rigs which allow for a wide range of shapes and sizes to be handled. Special rigs and screens can be made to accommodate specific contour and print formats.

ROTARY SCREEN

Rotary screen printing machines are used mainly in the production of high volume textiles, floor and wall coverings, coated vinyls and in label printing. The functional principles are very unlike those of conventional screen printing. Here the screen is in the form of a seamless perforated cylinder, made from a light metal foil, given strength and rigidity by the two metal tension rings that are fitted at each end. The squeegee is hollow, allowing ink to be pumped directly through it to the screen. As the screen rotates around the stationary blade, the printing medium is forced through the screen openings on to the moving web beneath.

Rotary screens are made in various grades, rather like conventional screen fabric. Generally speaking the lower the mesh count the thicker the gauge. For example, 100 mesh foil has a normal gauge of 0.09 mm (0.004 in), whereas a 17 mesh has 0.23 mm (0.009 in) gauge. By varying the mesh count it is therefore possible to vary the thickness of the medium deposited on the substrate. However, the main control in this respect is achieved by adjustment of the squeegee pressure on the press.

The stencil coating will also have an influence on medium deposit. Stencils are formed in the screens by direct photo-emulsion methods and by direct laser engraving. The photo-emulsion procedure is similar in principle to conventional direct stencil making but requires specialized coating and exposing techniques. The screen making process also requires specialized plant. Laser engraving is carried out using high energy CO_2 lasers which can only be used with metal screens.

The machines are made in a range of standard sizes, governed largely by standard substrate widths. The standard print width can vary from 600 mm (24 in) to 2600 mm (104 in). The circumference of the screen governs the length of the print repeat, which varies from 537 mm (23 in) to 1000 mm (40 in). The machines usually form part of a substantial plant investment and are designed and built to the customer's specifications.

CAROUSEL MACHINES

Based upon the hinged frame principle, these machines were originally designed for multicolour printing on to T-shirts and sportswear. They consist of multiple printing bases or 'garment platens' which can be rotated on a central pivot – hence the name 'carousel'. Above each platen is a printing head (also rotational) consisting of a hinged frame carriage, squeegee and flo-coater, the latter being mechanically driven on the more sophisticated automatic machines.

The printing cycle begins with a garment being slid over the platen. The first screen is then positioned over the platen for printing. After the first colour has been printed, the second screen is brought into register over the platen. The process is continued until all the colours have been printed. The garment is then removed from the platen for drying, usually by infra-red radiation.

Automation in garment printing

Automation in garment printing has spawned a wide range of highly sophisticated machine designs, with computerized control systems and precision register adjustment. There are three main design principles in common use.

Carousel machines

These are based upon a rotational principle similar to that described above, with garment platens rotating beneath fixed printing stations. Machines like the MHM and the M&R operate on this principle and can be configured with between 4 and 12 print stations, with infra-red flash curing and cooling units strategically positioned within the system.

The oval principle

Oval machines have the garment platens configured around an extended oval, with the print stations arranged in parallel along one or both sides of the oval. Like the MHM and M&R, these machines also have in-line infra-red flash curing and cooling units. This format of machine is exceedingly fast and is considered as the workhorse of the garment printing industry. Some very ingenious garment platens have been developed with a facility to accommodate all-over printing by allowing the garment platen to be 'flipped' over for printing on the back of the shirt.

This clever innovation allows both sides of a garment to be printed whilst it remains in place on the platen, thus providing precision control over registration.

M&R are currently developing a new generation of oval format garment machines, which will take garment printing into the next century, with increased control over registration, inking and flash curing.

The belt printer

This has been developed from flat-bed textile printing machinery. The machines consist of a long, flat printing bed, over which a full-width continuous neoprene belt is moved. The belt has an adhesive coating which allows the garment, or textile piece, to be held down for printing. The print stations (as many as eight screens) are arrange along the belt. In operation, the substrate is laid onto the belt and smoothed down so that it adheres. Precise lay position is achieved by aligning the substrate within a set of laser guide beams, directed down on to the belt. Alternatively, overhead projection may be used to gain lay position on the belt. The belt then advances the substrate under the first screen. Whilst this is being printed the next item is placed onto the belt. This is then advanced to the first print station, whilst the item just printed is advanced to the second print station, and so on. When all colours have been printed the item is transferred to the dryer and dried with either infra-red radiation or gas jet.

COMPUTER CONTROL

At the DRUPA 95 exhibition a number of machine manufacturers featured modular, computer controlled (CPC) screen presses on their stands. The CPC facility allows every operational function on the press to be controlled by computer. The press can be pre-set with job specific production parameters and these can be saved to disc for automated set-up on repeat runs. The modular design concept allows the printer to add units to the press, extending the line with four colour plus UV varnishing if required. Such innovation further exemplifies the dynamics of technology which is advancing the industry in line with the revolution in information technology.

7 Inks and solvents

Screen printing remains the most versatile of the printing processes. This is because of its ability to print on to an ever wider range of substrates and surfaces.

Of course to do this there has to be a range of inks to match the range of substrates. To give an indication of the scale, one major supplier lists over 50 different types of printing medium and at least half as many types of solvents and additives – and this does not include inks for ceramics and glass, thick film circuit printing or reactive textile dyes.

It is obviously impossible to deal here with every type of ink and medium available. However, the basic constituents which go into making screen printing ink will be described, also the main classes of ink and solvent types that are in current use in graphic screen printing. Other major classes of ink are considered in Chapter 12.

General properties

Screen printing inks are carefully formulated to conform to certain printing and finish specifications.

PRINTABILITY

Firstly an ink must be liquid enough to pass through the screen mesh without blocking or clogging up the small mesh openings.

RHEOLOGY

An ink must have specific flow and deformation properties which allow it to pass through the screen freely and then to form a solid film on the surface of the substrate. If an ink is too stiff it may not flow out enough after printing, leaving clearly visible mesh marks on the surface of the dried film. Early examples of screen printing exhibit this fault. On the other hand, if the ink flows too freely it may lack the necessary cohesion to form a firmly structured film on the substrate. Ink which lacks body will tend to 'bleed' at the edges of the film – this effect increases with the absorbency of the stock.

ADHESION

The ink must be capable of adhering firmly and permanently to the substrate. One of the reasons why there are so many different kinds of ink is that many surfaces, especially those made from certain types of plastic, will not readily accept conventional paper and board inks. These 'difficult' substrates usually require an ink which is formulated to bond physically and chemically to the surface.

DRYING

The ink must form a dry film after it reaches the substrate. Most inks are required to dry rapidly on the substrate whilst remaining stable (liquid) on the screen.

FINISH

The ink must provide the required finish characteristics. Depending on the formulation it may have a matt, semi-gloss or high gloss finish. The dry film must be resistant to scratching and scuffing. It should also be capable of receiving subsequent printings and finishing processes without crazing, cracking or peeling.

COLOUR

The pigment must provide richly saturated, 'clean' colours with good light and weather resistance. Inks formulated on single pigment colouration provide the cleanest (least degradated) colours. The colours should also be intermixable without loss of brilliance.

TOXICITY

The ink must conform to the current health and safety regulations. All inks must be clearly labelled and any hazardous substances contained in them must be clearly indicated on the label. There are strict EU and UK statutory regulations restricting the use of certain solvents and resin materials in printing inks. The use of lead and chrome-based pigments is also restricted, especially in inks that are used for food packaging, toy decoration and graphics instruments. All screen printing inks that are used for these purposes must be formulated and manufactured in accordance with the current statutory health and safety regulations. Ink suppliers will advise on the suitability of a particular ink range. It is the responsibility of the printer to check that an ink is suitable for the application it is used for.

Basic constituents of screen ink

Most conventional solvent-based screen printing inks contain pigment, vehicle, solvent, dryer, extender and modifier.

PIGMENT

This provides the colour and, in some cases, the opacity in the ink. Pigments are derived from organic and inorganic sources. Organic pigments are chosen for their inherent stability. Inorganic pigments are less costly and produce well saturated opaque colours. It is worth pointing out that the pigment in an ink is generally by far the most costly element in the formulation.

VEHICLE

This provides cohesion in the ink. It acts as a binder for the pigment, allowing it to be transferred through the screen on to the substrate. The vehicle also provides the adhesive properties in the ink, fixing the pigment to the printing surface. It consists of a viscous varnish-like medium which will reduce in a solvent and then form a solid, tough, flexible film when it dries. Many types of resin are used in the manufacture of screen printing ink; their selection is determined largely by the substrate type and finish requirements. For example, an ink that is used for paper and board may be formulated on an EHEC (ethyl hydroxyethyl cellulose) resin, whereas an ink for printing on to vinyl or acrylic materials will contain a vinyl/acrylic resin system. Special resin formulations which can be chemically cross-linked (cured) by exposure to ultraviolet light are used in the manufacture of UV-cured inks. Water-reducible polyester acrylates are used in the formulation of water-based UV systems.

SOLVENT

The majority of conventional screen printing inks dry by solvent evaporation. Solvents are usually added to an ink in complex mixtures, depending on their function and the properties they may impart. Often a solvent will be used for a particular function – for example, to improve the flow properties of the ink. However, its use may present drying problems because the reaction of the solvent with the resin system might inhibit solvent evaporation. It may therefore be necessary to add an additional solvent to the mixture to modify the adverse properties by increasing the evaporation rate. On the other hand, if a solvent with a high evaporation rate is used in an ink without any modification, the ink might dry very quickly on the substrate, but may also dry on the screen, rapidly causing it to block up and thus preventing continuous production.

Solvents are used to dissolve or 'cut' the resin components in the ink, so that they may be more easily mixed with the other ingredients. They are also used as diluents to reduce the ink's viscosity. In some inks they promote adhesion, as in the case of vinyl inks, where the solvent dissolves the surface of the substrate, allowing the ink to form a strong adhesive bond.

DRYERS

These consist of a combination of metallic salts: calcium, lead and cobalt. They are added to inks which dry by oxidation. Most of these inks are based upon alkyd resins which will form a very tough, flexible, durable film when they dry. Drying normally takes 6–8 hours at ambient temperatures. The drying process can be accelerated by stoving (drying in an oven) at 80–120°C (176–248°F) for 5–15 minutes.

EXTENDER

This is used to increase the solid content of the ink and improve its rheological properties. As mentioned before, the pigment solids in an ink are its most costly component. By adding an inert, colourless solid, such as calcium carbonate to the ink it is possible to increase its bulk without adversely affecting its printing characteristics. The extender may also increase the opacity of the ink. In addition there are extenders which can be used in transparent inks to increase their bulk value without affecting their ability to transmit light.

MODIFIER

This term is used for a whole range of additives that may be introduced into the ink to improve its press performance and finish qualities. Some screen inks, such as those that are based upon alkyd, vinyl or epoxy resins, tend to produce excessive bubbling during printing. This happens because air is introduced into the ink as it is pushed back and forth across the screen. Ordinarily the bubbles burst as the ink sheers away from the screen and the ink film flows out to form a flat, smooth surface. However, in some inks these bubbles are slow to disperse, resulting in a mottled, uneven surface to the ink film.

The problem can usually be eliminated by the addition of a flow agent, such as silicone. This lowers the surface tension of the ink and allows the entrapped air to escape before the ink film sets.

Anti-settle additives are introduced into inks containing heavy pigments and extenders. The additives prevent the heavy solids from settling out of suspension and migrating to the bottom of the ink can. Their addition improves the shelf-life of an ink.

Wax pastes are added to screen printing inks to improve scuff resistance. However, as with all modifiers, these must be added in correct proportions. Incorrect additions can lead to a reduction in sheen or gloss levels and loss of intercoat adhesion, colour on colour.

Plasticizers are added to certain inks to improve the flexibility of the dried ink film. They form an important component in the formulation of plastisol inks used in garment printing and inks used for transfers and decals, especially the dry or 'rub down' variety where the requirement is for the ink film to resist the excessive physical stressing which occurs during the transfer process.

Again, care is taken in the selection of plasticizers as they can create adhesion problems through delayed migration, leading to ink-film embrittlement (ink-film cracking) and intercoat adhesion failure, which may not manifest itself until some time after printing.

Inks for graphic screen printing

LONG OIL ALKYD INKS

These inks have replaced the old oil-based gloss inks. The alkyd resins on which they are based provide the high-build gloss finish, flexibility, and excellent durability associated with the older inks. Alkyd-based inks are soluble in white spirit and can generally be reduced (thinned) by 5–15%. They dry principally by oxidation, within 6–8 hours. When printed on to metal surfaces they may be stoved at between 80–120°C (176–284°F) for 5 minutes. Care should be taken to ensure that the ink film has dried completely before the work is stacked. Occasionally, the ink film can feel dry – indeed is dry on the surface – when it is still wet beneath. If work is stacked whilst in a semi-dry condition, 'set-off' (ink transfer between sheets) and 'blocking' (sheets becoming stuck together in the pile) can result.

When completely dry the inks provide a tough, high gloss finish. The highest gloss levels are achieved on surface-coated materials. They are suitable for printing on to paper and board and will exhibit good adhesion on some plastics. They may also be used for printing on to metal, glass, wood and transfer papers. Most major ink suppliers offer them. A typical formulation for an alkyd-based gloss ink might be as follows:

Constituent	%	Function
Titanium dioxide	14.00	pigment
Beta phthalocyanine blue	5.00	pigment
Calcium carbonate	20.00	extender
Long oil linseed alkyd	40.00	resin
Mixed naphthenate	1.00	drier
White spirit	19.00	solvent
Methyl ethyl ketoxime	0.20	anti-skinning additive

SYNTHETIC THIN FILM INKS

Sometimes referred to as 'poster' inks, these are based upon an EHEC resin system which is reducible in white spirit by 10–30%. They dry mainly by solvent evaporation. In normal workshop conditions they will air dry in 10–20 minutes. They may also be force dried in a jet air dryer, with drying times of 30–60 seconds. The drying rate of the ink can be increased by adding an accelerative (fast) thinner. The addition of a slow or retardant thinner will help to improve the ink's screen stability in hot shop conditions.

Synthetic thin film inks are suitable for printing on to all kinds of paper and board. They are formulated for poster printing – hence the name. However, they are also widely used for point-of-sale and display work. They can be printed on to wood and will adhere to some plastics.

They dry to a matt finish, but may be overprinted with screen varnish to provide a high gloss finish. Some of the major suppliers no longer offer these inks but do provide alternatives based upon improved solvent and resin systems. They are usually offered in the full range of colours, most of which will provide good opacity. The inks can also be made translucent by adding a clear extender base. Special ink types, such as metallics and fluorescent colours, are also available, as are four colour process inks.

Most suppliers offer a colour matching service; some include the range in their colour matching system. Coates Screen and Sericol Ltd both offer Pantone referenced computer matching systems. Other companies, such as Gibbon Marler, John T. Keep and Sons and Euroflex, offer very comprehensive dedicated computer-based matching systems.

A typical formulation for a thin film ink might be as follows:

Constituent	%	Function
Pale scarlet chrome	15.00	pigment
Calcium 4b	3.00	pigment
China clay	23.00	extender
High viscosity EHEC	6.00	resin
Pentaester gum	10.00	resin
White spirit	30.00	solvent/diluent
Aromatic hydrocarbon (160–180°C)	10.00	solvent
Propylene glycol monomethylether	3.00	flow additive

ULTRA-THIN FILM INKS

These inks are based upon ethyl cellulose resin systems, dissolved in volatile solvents. They have excellent screen stability, due to their ability to redissolve rapidly when rewetted. In practical terms the ink will remain wet while in the screen mesh; should it 'dry in' on the screen, it will quickly dissolve again after a few squeegee strokes. This important property facilitates short breaks in machine production whilst quality checks or press adjustments are made, obviating the need for a major press wash-up.

Ultra-thin film inks dry rapidly on the substrate, with rates of 3–8 minutes air drying in normal workshop conditions, and 15 seconds when force-dried at 50–70°C in a jet air dryer.

They are suitable for printing on to paper and board, including corrugated stock. They are reduced with special cellulose-based thinners, which is available in three types: fast (for accelerative drying), regular, and retardant (for improved screen stability in manual printing and in 'hot shop' conditions).

The inks dry to a semi-gloss finish on matt surfaced substrates, whilst on coated substrates they provide a gloss finish. They generally exhibit good opacity, the colours having exceptional clarity. The ink film thickness that can be achieved can be as low as 10 microns. This makes it possible to produce translucent colour effects, which give clear, strong undertones. This is particularly important in the production of colour process work for the point-of-sale and display market. Here, the brilliance and saturation of the colours that can be achieved by screen printing make it an attractive alternative to litho printing, which simply does not have the same three-dimensional 'punch' that is so important in the world of advertising and visual communications.

As with most other graphic inks, a full range of special finishes are available, including metallics, fluorescents and process colours. Suppliers offer a comprehensive ink matching service, and computer-based matching systems are also widely available.

A typical ultra-thin film ink might be made using the following formulation:

Constituent	%	Function
Primrose chrome	20.00	pigment
Ethyl cellulose	15.00	resin
Di-octyl phthatate	5.00	plasticizer
Aromatic hydrocarbon	25.00	solvent
Propylene glycol monomethylether	35.00	solvent

VINYL INKS

There is a wide range of vinyl inks suitable for both rigid and flexible materials. They are based upon vinyl and vinyl/acrylic resins, dissolved in aromatic hydrocarbons. Some of these solvents are extremely aggressive, like cyclohexanone, which provides a substrate 'keying' function by slightly dissolving the surface of the vinyl, thus allowing the ink to form a physical bond.

Vinyl inks dry by solvent evaporation. In normal conditions they will dry in 5–20 minutes. With jet air drying at 50°C, drying times can be reduced to 15 seconds.

The inks are thinned with a special vinyl thinner. As with other inks, a range of thinners is available to suit varying conditions and production requirements. Some inks and thinners can have an offensive smell and this can cause environmental problems both inside and outside the plant. The odour inherent in the dry ink film may also prove unacceptable to the client. Some suppliers offer low-odour vinyl inks. Developments in ink and solvent formulation will also be shaped by the tighter regulations that are consequent upon revisions to the Environmental Protection Act 1991 (see Chapter 10).

Vinyl inks are made in a wide range of finishes and special effects. These include gloss and matt finishes, metallic and fluorescent inks, and process colours. Most suppliers provide comprehensive colour-matching services and include vinyl inks in their computer-based colour-matching systems.

There are many applications for vinyl ink. They include self-adhesive stickers and labels, packing and containers, toys and gifts, point-of-sale advertising (especially in supermarkets and large retail outlets), shower curtains and flooring materials, surface and product decoration and many other specialist applications. They are suitable for printing onto a range of substrates, including PVC, ABS, CAB, acrylics, polystyrene and polycarbonate.

A typical gloss vinyl ink might be based on the following formulation:

Constituent	%	Function
Rutile titanium dioxide	27.00	pigment
Vinyl copolymer	19.00	resin
Methyl/butyl methacrylate copolymer	7.00	resin
Cyclohexanone	10.00	solvent
Aromatic hydrocarbon (124–180°C)	28.00	solvent
Aromatic hydrocarbon (160–180°C)	4.00	solvent
Non-migratory plasticizer	5.00	plasticizer

TWO-PACK CATALYTIC INKS

These inks are based upon epoxy resin systems, dissolved in a volatile hydrocarbon solvent. When the resin is mixed with a reactive polyamide catalyst, a printing ink with good screen stability and printability is produced.

The ink dries initially by solvent evaporation, surface drying in normal workshop conditions in 30 minutes. However, the catalytic process which causes the ink to set firmly on the substrate and form a solid and highly durable film is not completed until some days after printing. This curing process can be accelerated by infra-red stoving. Treatment with short-wave infra-red radiation can cure the ink in seconds; Sericol's Polyscreen PS, for example, will cure in 10–15 seconds at 100°C.

These inks are made especially for printing on to 'difficult' surfaces, i.e. those surfaces which reject most screen printing inks. They will exhibit exceptional adhesion to aluminium, brass and other metals; polyethylene, polypropylene and other plastics; glass and ceramics. The inks also have very good resistance to corrosive chemicals and solvents, and are used in packaging, industrial and electronics applications.

A range of surface finishes can be obtained, from high gloss to matt, depending on the type and amount of catalyst that is used when mixing the ink. A full range of intermixable opaque colours is available and these can be made translucent by the addition of a clear extender base. A typical formulation for a two-pack screen ink would be as follows:

Constituent	%	Function
PASTE		
Titanium dioxide	35.00	pigment
Epoxy resin	40.00	resin
Butyl cellosolve	25.00	solvent
CATALYST		
Reactive polyamide	70.00	resin
Butyl cellosolve	10.00	solvent
Aromatic hydrocarbon (186–214°C)	20.00	solvent

The two components are mixed together according to the manufacturer's instructions, to provide an ink with optimum adhesion and durability. One-pack catalytic inks like Unicat from Coates Screen and Unipol UF from Sericol are also available for use with pretreated polyethylene and polypropylene. Most major ink suppliers offer a range of specialist chemical curing inks for specific substrates and applications. Full colour ranges, special colours and finishes, and colour-matching services and systems are also offered.

ULTRAVIOLET CURING INKS

UV inks do not dry in the conventional sense of solvent-based inks. They are dried, or more correctly 'cured' (transformed into a solid film by chemical bonding of the vehicle molecules), through exposure to intense ultraviolet radiation, in the waveband region of 300–400 nm.

Their formulation is based upon novel ink chemistry. Chemically reactive resins are combined with a photoinitiator to produce a printing medium which has excellent screen stability. It will form a solid durable film with very good adhesion in a fraction of a second when exposed to intense UV light. The ink therefore provides an ideal solution to two major production problems in screen printing: screen stability and extended drying times. With UV inks it is possible to print the finest detail, since the screen mesh will not become blocked by drying ink during production. Since the ink dries almost instantaneously the press can be run at top speed.

UV inks are made for printing on to a wide range of substrates, including: paper and board, vinyls, polyester, polyethylene and polypropylene. UV formulations are also used in the production of printed circuits, packaging and product decoration.

Care must be taken in selecting the correct mesh and stencil system. Since there is no evaporation of solvent during the drying of the ink, the printed film remains 100% solid. This means that ink film thickness must usually be reduced by using finer screen meshes and thinner stencil coatings. Reducing the ink film thickness is also important in minimizing ink consumption, since UV ink is more expensive than conventional ink.

Reduced ink film weights are also essential in four colour process work, where thick ink films can produce heavy ink build-up in the mid tones, causing print failure on the third and fourth colours. Suppliers currently recommend monofilament screen meshes of 140–150 T. Semi-calendered meshes are also recommended in some applications (see Chapter 2).

Careful adjustment of the dryer is also necessary since not all colours will cure at the same rate. To be completely cured the ink film must be exposed right through to the substrate surface. If the top layer is cured and the underlayer remains unexposed, the ink will not adhere to the substrate. If the upper layer of the ink is overcured it will reject any subsequent printings. Generally speaking the more opaque the ink, the more difficult it is to cure. Varnishes and process inks do not usually present any problems.

Recent developments have encouraged the wider use and availability of water-based UV inks. The principle advantage of water-based UV is that it produces a thinner dried ink film deposit, resulting in improved colour reproduction in four colour process printing.

Thinner ink films are achieved as a result of the water in the system acting as a diluent, performing a similar function to that of the solvent in a conventional ink system. The water is evaporated away in the dryer, thus leaving a reduced ink film on the stock. Unlike solvent, water does not present any air pollution problems. The other major advantage is in screen cleaning and reclamation, where water is used instead of solvent, offering a further environmental advantage to the user.

At present water-based UV inks like Sericol's Aquaspeed, Coates Screen Concerto, Gibbon Marler's Watercolour UV and John T. Keeps's Aquatone and Aquaclear are available for paper and board substrates. For other surfaces, such as vinyl, coated polyesters, polyethylene, polycarbonate, glass, ceramics, coated and anodized metals and styrenes, conventional UV systems are used and are offered by most of the major ink suppliers.

UV inks are available with either a high gloss or a satin finish. There may be limitations on the colour range available, with most suppliers providing a matching service and some providing dedicated colour-matching systems. UV varnishes provide a crystal clear, high gloss finish and are often used to overprint litho work to provide added value to such things as corporate publications, product literature, prestige packaging and point-of-sale advertising.

Conventional UV inks are formulated from the three basic components, described as follows.

Photoinitiator This is the fundamental ingredient in UV inks. It accomplishes the initial step of absorbing the ultraviolet energy required to cause the formation of a reactive free radical which starts the polymer formation in the ink film. Several types of photoinitiator exist; each behaves differently, yet all of them bring about the same polymerization process. Each ink formulation, according to the end use requirements, will use an appropriate photoinitiator or photoinitiator combination.

Monomers These are single-unit building blocks upon which polymers are constructed. The most common type of monomers used are the polyether acrylates, which have the relatively low viscosity needed for screen printing applications. The monomer percentage in a formulation can influence properties such as chemical resistance and adhesion. Monomers are also used as diluents, to control viscosity, as a solvent for the prepolymers and for surface modification.

Oligomers These are short chains of monomers or prepolymers. Their high molecular weight makes them more viscous than monomers. They speed up the cure rate of the ink by reducing the time it takes to complete the full polymer chain. The final properties of the ink film are primarily determined by the nature of the oligomer used in the formulation. The most common oligomers are the epoxy resins, though polyethers and polyesters are also used to improve flexibility and adhesion.

A basic formulation for a conventional UV paper and board ink might be as follows:

Constituent	%	Function
Trioxide RTC-2	15.00	pigment
Epoxy acrylate	60.00	oligomer
Tripropylene glycol diacrylate	20.00	monomer
Photoinitiator	3.00	
Levelling and flow agents	2.00	

Emulsions formulated around the polyester acrylates have been used in water-based UV inks. A typical water-thinnable UV ink might be based on the following formulation.

Constituent	%	Function
Phthalocyanine blue	2.5	pigment
Polyester acrylate	78.5	oligomer
Butyl glycol	4.0	monomer
Photoinitiator	4.0	
Flow and levelling agent	2.0	
Water	9.0	

The principal advantages of UV systems

There are a number of advantages which accrue from using conventional and water-based UV ink systems. They may be summarized as follows:

- Almost instantaneous drying
- Ink does not dry on the screen
- No solvent emissions
- Low odour inks
- Compact dryers, save floor space
- Greener water wash-up with water-based UV
- High gloss finish available
- Very high gloss, water-clear finish for varnishes.

WATER-BASED INKS

The water-reducible printing pastes, commonly used in textile printing, have been available for many years. These media are formulated on acrylate copolymer resin emulsions, with the addition of white spirit to promote surface drying. Pigments are added to the emulsion binder by the user. The relatively high proportion of solvent (62% by volume) promotes drying and reduces film weight, giving a softer finish or 'hand' to the print.

Recently a number of ink suppliers have produced water-based inks for the graphic market. These inks are based upon similar pigmented emulsion systems, some of which contain very small amounts of solvent, whilst others claim to be 100% aqueous inks.

One of the main problems with using water-based ink systems for paper-based substrates is to control the effects of moisture absorbtion by the stock. If too much water is present, or if it is slow to evaporate from the printed film, then it will be absorbed by the stock, causing swelling and subsequent distortion and producing 'cockle'. This is usually characterized by an uneven rippling of the stock. If the ink film is too thick, this can cause the stock to curl at the edges, due to the swelling of the paper surface and the surface tension produced in the ink film as it dries and shrinks.

Water-based graphic inks are generally supplied press-ready; that is, they do not require thinning. However, they can be thinned either with a small amount of water (typically 2% by volume) or by adding a screen stabilizer to prevent the ink from drying in the screen. Most users do not thin the inks, simply because they are supplied in what appears to be a very low viscosity, exhibiting far higher flow properties than conventional solvent-based inks.

However, once on the press these inks tend to thicken very quickly. This is because the stabilizing agents in the ink are quickly lost through evaporation and printing, leaving the remaining ink on the screen to thicken and clog the screen mesh. To prevent this the screen should be charged at frequent intervals with small quantities of ink. In spite of its apparent low viscosity, thinning the ink can also help, although adding too much water will cause thin paper stocks to cockle. Some suppliers also recommend using a screen-stabilizing spray, which is sprayed on to the open areas of the screen prior to printing and after each stoppage. This helps to prevent thickening and 'drying in'.

Some water-based inks produce colours with good opacity, whilst others tend to be translucent. Some manufacturers offer only a limited colour range, whilst others like Coates Screen and Sericol offer a comprehensive colour range and dedicated colour-matching systems.

As with all new products there is a learning curve to be experienced before they can be used with the ease and confidence associated with conventional inks. When compared with solvent-based inks the new water-based systems perform very differently on the press. Care must be taken to ensure that ink film weights are kept to a minimum. Screens should have a minimum mesh count of 100 T/cm; 120 T/cm is the most commonly recommended. Stencil systems should be water/solvent-resistant, as even on the 100% aqueous systems screen clogging may require a solvent wash, which some water-resistant emulsions will not withstand. A sharp, medium shore squeegee and a round-bladed flo-coater should be used. Screen stability can be improved by using a heavy flo-coat to keep the mesh open. Repeated print and heavy flo-coating on to spoiled stock will usually open the screen, especially if fresh ink is applied. Increasing the weight of paper stocks will be necessary to prevent distortion and cockling where large areas of colour are printed.

The ink manufacturers are clearly committed to developing new, safer and environmentally acceptable products. Their aim in this is to keep the industry competitive by preventing the excessive costs which might be imposed upon the printer who is forced to use solvent-based products. It is clear that the environmental regulations on the use of solvents are going to become more constraining. It is therefore wise for the supplier and the printer to work together to safeguard their mutual interests.

A typical formulation for a water-based graphic ink might be:

Constituent	%	Function
Primrose chrome	15.00	pigment
Carboxylated acrylic emulsion	45.00	vehicle
Styrene/acrylic copolymer	15.00	vehicle
Ammonia	0.5	
Microcrystalline wax emulsion	5.0	
Silicone defoamer	0.5	
Levelling agent	1.00	
Dowanol DPM	4.00	
Water	14.00	

Solvents   A large number of solvents are used in the manufacture of screen printing inks and, as already indicated, they perform various functions. Solvents are also used by the printer to give the ink the particular printing characteristics required for the work in hand. They are also used for screen cleaning, reclaiming, and the adhesion of solvent adhered stencils. It will be helpful therefore, to describe these various solvents by classifying them according to their function.

THINNERS

Solvents, or more correctly diluents, are added to the ink by the printer to reduce its viscosity – screen inks are supplied with a viscosity of 50–100 poise. Most screen printing inks require thinning with an appropriate thinner (10–25% by volume). The addition of a thinner will generally improve the flow properties of the ink, increasing its screen stability and press performance.

FAST AND SLOW THINNERS

The evaporation rate of the solvents in a conventional solvent-based ink determines the speed at which the ink will dry. If the drying rate is too slow, special thinners can be used. Usually referred to as fast thinners, these consist of volatile solvents which have a relatively high evaporation rate and good rewetting properties. Conversely, slow or retardant thinners are added to the ink when it is drying too quickly and lacks the required screen stability. The fault commonly known as 'drying in' occurs when the ink begins to thicken up on the screen and sets in the mesh openings, blocking the image areas and causing print failure.

The problem usually occurs first at the stencil perimeter, especially where fine lines, highlight half-tone dots or small type matter are reproduced. This is because the stencil 'shoulder' (the very edge of the stencil) causes a very small amount of ink to remain in the mesh after the print stroke. This tiny halo of retained ink begins to dry in the period between print separation and flo-coating. Where an ink has poor rewetting properties a tiny 'beach' of set ink will form; where the stencil apertures are narrow this beach will build up rapidly, causing blocking and print failure. If a solvent with a lower evaporation rate is added, the ink thickens more slowly on the screen. Aggressive solvents, which promote rewetting, also serve to dissolve any ink retained by the mesh as the screen is recharged during the flo-coating stroke.

GEL REDUCERS AND RETARDERS

These are thixotropic additives which improve the printing characteristics of the ink without affecting its viscosity. They are particularly useful in fine line and half-tone printing where increased flow in the printed film may result in loss of detail in the mid tone and shadow areas, due to excessive dot gain. Gel additives improve the printability of the ink without affecting the flow characteristics of the printed film.

FLOW THINNERS

These are added to the ink to improve its surface finish and to prevent the effects of bubbling in the ink. Certain inks and print mediums, particularly process inks and overprint varnishes, have a tendency to 'mottle' (produce an uneven ink film surface). The addition of a flow thinner will minimize this effect by lowering the surface tension in the printed film, allowing any air bubbles to burst on film sheering, and accelerating the flow-out in the printed film.

HOLD-OUT THINNERS

Ultra-thin film inks containing a very low percentage of solids tend to be absorbed into uncoated papers. This often results in an uneven ink film and poor finish with certain areas appearing darker than others. The problem can be minimized by adding a hold-out thinner to the ink. This improves the film-forming characteristics of the ink and prevents excessive substrate absorption.

The problem is particularly common when printing on to uncoated cover board materials, where the surface is particularly porous and absorbent. In such cases the best results will be achieved by aiming for increased ink deposit with a low count screen mesh (preferably HD), a thick stencil, 25–40 micron capillary film, a round-bladed squeegee and a high viscosity ink. Improved hold-out can also be achieved by doubling the print stroke, i.e. printing a second film directly after the first.

ANTI-STATIC ADDITIVE

This is added to an ink when printing on to substrates which are prone to the generation of static charges. This is a common problem with most plastics and may occur with some paper and board substrates, especially calendered and coated papers. It usually results in the print failing to release from the screen; in some cases the sheet will be drawn back to the screen by the presence of the static charge after the printed sheet has been released.

Another common effect is 'spidering' or 'cobwebbing' at the edges of the ink film. This occurs as the ink film sheers away from the screen; the charge present on the stock pulls the stringing ink out over the surface of the sheet, causing what looks like a spider's web. The addition of an anti-static agent helps to reduce the charge on the screen and minimizes the effects of any static that may have built up on the stock.

SCREEN WASH

This is the generic name for the general purpose screen-cleaning solvent that most ink manufacturers supply. It consists of a mixture of very potent solvents, such as cyclohexanone. Screen washes are formulated to provide powerful film wetting and dissolving properties, and must be effective across a wide range of resin systems. Some screen washes will dissolve even the most stubborn ink residues, and when used in combination with a concentrated alkaline paste they will remove even the most resistant ink and stencil combinations, leaving the screen completely stainless.

Due to these very aggressive properties great care must be taken when using them. Certain stencil materials are adversely affected by strong solvents; gelatine products will become brittle after repeated treatment, and may break down if care is not taken. Some of the solvents that are contained in these cleaning agents are classified under EU regulations (Council Directive 73/173 and 77/728) as 'Harmful Substances'. Cyclohexanone, for example, is classified as a class II/c substance, and if more than 10% of it is contained in any printing medium or ancillary product then it must be identified on the label.

Most suppliers are now offering new low hazard screen washes, which present more environmentally friendly chemical properties and a lower health hazard for the user. All such products must by law be supplied with a safety data sheet, and those which present a health or environmental hazard must carry a hazard warning label (see Chapter 10).

Health and Safety Note:

Inks, solvents and auxillary products must be handled in strict accordance with the manufacturer's health and safety data sheets. This is a requirement of the law, under the Control of Substances Hazardous to Health, COSHH. Ensure that wherever these products are used there is adequate ventilation and extraction of fumes and vapours. Always avoid the inhalation of solvent vapours and where necessary wear protective gloves to avoid skin contact.

Printing 8

Before the screen is ready for printing, all non-image areas that remain open must be blocked out with an appropriate screen filler. Any pinholes or damaged areas of the stencil are also filled at this stage.

Screens which carry indirect stencils are usually blocked out with filler immediately after the stencil has been transferred to the screen. Filling the screen while the stencil is still wet improves the dimensional stability of the screen, since both stencil and filler dry together and any differential in shrinkage will be evenly compensated for over the entire screen. If the stencil is allowed to dry before the screen filler is applied, then stress will be exerted on the stencil as the filler dries, causing distortion to the image, which can lead to registration problems.

Screen filler is best applied with a card or plastic scraper. The aim is to apply a thin and even coating, completely blocking the open areas of the mesh surrounding the stencil. The filler flows through the mesh openings to the other side of the screen and it is best, therefore, to apply it with long continuous strokes, working in one direction around the screen, thus avoiding any repeated applications in one area. If the filler is allowed to build up on the screen it will prolong the drying period and may adversely affect the printing quality of the screen by causing excessive shrinking.

The filler can be force dried with warm air. The so-called 'flash-dry' fillers contain volatile solvents which cause the filler to dry as it is applied to the screen. However, these rapid-drying fillers are suitable only for short run work, as they lack the resistance of the slow-drying screen fillers and are therefore not to be recommended for print runs in excess of 1000 copies.

Screens carrying gelatine-based stencils must not be dried with warm air above 30°C (86°F); for optimum results, indirect gelatine based stencils should be allowed to dry naturally. However, synthetic polymer stencils may be force dried at 40°C (104°F). Where a fan is used it should never be positioned closer to the screen than 30–45 cm (12–18 in) as this will cause uneven drying.

Screen fillers   There are a number of different screen fillers available; some are water-soluble and made for use with solvent-based inks, whilst others are water-resistant, for use with water-based inks. The choice of filler will be determined largely by the ink type in use and the length of print run.

FLASH-DRY FILLER

This is a rapid-drying water-soluble screen filler. Whilst it is formulated for use with solvent-based inks, it has a relatively poor resistance to aggressive cellulose and ketonic solvents. It is used primarily for short run work. It can be quickly removed with cold water. It may be used for spotting-out, but is not suitable for retouching or hand-rendering.

SLOW-DRYING WATER-BASED FILLER

This filler is suitable for all kinds of solvent-based inks. It is supplied in a regular viscosity and is usually applied with a scraper. It can also be thinned by 20% with water and applied with a brush for retouching or autographic dry brush techniques (see Chapter 13). High viscosity screen fillers are available for use with low mesh count screens. When dry, these screen fillers provide a very tough and flexible screen blocking film, which makes them especially suitable for long run machine production and/or repeat run work. The filler is removed from the screen with warm water.

SOLVENT-BASED FILLER

Solvent-based screen fillers are used in conjunction with water-resistant stencil systems when printing water-based inks. The filler can be applied with a scraper or with a brush. It may be used as a temporary block-out in multicolour work, where multiple colours are planned on the same screen. Most solvent-based fillers are formulated on ethyl cellulose resins in a volatile solvent to provide rapid drying. They are normally removed with screen wash.

Health and Safety Note:

As with all solvent-based products, flash-dry and solvent-based fillers must only be used in a well ventilated working environment. Always avoid inhalation of the solvent vapours and wear protective gloves to avoid skin contact.

The edges of the screen frame are usually sealed to the mesh with an adhesive tape; gummed paper, waxed or polyester self-adhesive tapes are commonly used, the latter providing the more durable seal. The main concern is to provide a complete and durable screen seal which will not leak or break down during printing. There is nothing more frustrating and time wasting than having a leaking screen to patch up in the middle of the print run, especially when using water-based inks.

The standardization of screen frame sizes and print areas in machine printing allows for a rational approach to screen filling. Machine printing screens are usually pre-masked during or shortly after tensioning. This is done by blocking the screen mesh with a permanent screen filler to within 2.5 cm (1 in) of the effective printing area. Solvent-resistant screen adhesive or 'liquid tape' is used to seal or caulk the frame to the mesh so that a permanent, flexible seal is achieved in a 'once only' procedure.

Sealing the screen

The squeegee performs a very important function in screen printing. It is used to force the ink through the screen mesh and stencil on to the printing stock below. This process of ink transfer is complex, involving a number of variables which operate together in a dynamic relationship. The main variables involved are:

The squeegee

- the squeegee angle of attack;
- the primary and secondary forces exerted on the squeegee;

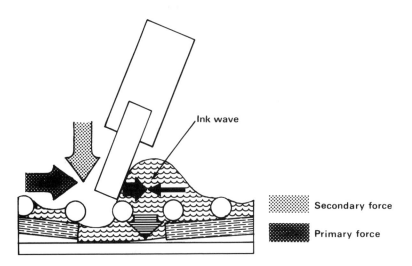

Ink wave

Secondary force

Primary force

Fig. 52 Sectional view of the squeegee forcing ink through the screen and stencil on to the printing stock.

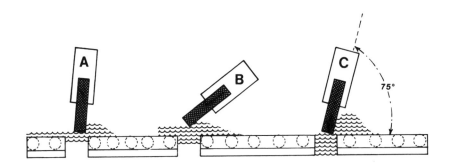

Fig. 53 Sectional diagram showing the effect of varying the squeegee angle.
(a) The squeegee is too upright and loses contact with the screen.
(b) The squeegee is too flat, resulting in displacement of the secondary force and a loss of contact with the screen.
(c) An angle of 75° produces an effective pressure wave, forcing the ink through the screen and stencil.

- the squeegee blade profile;
- the shore hardness of the blade.

As indicated in Fig. 52, the ink is pushed through the screen and stencil by the forces created in it through the action of the squeegee during the printing stroke. The squeegee is pressed down into contact with the screen (secondary force) whilst it is held at an angle of about 75°. During the printing action the squeegee is moved across the screen, creating a pressure wave in the ink. The pressure wave is caused by the primary force exerted on the ink through the motion of the squeegee and the resistance to this force by the ink. The resulting pressure created in the ink wave causes the ink to move in the direction of least resistance, principally through the screen image openings.

The most effective angle between the squeegee and the screen is 70–78°. If the angle is greater or less than this, the pressure in the ink wave will fall and print failure may occur.

SQUEEGEE BLADE PROFILES

The dynamics created in the ink transfer process are very much determined by the rheology of the ink and a principal factor in this is its viscosity. As we have seen, the viscosity of screen inks can vary between 50 and 100 poise. Some screen inks, like the high opacity 'flash white' plastisols used in garment printing, exhibit high levels of viscosity, whereas water-based graphic inks have very low viscosity. Between these two extremes there is a wide range of inks, each with its own rheological

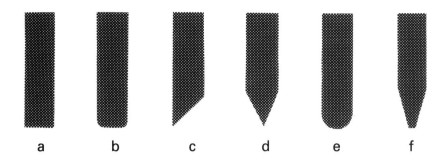

Fig. 54 Squeegee blade profiles (see below).

properties. To cope with such variability, manufacturers have developed a wide range of squeegee blade profiles and shore hardness.

(a) The square-edged blade is used for a wide range of printing applications where a thin ink deposit is required, for example in four colour process work.
(b) The rounded square-edged blade is used in situations where an increased ink deposit is required, for increased colour opacity or gloss level on an uncoated stock.
(c) The single bevel-edged blade is used for printing on to non-absorbent surfaces such as glass or metal.
(d) The double bevel-edged blade is used for direct printing on to curved surfaces, such as containers.
(e) The round-edged blade is used in textile printing to provide increased dye penetration, forcing the printing medium through the screen in two or more printing strokes.
(f) The double-sided flat-edged bevel blade is used in direct ceramic printing.

POLYURETHANE BLADES

Polyurethane squeegee blades have replaced rubber blades and are now used throughout the industry. They are made in a wide range of grades and sections. Their high resistance to abrasion makes them particularly suitable for machine printing. The precision-cut blade profile will retain its edge over long periods of use without the need for frequent sharpening or reshaping.

Unitex, who manufacture squeegee blades, supply a wide range of grades, all of them classified and colour coded to make identification and selection a simple matter. For example:

Grade	Hardness Shore A°	Colour
PU500/1	55–60	Yellow
PU500/3	60–65	Red
PU500/3/4	65–70	Red
PU500/4	70–75	Green
PU500/8	75–80	Blue
PU500/9	80–85	Brown
PU101/9	85–90	Brown

TRIPLE DUROMETER BLADES

Multilayer squeegee blades, like the Serilor 3 blade, available from Sericol Ltd, provide a combination squeegee blade composed of two outer print layers of either 65° or 75° shore with a central stiffening core of 95° shore. This combination gives the printer the responsiveness of a soft to medium hard blade without the undesirable flexing created by increased secondary force squeegee pressure. The harder 95° shore core provides the necessary structural rigidity to resist flexing under increased squeegee pressure, making these blades particularly useful in large format, high speed flat-bed and cylinder machines. The blades are also useful in critical four colour process printing and in applications where close tolerance printing is required.

HAND-PRINTING SQUEEGEES

There are various designs of hand-printing squeegee. The basic design consists of a wooden handle, shaped to facilitate a firm and comfortable grip. The handle is rebated to accommodate the squeegee blade, which is usually held in place by countersunk screws, positioned alternately on either side at intervals of 4–5 cm. It is a good idea to seal the blade into the handle to prevent ink from seeping into the blade rebate – a fault which can cause problems of colour contamination when changing from dark to light colours.

Some of the better squeegee designs are of lightweight aluminium construction with two blade-clamping jaws which can easily be loosened to allow the blade to be removed for cleaning, or changing whenever required.

Fig. 55 Hand-printing squeegee, flo-coating blades and machine-printing squeegee (left to right).

MACHINE-PRINTING SQUEEGEES

Squeegees that are used in machine printing are available in several different designs. Machine manufacturers supply squeegees designed for use with their machines. Essentially they consist of an aluminum blade clamp, having two halves, held together by a series of countersunk bolts. The bolts are easily loosened with an allen key to release the squeegee blade for cleaning or replacement. The blades used in machine printing are usually smaller in section than hand printing squeegee blades, i.e. $25\text{--}35 \times 5\text{--}7$ mm.

Squeegee maintenance

The condition of the squeegee has an important influence on the quality of the print that is made with it. If the squeegee is not prepared correctly before printing, the print may lack the clarity and definition required; if the blade has sustained damage it may cause streaks in the print; and if the blade has become unseated from the clamp or handle then it may produce uneven coverage or cause large areas of the print to fail or flood with ink. Before each operation the printer should run the following quality check:

- Check that the squeegee is clean, particularly where the blade seats into the handle. If ink has seeped into this area, the blade should be removed and thoroughly cleaned.
- Check for any nicks or cuts in the blade. If the printing edge is damaged the blade should be redressed; if the blade is polyurethane it may be quicker to turn it so that the damaged edge is seated in the handle.
- Check for wear; a worn squeegee blade will not print efficiently.

Worn blades should be redressed on a blade grinder or turned as described above.

- Check that the blade is seated correctly in the handle. Hold the squeegee with the printing edge resting on a flat surface. Look carefully along the edge of the blade; if any light is seen between the blade edge and the surface that it rests on, the blade is not flat; it will require either reseating or redressing.

Making ready for printing

In every printing process there is an established systematic procedure which is followed when setting up equipment or machinery for printing. This procedure is known as 'make ready'. The exact method that is adopted will be determined by the application and the type of equipment or machinery that is being set up. However, there are a number of essential procedures which are common to most situations.

The example described below would be suitable for most hand-bench equipment and semi-automatic sheet fed machines. When making ready on ¾ semi-automatic and fully automatic flat-bed and cylinder machines, the general procedures would be the same as described here, though there are many points of detail which simply do not apply. All that can be done here is to allude to the main points of difference, as space does not permit a more detailed description related to individual machine requirements. For further detail on specific applications, such as garment printing, see Chapter 12.

Steps 1–8 of the make ready procedures are as follows.

1. THE LAY SHEET

Drawing an accurate working layout of the job is the first step in making ready for printing. In some cases this is done by the layout artist or planner before the job reaches the printer; in certain circumstances the printer may do it. In either case it is essential that the person responsible has all the relevant information required to set the job up on the printing equipment or machinery.

The essential information required on the lay sheet is as follows.

- The exact imposition of the work should be clearly indicated. The lay sheet is usually drawn up on the stock on which the job is to be printed. The imposition may be indicated by register marks or targets. Trim and bleed marks may also be indicated.
- The printing sequence should be indicated.
- The lay and gripper edges should be indicated.
- On hand-bench work it may be necessary to indicate the print stroke direction.

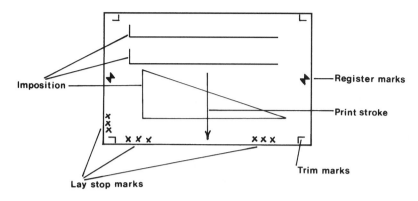

Imposition

Register marks

Print stroke

Trim marks

Lay stop marks

Fig. 56 A lay sheet.

2. LOCKING THE SCREEN FRAME

Before locking the screen frame into the screen carriage it is necessary to establish the lay edges, which should be indicated on the lay sheet. In machine production the work is usually planned on the screen in relation to the gripper and side lay positions on the press. It is possible to make register adjustments on the press but these are usually kept to a minimum by pre-registering the image on the screen.

The screen frame must be locked securely into the screen carriage; any movement during production would result in registration errors.

3. SETTING REGISTER AND OFF-CONTACT ADJUSTMENTS

The register adjustments on the printing equipment should be equalized to allow for maximum adjustment in all directions. The off-contact adjustments should be set at zero so that any adjustments that are made can be done in a controlled manner. This is especially important in close tolerance multicolour and four colour process work, where screen tension and off-contact control require careful measurement and control.

4. REGISTERING THE LAY SHEET

The lay sheet is positioned on the printing base so that when the screen is lowered the registration targets will align exactly with those on the stencil. In hand-bench operation an overlay sheet is sometimes used to ascertain lay position. In this case a sheet of transparent acetate or polyester film is taped to the printing base, a print is taken on the overlay, and the lay sheet is then slid beneath the printed overlay to reference the precise lay position. This method is useful in that it allows for any distortion which may occur as a result of the stressing caused by the squeegee on the print stroke.

5. FIXING THE LAY STOPS

On some semi-automatic machines, and on all hand-bench equipment, the lay stops (small raised sheet guides, used to position each sheet of stock precisely under the screen) are usually fixed on to the printing base as required, every time the equipment is made ready. Lay stops can be made in a variety of ways. They may be cut from the printing stock itself, or made from several layers of adhesive tape, placed at the edges of the lay sheet. However they are made, they must conform to the following basic requirements:

- They must be securely attached to the printing base.
- They must stop the sheets efficiently and facilitate fast and accurate feeding to lay.
- They must not be thicker than the printing stock.
- The stops should be placed at three control points: two on the long edge and one on the short edge of the sheet. This three-point configuration is an absolute prerequisite for accurate and rapid sheet handling.

Once the lay stops have been fixed down their positions are carefully recorded on the lay sheet. In subsequent printings the lay stops are positioned with reference to the positions indicated on the lay sheet, thus ensuring consistent sheet handling from one colour to the next throughout the entire job.

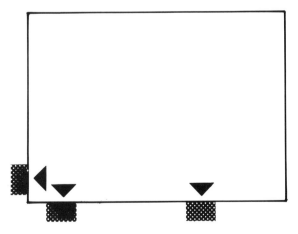

Fig. 57 The 'three point' lay stop configuration.

6. MASKING THE VACUUM BASE

Any area of the vacuum base that is not covered by the printing stock must be masked off before printing commences. If the vacuum is not masked the print release facility that it provides may be adversely affected. Incomplete or slow print release can result in a loss of print definition; it may also cause 'slurring', or 'flooding', and may produce print release marks on large solids.

The vacuum base is usually masked off with newsprint, to within 25 mm (1 in) of the edge of the printing stock. When very light or soft stock is used it may be necessary to reduce the vacuum pressure, since this can cause the vacuum holes to be reproduced in the ink film. A good way of preventing this is to cover the vacuum base with a light tissue paper or fine count screen mesh – garment platen adhesive can be used to hold the material in place. This will help to diffuse the vacuum pressure over the area of the print.

7. ADJUSTING OFF-CONTACT DISTANCE

Most applications require the screen to be out of contact with the surface of the print stock. This facilitates rapid ink film sheering and allows the print to release rapidly from the screen, thus preventing any tendency for the ink to flow laterally between the underside of the stencil and the surface of the printing stock.

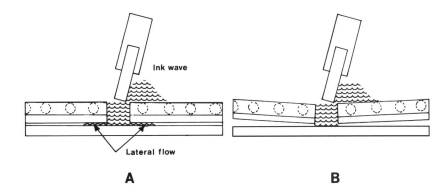

Fig. 58 The off-contact principle.
(a) Ink flows laterally between the underside of the stencil and the printing surface.
(b) The off-contact principle allows the screen to release from the print immediately, thus preventing any lateral flow of ink.

The amount of off-contact distance required will be determined by the following variables:

- The print area
- The tension of the screen
- The viscosity of the ink
- The nature of the image.

Print area

Large solids generally require more off-contact than is necessary when printing line and text work. The reason for this is that the greater the area of ink contact between the screen and the printing surface, the greater will be the resistance to their separation.

Screen tension

The tension of the screen has a direct effect upon the rate of print release. It is the screen's resistance to deformation that determines the speed at which it will release from the print. If the tension of the screen is low then its resistance to deformation will also be low, causing a slow or incomplete print release after the squeegee passage. In order to increase the rate of print release the off-contact distance must be increased. Excessive increase in off-contact can often lead to screen and image distortion, resulting in a loss of dimensional stability and poor registration. Ordinarily a correctly tensioned screen will require a minimal amount of off-contact. In order to minimize image distortion, the off-contact distance should always be as low as possible, consistent with rapid print release and high image definition.

Ink viscosity

The viscosity of an ink also has a direct effect upon the rate of print release. Viscous screen inks usually exhibit a high degree of tack and tend to resist the sheering effects which take place as the screen separates away from the print. When printing with highly viscous inks it is usually necessary to have an increased off-contact distance; in some cases as much as 1.5 cm may be required. On the other hand, when the print release is slow or incomplete it may be improved by reducing the viscosity of the ink with the addition of an appropriate thinner.

The image

The nature of the image on the screen can also influence the off-contact requirement. For example, when printing negative detail out of a large

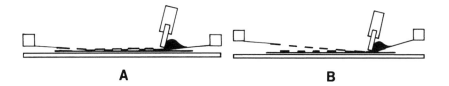

Fig. 59 Off-contact adjustment.
(a) The print fails to release from the screen.
(b) The increased off-contact distance causes the print to release from the screen immediately behind the squeegee.

solid it may be necessary to increase off-contact distances in order to retain print definition. In some circumstances the off-contact distance at the rear of the screen may have to be greater than the setting at the front of the screen or vice versa. Machines which incorporate 'lift-off' allow for the off-contact distance to be variably controlled during the printing stroke, thus ensuring effective print release whilst minimizing screen/print distortion.

8. PROVING

At the proving stage a small amount of ink is distributed across the screen in front of the squeegee. In machine operation the squeegee and flo-coater blade pressures and angles are set before the ink is placed on the screen. The squeegee blade pressure should be enough to force the screen into contact with the surface of the stock. The flo-coater blade should be adjusted so that its coating edge is in contact with the screen for the flo-coat stroke. At the proving stage both squeegee and flo-coater are set at minimum pressure, adjustments being made when the screen is carrying ink.

As the first print is made the printer carries out the following performance checks:

- Squeegee pressure and angle
- Print release
- Flo-coating angle and pressure
- Print quality (image fidelity and registration).

The necessary adjustments are made and further proofs are taken until the printer is satisfied with the print quality. In machine operation further adjustments are made as the printing speed is increased to meet the production requirements. For example, it may be necessary to increase the off-contact or lift-off to maintain rapid print release. Any such adjustment would invariably mean that the squeegee pressure must also be adjusted. Increases in off-contact and squeegee pressure will cause increased stressing of the screen, with a disproportional stress in the printing stroke direction, causing elongation to the print. These critical settings must be consistent throughout all colours, screen to screen, to minimize registration problems.

At the proving stage the printer may also be required to make final checks on the accuracy of a colour match. It is usually necessary for the print to be checked and passed for colour, print quality, imposition and register before the production run is begun. The printer should only 'run on' when the proof is returned with a signature from the production manager indicating that it has been passed. This proof copy is then retained as the standard for quality control checks. In some circumstances, the proof must also be approved by the customer prior to production.

In machine production the printer will also have to check that the prints are drying correctly. This may involve a series of adjustments to the dryer, the press and the screen ink. In the following chapter the methods and equipment used in the drying of screen printed matter will be discussed.

Ventilation and extraction

It is important to ensure that solvent vapours and fumes are extracted from the working environment and that adequate ventilation is provided wherever potentially hazardous solvents and chemicals are used. This is particularly important at the press, where solvent vapours are produced as the ink is spread back and forth across the screen and coated on to the stock. In a situation where space racks are in use, solvent vapours often accumulate and quickly reach unacceptably high concentrations. A local extraction system at the rear of the press (drawing vapours away from the operator) and behind the space rack (removing vapour from the drying prints) can, with the addition of an effective general extraction/ventilation system, solve the problem.

The Health and Safety Executive publishes guidelines for the screen printing industry. These give detailed recommendations for extraction and ventilation and they outline the need for local on-press ventilation. HSE inspectors will require assurance that extraction and ventilation systems are effective. They may require air tests to be undertaken in areas where potentially hazardous solvents and chemicals are used. Regular testing and maintenance of the extraction and ventilation systems will also be required and records of this must be made available to inspectors. In certain circumstances, they will also require regular medical checks for employees who come into contact with substances which constitute a potential hazard to health. Here again, records must be made available to the inspectors (see also Chapter 10).

Drying screen printed matter 9

Screen printing has always been distinguished by the thick ink film deposit that it can produce. Indeed this characteristic has long been regarded as its principal advantage. Yet this aspect of the process loses some of its appeal when it comes to drying the ink film. A thick ink film can take a lot of drying!

According to their particular formulation, screen printing inks dry by one of the following mechanisms:

The mechanisms of drying

- Oxidation
- Solvent evaporation
- Infra-red curing
- Ultraviolet curing.

Each of these mechanisms will be described in turn, giving examples of the kind of equipment currently used in both manual and machine production. Recent developments such as radio frequency (RF) drying and the use of catalytic technology in radiant gas dryers will also be outlined.

The early oil-based screen printing inks dried by a process known as oxidation. The inks were formulated with stand oil vehicles, such as linseed and tung-oil. These oils have the property of drying to form a hard flexible film when exposed to the air for extended periods. To speed up the drying process metallic drying salts (cobalt, lead and calcium) are added to the ink. These additives promote oxidation in the ink film, giving it a drying time of 6–8 hours.

Oxidation

Modern alkyd-based gloss inks have been formulated to provide more rapid drying and improved surface finish and flexibility. They dry by oxidation. When printing on to metal or glass the inks can be dried by stoving them in a drying oven at 80–120°C (176–248°F) for 5–15 minutes,

Fig. 60 The space rack.

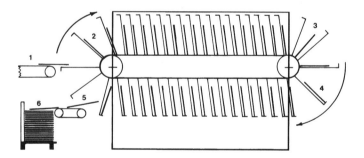

Fig. 61 The wicket dryer.
1. Print delivery.
2. Print is transported into the drying chamber.
3. Print drops into the tray below.
4. Print is trapped by the tray lip.
5. Print is delivered on to the stacker belt.
6. The stacker belt delivers the dry print on to the autopile unit.

or they may be dried by infra-red radiation. When printing on to heat sensitive materials, such as paper, board or plastics, the prints must be dried in drying racks; wicket drying equipment is also used to shorten drying times.

THE COUNTERSPRUNG SPACE RACK

The 'space rack' is one of the most common forms of drying system used in the screen printing industry. It consists of a stack of light wire-framed trays (50–75). The trays are hinged at the rear to a vertical frame, where they are counterbalanced with strong springs. The whole rack is supported on four heavy duty castors which allow the rack to be manoeuvred around the print shop.

Solvent evaporation

Many graphic screen printing inks dry by solvent evaporation. In manual operation the wet prints are placed on space racks where they will dry unassisted in 10–20 minutes. In machine production the drying process is accelerated with the assistance of various types of mechanized drying device. The 'wicket dryer' is one of the simplest forms of mechanized drying in current use.

THE WICKET DRYER

The wicket dryer consists of a number of light wire trays arranged horizontally or vertically (depending on the design) and linked together on a chain drive. Wet prints are delivered into the empty trays from the screen press, transported around the drying loop and off-loaded on to the stacker, situated beneath the print delivery point.

The main advantage of this kind of dryer is that heat sensitive stocks can be dried slowly at low temperatures, while maintaining relatively high press speeds. Most of these dryers have provision for warm air print ventilation and solvent extraction.

THE JET AIR DRYER

The jet air dryer is widely used with evaporative inks. Here the wet prints are transported from the press on a conveyor belt through long drying tunnels where the evaporating solvent vapours are driven off by strong jets of air. The solvent-laden air is removed by extraction fans so that a constant stream of dry air is supplied to the drying chamber.

Most dryers have two or more separate sections. The first section

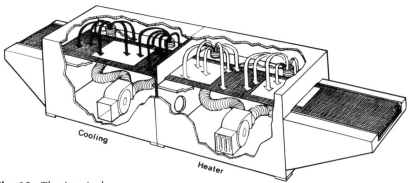

Fig. 62 The jet air dryer.

provides controlled hot air which is directed at the wet ink film in small powerful jets, the effect being to maintain rapid solvent evaporation. Some dryers may have two heater stages. The second section supplies cold jet air to cool the ink film and the stock so that it may be safely stacked without the problem of 'set off'. In some cases there may be two cooling stages, one of which may contain a humidifier to condition the stock after drying.

The main controls on this kind of equipment are: the belt speed (which is determined by the speed of the screen press) and the temperature of the heater section. In some cases it may be possible to run at maximum speeds, using elevated drying temperatures and a fast belt speed, whilst at other times it may be necessary to lower the temperature in the heater section and run at slightly slower speeds. Any adjustments that are made will be determined by the heat sensitivity of the stock, the dimensional tolerances of the work and the drying rate of the ink used.

Infra-red (IR) curing   Many screen printing inks, from metal decorating enamels to textile plastisols, are dried (or, more accurately, 'cured') with infra-red radiation techniques. In most cases the inks are based upon resin systems which will fuse when exposed to intense IR radiation. The process is called 'curing' because the ink's resin system cross-links on exposure to electromagnetic radiation in the infra-red wave band (540–640 nm), causing the liquid ink to fuse into a solid film. A fully cured ink film usually exhibits high resistance to subsequent treatments, such washing, abrading or stressing.

Infra-red sources are designed to provide radiant energy in one of three distinct wave bands:

- short wave IR (0.6–2.5 microns)
- medium wave IR (2.5–3.3 microns)
- long wave IR (3.3–5.0 microns).

Generally speaking, the short wave region operates at elevated temperatures with quartz halogen emitters running at 2200°C. Short wave IR dryers can reduce drying times from hours to seconds. They are mainly used for curing non heat-sensitive materials but some textile dryers also employ short wave IR, usually in combination with jet air drying to keep the heat-sensitive substrate from scorching.

Medium and long wave IR emitters operate at much lower temperatures (800–950°C) and are therefore more suitable for heat-sensitive substrates.

THE INFRA-RED DRYER

The most widely used form of IR dryer is the conveyor dryer. This consists of a heat-resistant glass fibre conveyor belt which transports the wet prints beneath the IR emitters. The emitters are usually housed in air-cooled or water-cooled reflectors, designed to provide a divergent beam of radiation which can overlap to provide an even distribution of radiation and prevent 'hot-spots'.

Many IR dryers employ jet air drying to remove the evaporating solvents or water from the ink. Cold jet air is also used to cool the cured ink film and to prevent any scorching that may occur when curing heat-sensitive substrates. The distance between the IR emitters and the substrate can be adjusted, usually in conjunction with the belt speed settings. Care must be taken when curing heat-sensitive materials since certain colours will absorb more IR radiation than others, and incorrect adjustment of belt speed or IR emitter distance can cause either scorching or inadequate curing.

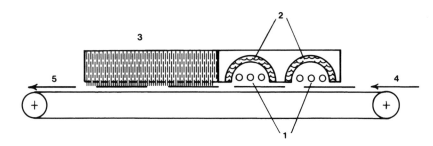

Fig. 63 The infra-red dryer.
1. IR emitters.
2. Water-cooled reflectors.
3. Jet air cooling section.
4. Delivery from screen press.
5. Delivery to stacker.

GAS DRYERS

Gas dryers have been used in the textile industry for many years. Recently there has been an increased interest in gas dryers for use in garment printing. The main advantages of gas as opposed to the conventional IR dryer are:

- energy cost savings
- responsive radiant control
- suitability for use with water-based inks.

EVALUATING DRYING PERFORMANCE

Production test devices, such as cure test strips and energy probes, can be used to establish control data for the dryer and job-specific dryer settings. These devices allow the printer to ascertain the temperatures and levels of radiation attained inside the dryer so that the appropriate adjustments may be made to radiant energy, heat and belt speed. Temperature probes (or 'doughnuts', as they are often referred to) provide the printer with an exact drying profile, detailing the temperatures throughout the drying chamber. The device consists of a heat sensor ring ('doughnut'), connected via a cable to a digital display. As the ring is passed through the dryer, the ambient temperatures are transmitted to the digital display. In this way an exact drying history can be recorded, allowing for precise adjustments to be made to the dryer before and during production.

RADIANT HEAT (CATALYTIC) DRYERS

Recent developments in the design of gas drying equipment have lead to the introduction of a dryer which is said to provide a cheaper, more energy efficient and environmentally acceptable solution to the problem of drying screen printed matter.

The main advantage of the system is that it utilizes the calorific energy in the solvents which evaporate from solvent-based inks during the drying process. Drying is effected by solvent removal heat (SRH) panels which direct radiant heat to the print as it passes through the drying chamber. The evaporating volatile organic compounds (VOCs) are attracted to the catalyst panels, where they are incinerated to provide heat energy, which in turn provides the radiant energy required to increase evaporation rate and dry the print. The more solvent the catalyst consumes, the less gas energy is required to heat the radiant panels.

It is claimed that this drying system provides energy savings in the order of 70% when compared with other conventional drying systems. The other main advantage is that virtually all the VOCs produced in drying the ink are consumed, leaving only warm air to be vented to the atmosphere.

The manufacturers, Solban Ltd, have built a number of systems for the textile printing sector. The SRH panels can be made in a variety of sizes and shapes to accommodate all forms of dryer design, from flat tunnels and vertical towers to static 'hot box' construction. The speed of the drying process also makes the system especially suitable for drying water-based inks, where drying times of 90 seconds are quoted.

Ultraviolet (UV) curing is based upon the principle of photopolymeriza-tion. The photochemistry of polymers is a well established area of research in the chemical industry. Its application in the formulation of adhesives, surface coatings and printing ink is also well established. Recent developments have produced new water-based systems which have special relevance for the screen printing industry.

Ultraviolet (UV) curing

UV ink systems are based upon specific types of photosensitive resins which will chemically cross-link when they are exposed to intense UV radiation. The spectral region that is most effective lies between 300 and 400 nm; radiation below 300 nm lacks the necessary penetration to cure the ink film right through.

The curing process proceeds by what is termed free radical chemistry. Ultraviolet radiation provides the energy required to start the chemical reactions which bring about polymerization of the resins in the ink system. There are three stages in this reaction process: photoinitiation, polymer propagation and polymer termination.

Photoinitiation

The process begins with the creation of reactive free radical intermediates, formed by the action of UV radiation.

Polymer propagation

The free radical intermediates react with the monomers to form a longer free radical intermediate. After many propagation steps a very long polymer chain is formed.

Polymer termination

When the monomers have reacted, only the free radicals remain to react with themselves. At this stage a stable polymer is formed.

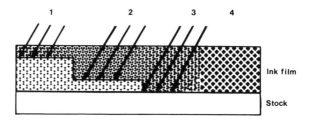

Fig. 64 The four phases of UV curing (see below).

The phases of UV curing

There are four distinct phases through which the UV ink must pass before it is completely cured.

1. The top surface of the ink film cures first of all. This has an important influence on the finish of the ink film. This layer is affected by oxygen in the air which can slow down the curing process.
2. The bulk of the ink film is cured as UV radiation penetrates deep into the ink film structure. During this stage a flexible polymer is formed throughout the film.
3. The UV radiation produces polymerization at the substrate surface, promoting firm adhesive bonding. Good adhesion is primarily affected by cure time, light intensity and the shrinkage that occurs within the film as polymerization proceeds.
4. A post-curing process occurs after the ink film has been removed from the source of radiation. Typically the ink film is in an immobile semi-plastic state after curing. The further chemical reaction that continues to occur for up to 24 hours after exposure improves adhesion and increases surface hardness.

A number of different types of UV dryer are available. Some are designed to fit on to existing jet air and infra-red drying equipment; others are self-contained units which can be operated singly or as a module in a large combination dryer.

The basic dryer consists of a heat-resistant glass fibre conveyor belt which transports the wet prints beneath high intensity mercury vapour lamps. These lamps can reach temperatures of 700°C and must therefore be cooled, usually with cold jet air. The lamp's reflector must also be prevented from overheating and this is done by cooling it with cold water, circulated from a refrigeration unit. Some dryers are fitted with IR filtration, which consists of deionized water recirculated in optically-designed quartz tubes. These filter out the IR radiation generated by the mercury vapour lamps, reducing the heat generated on the stock and thus preventing the stock and ink film from overheating. Such systems have

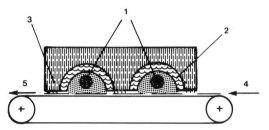

Fig. 65 The UV dryer.
1. Mercury vapour lamps (UV).
2. Water-cooled reflector.
3. Cold jet air cooling.
4. Delivery from screen press.
5. Delivery to stacker.

been designed for use with heat-sensitive materials, such as vinyls and plastic foils which tend to shrink and buckle when exposed to elevated temperatures.

The cure rates of UV inks can vary considerably depending on the formulation, colour and ink film thickness. The main controls provided by the dryer consist of UV emission intensity (most dryers are fitted with multiple lamps which can be independently adjusted) and exposure time, which is determined by the speed of the conveyor belt.

All UV dryers must be fitted with adequate shielding to prevent accidental emissions of UV radiation. Manufacturers are also required to fit electrical interlocking devices which automatically cut off the power to the lamps when the curing head is opened. Thermal cut-out devices are also fitted to prevent overheating due to a fault in the lamp cooling systems.

UV dryers produce a certain amount of ozone, a highly reactive poisonous gas. The gas is created at the surface of the lamp where the UV radiation breaks down the oxygen in the air. Most dryers are fitted with a fume extraction system which ducts the ozone away to the outside atmosphere. Current developments in EU environmental law concerning the production of ground-level ozone may bring about new regulations controlling the emission of ozone from UV curing installations.

FLASH-DRYING UV

Recent innovation in UV drying technology has produced UV lamps which operate on the flash-drying principle. As the lamps only operate for a fraction of a second, when each printed copy passes beneath them, they run at low temperatures and thus do not produce the harmful ozone

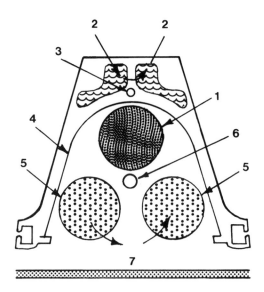

Fig. 66 The Kool-Cure UV Curing Head. (Courtesy of Ultra-Violet Products Ltd.)
1. Mercury vapour lamp (200 watt per inch)/.
2. Water-cooled reflector.
3. Lamp air cooling.
4. Replaceable reflector liner.
5. Aqua-optic IR filter.
6. Substrate air cooling.
7. Substrate.

gas produced by conventional UV lamps. In addition to this they also consume only a fraction of the energy used in conventional UV systems. Further evidence of the advances are apparent in almost every area of the process.

Health and Safety Note:

It is important to ensure that solvent vapours do not accumulate in the working environment. Health and Safety Executive inspectors will require assurance that extraction and ventilation systems are effective. Where potentially hazardous solvents and chemicals are in use they may require air tests to be carried out. Regular testing and maintenance of the extraction and ventilation systems will also be required and records of this must be made available to the inspectors. In certain circumstances, all employees who come into contact with potentially hazardous substances must be given periodic health checks. Here, too, the records must be made available to HSE inspectors (see also Chapter 10).

At a recent screen printing exhibition the Italian screen printing machinery manufacturer Siasprint introduced a new dryer which utilizes the electromagnetic radiation of the radio frequency wave band to dry water-based inks. The technology has been used for some time to dry water-based adhesives and coatings in the paper industry. Tests carried out in screen printing applications have shown that RF can be used with equal success on many other substrates, including textiles and plastics such as PVC.

The principle of RF drying is the same as that used in microwave ovens. In the RF dryer the water present in the printed ink film is heated by the action of the high frequency energy present in the microwaves, transmitted from the RF emitters. The capacity of a substance to absorb RF energy is technically termed the loss factor. Water has a high loss factor – some 100 times higher than that of any other material – which makes it particularly suitable for RF drying.

The manufacturers of RF dryers claim that there are significant benefits to be gained by using RF in place of conventional jet air or UV drying systems.

- RF only heats the water in the ink film and therefore targets energy where it is needed.
- Since water has a loss factor 100 times higher than any other material, the ink is selectively heated and dried instantaneously without heating the substrate.
- Since only the water in the ink is heated, distortion of the stock is minimized.
- RF dryers are more energy efficient, saving up to 65% of energy costs when compared with conventional jet air and UV systems.
- Drying speeds are comparable with UV.
- RF dryers are compact, typically 3.9 m in length.
- RF dryers do not produce any harmful emissions.
- RF dryers do not produce any radiated heat.

The use of water-based ink in place of conventional solvent-based ink is discussed elsewhere (see Chapter 7: Inks for graphic screen printing). Radio frequency drying and the development of water-based ink systems still requires wider adoption by the industry before being accepted as practical, realistic alternatives to the more conventional drying systems currently in use.

Much of this development will depend on the continuing impact of new EU environmental regulations adopted by the UK under various Acts of Parliament such as the Environmental Pollution Act 1990. This, and other relevant industrial legislation, is treated in the next chapter.

Radio frequency (RF) dryers

10 Health, safety and the environment

During recent years there have been several important changes in UK legislation relating to industrial processes. This chapter reviews these changes and outlines their impact on the screen printing industry. The intention is not to detail the provisions contained in the new systems of legislative regulation, but rather to highlight the main areas of concern and identify the agencies responsible for their implementation and enforcement.

Drivers of change
Changes in the law related to industrial processes are the result of a growing general concern with controlling and reducing the impact which the modern consumer society has upon the environment. These concerns are focused through various channels: local pressure groups concerned about a particular industrial plant and its impact upon the local environment; industrial health research bodies concerned with monitoring the impact of industrial processes upon the health of workers and those who live in the industrial locality; trade union health and safety committees concerned with the health and safety of their members; national bodies concerned with protecting the environment and wildlife; international organizations such as Greenpeace, Friends of the Earth and the World Wildlife Fund, concerned with monitoring the environment and the protection of wildlife across the globe; and, most importantly, the departments of government, charged with the responsibility of responding to national and international pressure.

Major industrial disasters such as Bhopal and Chernobyl are exceptional and dramatic examples of industrial hazards which heighten public awareness as to the dangers which can arise through industrial malpractice and negligence. Frequent reports of the effects of so-called 'greenhouse gases' and the depletion of the ozone layer through the emission of CFCs also raise the general level of public anxiety and keep the issue of the environment as a pressing concern for everyone.

Much of what has been reported about the effects of global warming is based upon predictions drawn from computer modelling, which may or may not be proved in practice. However, our present understanding of the environmental impact of many industrial chemicals and processes is limited and the production of new chemical products is taking place at an ever increasing rate. This being the case, the consequences of ignoring such predictions are so serious that international agreements have been reached on finding ways to reduce the level of hazard created by the modern industrialized world.

Concern for the environment is a highly political issue. Political parties across Europe, actively seeking to influence governments, bring pressure to bear upon those responsible for developing and implementing national and international policy. Much of the recent UK legislation has directly or indirectly resulted from such pressures, brought to bear through the EU legislative mechanisms of directives. All member states (the UK being one) are required, as signatories to the various treaties establishing the EU, to relinquish sovereignty in relation to laws on certain subjects. Specially created institutions have been established with responsibility for drafting EU directives which all member states are bound to implement in precedence to domestic laws. In the UK these directives and 'daughter' directives have been embodied with the framework of Acts of Parliament, which form the basis of the UK legal system.

The two Acts of Parliament which contain the areas of principal concern here are:

- Health and Safety at Work, etc. Act 1974 and subsequent related legislation
- Environmental Protection Act 1990.

Health and Safety at Work, etc. Act 1974 (HSW Act)

Like other pieces of industrial and environmental legislation, this Act of Parliament provides a framework within which detailed legislative regulations, rules, orders etc. are formulated. Drawn up in 1974 as a result of the Robens Committee Inquiry, the HSW Act consolidates earlier legislation spread across several separate Acts of Parliament, dating as far back as 1875. It places a number of general duties on both employer and employee. It also empowers government ministers to issue regulations to deal with specific areas of concern. Importantly it requires the employer to demonstrate how the duties imposed by the Act are to be fulfilled within the organization. It also imposes a clear responsibility on the employee to conform with the established health and safety procedures within the organization and to ensure that actions do not present a health and safety hazard to the worker or to others. Thus the new Act places a duty on everyone in the organization to act in accordance with a set of established Health and Safety Regulations and to take full responsibility for their actions in this respect.

A new government agency, the Health and Safety Executive (HSE), was established to promote health and safety at work. HSE inspectors are appointed to monitor health and safety procedures. They are given powers to enter the factory, inspect plant, observe processes and gain access to any relevant documentation. Should any hazard be identified they are empowered to issue an Improvement Notice which requires remedial action to be taken by the company within a specified time. In more serious cases Prohibition Notices may be issued which require immediate suspension of an operation until the hazard has been removed.

The Act also places a responsibility on employers to look after the health, safety and welfare of those outside their employment who might be affected by the activities engaged in by the company. This involves the handling, use and storage of hazardous chemicals and the emission of noxious or offensive substances into the atmosphere – not just those activities which constitute a potential hazard to health.

Importantly the Act established the principle that primary responsibility for accident prevention and combating occupational ill health resides with those who create the risk. In practice this places responsibility on everyone involved at the workplace for achieving high standards of health and safety. The Act requires that the employer's duties are to be carried out *so far as is reasonably practical*. Special mention is made regarding the management and implementation of health and safety policy within an organization through the establishment of a Health and Safety Committee.

Many of the provisions in the HSW Act have been replaced by the implementation of the new EU Framework Directive and 'daughter' directives embodied in the Management of Health and Safety at Work Regulations 1992, which came into force on 1 January 1993. The Regulations reinforce the principles contained in the HSW Act by detailing in a much more prescriptive way the responsibilities of the employer for the management of health and safety matters in the workplace. The Control of Substances Hazardous to Health (COSHH) Regulations exemplify the underlying philosophy which is shaping much of the legislation coming from Brussels. The basic aim is to encourage self regulation and control.

The COSHH Regulations and the management role

As stated above, there has always been a responsibility placed upon the employer to control the use of substances which may present a potential hazard to the health of employees or others who may be affected by their use in the workplace. What COSHH does is to establish principles upon which the development of health and safety policy and subsequent actions should be based. These principles require the employers to:

- assess the level of hazard presented by a substance and/or the process in which it is used;

- eliminate the hazard by using a safer alternative;
- prevent or minimize the risk where no alternative is available or practicable;
- protect the employees against the risk.

More clearly than ever before these regulations specify the requirement to demonstrate that health and safety is being managed in a formal and organized way which is characterized by: effective planning; data collection and dissemination; organization and control; training; and the monitoring and review of preventive and protective measures. In all companies employing more than four persons the arrangements for the management of health and safety matters must be formally recorded and this information made available to the HSE inspectors upon request.

Again, what is new here is the onus being placed upon the employer to demonstrate a proactive interest in health and safety matters. Where an employer is not competent to undertake this task, a person or persons must be appointed to assist in the discharge of the responsibilities placed upon the employer under the Act. In this respect there are specific requirements related to training and instruction and the dissemination of health and safety data to all employees.

Companies employing more than five persons must produce a written statement of health and safety policy. The policy must clearly indicate the implications of the Act and detail responsibilities related to the processes and activities carried out at the plant. The policy should be seen as a basis for clear understanding and agreement between management and workers of common interests and responsibilities for health and safety matters. In particular the employees should be able to determine from the policy how they fit into the health and safety structure: what their individual duties are, where they are to seek advice, where to report an accident or potential hazard and how to obtain first aid or other assistance in the event of an accident.

The Health and Safety Executive publishes a number of free leaflets advising employers on health and safety management. There are also guidance notes for small businesses.

Under the HSW Act, the employer is required to establish a safety committee. Its composition is formed by members from all major departments within the plant. Depending on the size of the company, the health and safety manager may be supported by key health and safety contacts with responsibility for the various areas of the plant. The safety committee takes collective responsibility for monitoring and reviewing health and safety procedures, meeting at regular intervals and reporting through its chairperson to the board of directors. It will have responsibility for reviewing health and safety data and considering information on new, safer products and processes. Its terms of reference should embody the principles noted earlier, the first being to eliminate the hazard by using an alternative product or process; in all its deliberations this basic principle will always be before it. Its terms of reference will include the following items:

- Examination of accident reports
- Recommendation on policy for accident prevention
- Monitoring of fire alarm procedures
- Reporting on fire drills and training
- Health and safety training
- Studying health and safety data sheets for raw materials
- Keeping abreast of new legislation.

Training

Training is an important aspect of effective health and safety management. Good training policy and procedures should:

- assess the potential hazards associated with every process;
- identify areas where potential risks occur;
- establish safe working practices;
- draw up training procedures and programmes of induction for new employees;
- ensure that effective training is implemented and regular assessment is made against the established procedures.

Training in health and safety is provided by the Trade Unions, who run courses on a regular basis. The HSW Act clearly states that instruction, training and good supervision are essential. Effective health and safety management will promote training as a key element in the successful implementation of the company health and safety policy.

Safety in the handling and storage of inks and solvents

Under current EU and UK health and safety legislation, all inks and auxiliary products that contain any substances likely to be harmful to the user must carry labels clearly identifying these substances. Manufacturers are also required to issue clear instructions regarding the use of their products. These must specify the nature of the hazard presented.

For example, some UV formulations may be irritating to the eyes and skin. In this case the manufacturers must indicate that the product contains irritant substances and will advise the user to wear protective goggles and gloves to prevent accidental contact. The product data sheet will provide further detail and advice on appropriate action to be taken in the event of accidental eye or skin contact.

The company using the product is legally obliged to make this information known to all those who come into contact with the product. Health and safety data sheets are usually held centrally by the health and safety manager, who is charged with the responsibility of updating and disseminating such information, through the processes of auditing and health and safety training.

If in any doubt about a product, obtain the relevant published instructions from the supplier before permitting its use. All such information must be available for inspection by the Health and Safety Inspectorate, and the relevant regulatory bodies, where these are concerned.

Manufacturers and suppliers do all they can to ensure that their products are as safe as possible. However, it must be realized that inks, solvents and screen cleaning products are not benign substances. They are industrial products and must therefore be used according to correct industrial practice.

GUIDELINES ON INDUSTRIAL HYGIENE AND SAFE WORKING PRACTICE

Generally speaking, most inks and solvents and auxiliary products that are used in screen printing do not present any dangerous level of health hazard when handled with care and common sense. However, they can only be regarded as 'harmless' when handled with due regard to the following principles of industrial practice.

- When used in accordance with the manufacturer's product literature and health and safety data.
- When reasonable standards of cleanliness, tidiness and storage are maintained.
- When handled without abuse or carelessness.
- When the persons handling them are properly instructed.

The minimum requirements for the maintenance of good standards of industrial hygiene and safe working practice are contained in the following elementary guidelines.

1. These products should never be allowed to enter the eyes. Prolonged and repeated contact with the skin should be avoided. Many solvents and inks will remove the natural oils from the skin and cause local skin irritation if prolonged contact is permitted. Protective clothing should always be worn when these products are handled.
2. Splashes of these products on the skin or in the eyes should be treated promptly by washing with copious amounts of clean water. In cases of eye contamination, medical attention should be sought at once. (The HSW Act recommends that eye wash stations be located in areas where potential hazards exist.)
3. Ingestion of these products should always be avoided. Food and drink should not be stored, prepared or consumed in areas where inks and solvents are used. Smoking in these areas should also be prohibited.

4. Inhalation of these products as particles, dust, fumes or solvent vapours should be avoided either by using efficient local ventilation/extraction or by using masks or dust respirators, as may be determined by circumstances.

5. All areas where these products are mixed, blended or applied must be adequately ventilated.

6. There should be facilities for changing and cleansing protective clothing and equipment and these items should be replaced when necessary.

7. Washing facilities should be available near to the area in which the products are being used. Personnel should be encouraged to wash before taking food and before using toilet facilities. It is important to stress that ink should be removed from the skin with an industrial hand-cleaner. Hands should be washed thoroughly with soap and water, paying special attention to the finger nails. Under no circumstances should solvents be used to remove ink from the skin.

8. Spillage of inks and solvents could be hazardous and must be cleaned up at once. Care must be taken at all times to prevent solvents and inks from entering the drains or sewage systems. To allow this to occur is an offence.

9. Any used cleaning materials, such as rags and paper wipers, must be treated as a fire hazard and should be placed in appropriate waste disposal containers. These should be removed from the production area at least once a day, or at the end of each shift. Illegal storage of controlled waste is an offence under the Environmental Protection Act 1990 Section 33(1)(c).

10. All inks, solvents and auxiliary cleaning products must be handled in accordance with the manufacturer's instructions.

11. The disposal of waste should be in accordance with the regulations made under the Environmental Protection Act 1990 (pg. 159).

STORAGE OF INKS AND SOLVENTS

All printing inks and auxiliary products should be stored in well ventilated buildings or in areas set aside for this purpose and suitably located in case of fire. Products that are based upon volatile flammable solvents must be stored in accordance with local regulations relating to the particular constituents.

FIRE RISK

Solvent-based screen inks and their diluents do present a degree of fire hazard. The level of hazard will depend on the particular constituents of the product. The flash point of each product should be clearly indicated on the label. If the product presents a particularly high degree of hazard, appropriate instructions will be given on the label and in the product handling and storage instructions. Whilst water-based inks do not present a fire hazard, if they are exposed to high temperatures for a prolonged period the water may evaporate to yield a residue that may burn.

If these products do become involved in a fire, the nature of their chemical composition in respect of pigment, resin, solvent and other components may be such that they will produce noxious or flammable fumes. For this reason storage locations should be chosen so that, in the event of a fire, there is a safe and ready (preferably external) access for the fire-fighting services and a minimum risk of noxious fumes reaching other areas. Screen inks and auxiliary products should never be stored next to direct sources of heat.

The Environmental Protection Act 1990

The Environmental Protection Act 1990 (EPA) is just one of several new Acts of Parliament which have been drafted in response to the UK's commitments to the EU and international treaties on the protection of the environment. Other Acts include the Water Industries Act 1991, the Water Resources Act 1991 and the Clean Air Act 1993, all of which directly or indirectly have implications for the printing industry. It is also important to recognize that the law relating to the environment is a rapidly developing and evolving aspect of the modern industrial scene. The regulations placed upon a process today may very well change within 6–12 months. We have to accept the fact that the underlying philosophy of the environmentalists is to achieve a continuing reduction in industrial pollution and in waste and energy consumption. This is an established aim underpinning the EU legislative process. It is also enshrined in the international treaties agreed at the 1987 Montreal Summit on the Protection of the Environment. It is something with which we must come to terms if we are all to survive and prosper in a safer and more healthy world.

How can the goal of continuous reduction be achieved? Several methods have been devised to encourage and coerce us into a greener way of life. For example:

- Drawing up tighter and tighter controls on the use of ecotoxic and potentially harmful substances.
- Encouraging the development and use of new 'green' products and processes such as water-based inks and low toxicity solvents.
- Applying the principle of 'the polluter pays' – the cost of pollution control can be prohibitively high, both in terms of recovery and waste disposal and also in the administration necessary in its management.

- Using the power of the market, identifying effective environmental management with quality (the 'green is good' principle).
- Applying the negative pressure of fines and bad publicity consequent on prosecution under the law.

Like the HSW Act, the EPA is a framework Act composed of delegated legislation in the form of rules and regulations, each of which has the legal force of an Act of Parliament and together comprise the statutory law. The EPA is a development of the earlier Control of Pollution Act 1974, modifying and redefining many of the provisions made therein. The main areas of substantial change of relevance to the screen printing industry are in the regulations relating to air pollution and waste management.

AIR POLLUTION CONTROL (APC)

Part I of the Environmental Pollution Act 1990 introduces two new regulatory systems:

- Air Pollution Control (APC), which is the responsibility of the local authorities (district or county councils), who will apply the law in regulating the control of emissions (solvents, dust particles, noxious smells) into the air.
- Integrated Pollution Control (IPC), which applies to the larger more polluting industries and covers emissions to air, water, sewers and land. The enforcement of IPC is the responsibility of Her Majesty's Inspectorate of Pollution and the local river purification authority. Currently IPC has little relevance to the printing industry.

The relevant part of the Act is contained in the Environmental Protection (Prescribed Processes and Substances) Regulations 1991 (SI 1991/472). Part B lists the prescribed processes covered by APC, with printing referred to at Section 6.5 as 'Coating Processes and Printing'. For a process to be covered here it must comply with a number of requirements:

1. The process releases into the air particulate matter in the form of grit, dust or fumes, or any volatile organic compound (VOC). It is important to note that 'air' refers to air inside the factory as well as outside it.
2. The plant uses either:
   (a) 20 tonnes or more of printing ink, paint or other coating material that is applied in a solid form annually; or
   (b) 5 tonnes or more of organic solvents annually, including solvents used in cleaning and for other purposes in addition to those contained in surface coatings.

(Note that the above calculation in relation to solvent usage is the subject of governmental review. Currently, the published Government view is that account need only be taken of the solvents consumed in the process, and not those which may be recycled or sent for disposal. However, EU Directives are currently being drafted, tightening the control of solvent usage, and this may well lead to a lowering of the quantity thresholds which will result in more companies being brought within the scope of APC. In 1993 the Department of the Environment published a UK strategy for reducing emissions of VOCs and ground level ozone. In relation to the printing industry, the strategy proposes a 49% reduction in VOC emissions between the 1988 base-line and 1999. This document does not take into account the proposed EU Solvents Directive. The recent Directive 92/72/EEC on Air Pollution by Ozone is concerned with monitoring ground level ozone across the EC and assessing its impact on human health. Other proposed Directives will seek to establish air quality laws. Although their impact is indirect, these new Directives set out to create further reductions in the use of solvents and will eventually lead to increased regulation through the UK legislative framework.

Whether or not a company will be subject to the Regulations contained in Part I of the Act will depend largely on its size and the nature of the processes and volume of materials it uses. Much of the screen printing industry consists of small companies, employing fewer than ten persons. Most of these companies will not be covered by APC. However, they will still be required to comply with:

- Part III of the Environmental Protection Act 1990, which deals with statutory nuisance (this covers such things as noxious smells, smoke and noise).
- The Clean Air Act 1993, which covers emissions of smoke, dust, grit and fumes.
- The civil law relating to air pollution.

Therefore, whilst the small screen printer employing, say, just eight people and producing self-adhesive vinyl stickers may be exempt from APC, the folks living next door may not be happy with the smells coming out of the extractor units along the side of the workshop; and the new screen cleaning unit at the rear of the premises does little to enhance the peace and quiet previously enjoyed by those gardening in the adjoining allotments. All of those living within the vicinity of the factory have the right under the law to seek protection against any nuisance caused as the result of industrial and commercial activities undertaken there. In this case the small printer may very well find that activities hitherto outside the law are no longer so. With public awareness in matters relating to the environment growing all the time, only the foolhardy will continue regardless of change and in ignorance of information which is vital to their existence.

Processes which at present enjoy exemption from APC are listed in Process Guidance Note 6/32 and include:

- sheet-fed screen processes;
- rotary-fed screen process not using toluene or xylene;
- ultraviolet and infra-red cured ink systems.

Exemption is always a matter of degree and depends on the scale of the operation, location and to some extent the attitude of the local authority. If the printer is in any doubt about the emissions from the plant, the wisest action is to contact the local authority for advice. It is a misconception to see the regulatory bodies as the enemy, ready to pounce on the unsuspecting with prohibition notices and fines. Their role is as much an advisory one as it is a policing one.

A sensible first step would be to seek advice from the industry's professional body, the Screen Printing Association UK Ltd (SPA), which monitors all aspects of the industry and maintains extensive data bases on such things as health and safety, environmental legislation, training, and the achievement of BSI and ISO quality standards. There are also independent organizations providing advice and information relating to environmental law. These will often publish details of legal actions which establish case law. In cases where there is no relevant Act of Parliament, the courts may also make law through trying certain cases – for example, in establishing the principles of civil liability for environmental harm. This is known as case law. Case law is also important in interpreting and defining the meaning of Acts of Parliament by providing examples of their application. This is especially important where new legislation is being enacted, as is the case with much of the current environmental legislation.

A company which finds that it is covered by APC must apply to the local authority for an authorization. This will require a detailed specification of the processes involved, substances consumed and methods adopted to control emissions. The application must be published in the local press. The local authority will set conditions on the authorization which require the company to demonstrate that the 'best available techniques not entailing excessive cost' (BATNEEC) are applied in controlling and minimizing the emissions.

These conditions also require the company to demonstrate continuous improvement as better techniques become available. There are fees charged in respect of the application and an annual charge is made for the authorization. The conditions attached to the authorization may be changed at any time, reflecting changes in the Regulations under APC. The local authority may revoke an authorization at any time should the company fail to comply with the established conditions or any new conditions imposed.

In line with EU policy on public access to information relating to the environment, local authorities are required to provide public registers detailing information relating to any authorizations granted – this includes monitoring information. Local authorities have been granted strong powers of enforcement backed by a range of offences which carry high potential penalties, with fines currently in the range of £5000–20 000 depending on the nature of the offence. Where a case is tried in the Crown court there is an unlimited maximum fine and a jail term of up to two years. Appeals against local authority decisions can be made to the Secretary of State; there is, however, little experience to date of such appeals being upheld.

WASTE MANAGEMENT

Part II of the Environmental Protection Act 1990 is concerned with the regulation of solid waste disposal and the licensing of waste management (i.e. contractors providing waste disposal services). From April 1992 all those involved in industrial and commercial activities wherein solid waste is produced (controlled waste) are made legally liable under a Duty of Care to ensure that safe and environmentally acceptable methods of waste disposal are adopted.

The most important aspect of the Duty of Care is that it embodies the principle of 'cradle to grave' responsibility for 'controlled' waste, i.e. that which is a by-product of the process: soiled wipers, spoilage, off-cuttings and trimmings, scrap materials or equipment. This means that the producer of the waste is responsible for its disposal and is legally liable to ensure that this is done in a way which is compliant with the specifications made under the EPA Duty of Care as specified by the local authority waste management department. This responsibility may not be delegated to a third party, i.e. the waste disposal contractor. It is, therefore, the responsibility of the waste producer to ensure the following:

- That the waste disposal contractor is properly licensed to transfer and dispose of the waste. This means obtaining a list of licensed contractors from the local authority waste management department; the SPA will also advise in this matter. It is important to ensure that the waste disposal contractor is licensed for both transfer and handling/management, since separate licences may be issued for each of these functions.
- That a waste transfer note is completed and signed and that copies are kept by all parties. This provides a detailed description of the nature of the business, the substances contained in the waste, their chemical analysis, the processes used in producing the waste, and the type of packaging. Special waste must be separately identified and placed in special waste containers.

'Special waste' is a category of controlled waste consisting of substances which constitute a danger to life or have a flash point below 21°C. Although most screen printing inks and solvents are not now classified as special waste, the current EU Draft Directive on limiting solvent usage includes irritant substances (some UV resins) and raises the solvent flash point threshold to 55°C. This means that all solvent-based inks and those inks which contain irritant substances will be regarded as special waste and will therefore require special waste disposal arrangements (landfill, which is widely used in the UK, will no longer be permitted). If in doubt consult your supplier, the SPA and the local authority waste management department. Some suppliers, like Sericol Limited, now provide a comprehensive waste management service.

Water pollution – Water Industries Act 1991

Another area of principal concern, relating to the Water Industries Act 1991, is the control of solvent- and chemical-contaminated water which enters the sewers. The water treatment companies are charged with the responsibility for treating waste water. Where this is polluted by industrial effluent the polluter will be required to pay by obtaining an authorization from the water company; failure to do so will result in prosecution. It is illegal to dispose of industrial solvents and chemicals in the drains without authorization to do so.

Many screen printers still appear to be blissfully unaware of the restrictions imposed upon them by this Act and other related legislation. Again, information is provided through the SPA and by the local water companies responsible for water treatment.

Environmental law is a rapidly developing aspect of the contemporary industrial world. It is not yet clear how it will constrain the growth and development of the screen printing industry but one thing is certain: it is here to stay. The regulations it places upon the printing industry are likely to become more tightly drawn and more complex in their implementation. As yet enforcement appears to be slow to take a grip, since the administrative mechanisms and resources needed for practical implementation always take time to become established. However, this does not mean that the industry can simply relax and wait for the regulator to come knocking at the door. The law is there and non-compliance is an offence – and the law does not regard ignorance as an excuse.

These changes in the law serve to exemplify the nature of the contemporary world in which we live. It is a world characterized by rapid, complex and dynamic change, a world where more than ever before we need to have access to information if we are to survive and prosper. For this is the information age and our ability to survive and prosper is dependent on our ability to know, to understand, to apply our knowledge and to adapt to change.

The dynamics of change 11

To operate effectively in this fast moving-technological world it is necessary to understand the nature of change and how its dynamic influence will impact on the processes, services and products provided by the industry. This chapter deals with the nature of change; it outlines some of the main features and describes the problems it can create. It will also indicate how those in the industry might learn to respond to change in a new and positive way – indeed, how change may be grasped as an opportunity rather than being avoided or resisted as a threat.

Change is a phenomenon which most people find uncomfortable, sometimes threatening, especially when they do not expect it, or cannot understand it. In most cases the natural reaction is to resist it or to pretend that it is not really relevant. This is because we are conditioned through our very earliest experiences to look for continuity and to be wary when presented with the new and unfamiliar.

It is a commonly understood fact that as people grow older they find that changes, such as moving house or changing their job, can impose considerable psychological stress. This can be caused by unfamiliar surroundings, the need to establish new relationships at work or with neighbours, the need to demonstrate skills and ability, or the need to regain self-esteem and the respect of fellow workers and colleagues. In extreme circumstances, when these needs are difficult to satisfy, such unsettling experiences can lead to breakdown and illness.

It is therefore to be expected that changes in our working experience can also cause problems. For example, learning to use a new process or a new machine can cause feelings of anxiety and stress. This is especially true for those who have worked in one particular situation for a number of years and are then expected to undertake a new set of tasks, requiring new skills.

I can recall my own experiences when moving to a new job after completing my apprenticeship as a technician in a hand-bench print shop. I remember vividly how nerve-racking it was during the first few weeks, coming to terms with the new world of machine printing, having spent the first four years of my working life learning the gentle art of the squeegee. Suddenly it was all button pushing, setting squeegee pressures and flo-coaters, dwell-times, lift-off adjustments, drying temperatures and belt speeds And the noise and the pace of the new job made the old job seem like another world – far more relaxed and humane.

At 20 years of age I soon picked things up. How different it might have been were I to have been in my early 50s. In those days there were no computers, no electronic control systems, no digital imaging. There was full employment. The industry was changing and growing, but at a pace which did not appear threatening. Today the pace of change seems to move at an ever increasing speed. And it is not just the speed, but the nature of change which makes it often so difficult to cope with. This is because change is multidimensional; it is a dynamic force and therefore complex in its effect.

This can best be understood by looking at some examples of changes now taking place in the industry. Consider the impact of the new Environmental Protection Act, outlined in the previous chapter.

It is clear from what has been said that suddenly the screen printing industry, like the rest of the printing industry, is having to contend with a whole new set of complex and restrictive regulations. It is also clear that the situation is not going to become easier, since more regulations are on the way which will tighten the limits on what we can and cannot do even further.

The first principle of effective environmental management is to try to find an alternative product or process that does not require complex and expensive authorization and monitoring in its use. The second principle is to demonstrate continuous improvement – in fact, to be able to demonstrate not simply responsiveness to change but proactive engagement in the process.

Materials suppliers and equipment manufacturers are of course acutely aware of the implications for their products and services. Limiting the use of solvents has encouraged ink manufacturers to search for safer more ecologically acceptable solvents and chemicals. Much research and development has been and is being invested in new water-based ink systems, both conventional and UV curing. Indeed, most suppliers have grasped the challenge as an opportunity to gain a marketing advantage in supplying new, greener products. Some suppliers are also extending the supplier links in providing a 'cradle to grave' service for their products which includes waste disposal. This does two things: it reassures the user that compliance with the law is effectively taken care of, and it strengthens the user/supplier chain, thus satisfying both needs. This in turn leads to a more stable and confident industry which encourages further investment and leads to further growth.

Machinery manufacturers are also investing research and development resources into new technology for screen cleaning and reclamation and in the development of new drying systems which control solvent emissions and reduce energy consumption. Such development is of course taking place across the whole of the printing and surface coatings industries. As with much R&D activity there are spin-off developments which can find applications beyond those original intended. This is often the case in the development of raw materials used in inks and screen emulsions and in drying technology.

However, in order for manufacturers and suppliers to commit resources to the development of new products and equipment there has to be the confidence that a market exists to purchase them. In other words the industry must demonstrate a willingness to respond to the changes made possible by the such developments. Failure to do so will cause the suppliers to take a more cautious and conservative stance which carries the risk that the industry will begin to fall behind other industrial areas where R&D investment is made with more confidence.

A good example of this may be seen with the development of water-based ink systems. The first water-based UV ink systems were developed in Australia some ten years ago. The chemistry and drying technology developed further as a result of its acceptance by the Australasian screen printing industry. Water-based UV inks have only recently been offered in this country as a serious alternative, mostly in the areas of four colour process printing. Such reluctance to take on new products and processes may be symptomatic of the conservatism of British industry, on both sides of the supply chain. However we like to view it, it is evidence of a resistance to change which can be identified throughout many levels of the industry, from senior management to the janitor.

Most new products require the user to learn how best to use them. If this was not the case, there would be little reason for introducing them in the first place. The introduction of conventional water-based inks is a good example. Most of these new products require a totally different approach to printing than is the case with conventional solvent-based ink systems. Care must be taken in selecting the screen mesh, the stencil system and the paper stock. The techniques used in printing must also be revised in order to achieve satisfactory results. Some of the conventional water-based inks do not provide the high colour opacity obtained with most solvent-based systems. It is therefore essential to advise clients so that slight modifications in design and origination may be undertaken to take this into account.

As with all new products and processes, a learning curve is necessary. Time must be spent in learning to make the most effective use of them, which means investing time in gathering information and conducting tests in production conditions. Most manufacturers and suppliers want the industry to give their new products a fair trial. They have a vested interest in recovering the investment in R&D and in ensuring that the industry is able to adapt to the changes which new legislative regulations are bringing about. Their own survival depends upon this.

As the saying has it – no screen printer is an island. We are all affected by the processes of change and the way we respond to them will impact upon others. The more unwilling we are to stay abreast of developments and the more we wait for others to try new products, the more we put ourselves and our industry at risk. This is not to say that every screen printer has to try every new product that comes on the market. It simply means that we must make a conscious effort to ensure that we keep our own operation and our industry always in the forefront by being alert to change and proactive in our engagement with it – to see change as a challenge to our imaginative and creative intelligence and to embrace it as an opportunity, rather than shun it as a threat.

To survive and prosper in the modern world we must learn how to understand the nature of change, both in its direct impact upon us in our everyday working environment and in the broader technological, economic and political dimensions. We must try to encourage a change in attitude in those who work for us. How often do we find that new products used successfully by our competitors have been rejected simply of the basis of production staff prejudice?

We are all familiar with the stereotypical responses: 'We've always done it this way,' or, 'It works all right, so why change it?' or, 'This is just change for change's sake.' How do such attitudes come about? What is it that gives rise to such negative and blinkered responses?

Very often negative attitudes arise from the way in which change is introduced. As noted earlier, people do not like change; they seek continuity. It might be said that this is because people are essentially lazy. To do something new requires additional effort and greater concentration, and usually involves a degree of uncertainty. However, all of these experiential attributes of the new can also be pleasurable. There is a sense of excitement about trying something new – the unexpected, both in the way a new product or process works and in the achievement of actually getting it to work. The effort and concentration needed can serve to heighten the sense of achievement by raising the level of challenge experienced in the engagement with something new. The possibility of achieving results over and above those previously achieved creates the potential for reward through effort. New products, machines and processes are very often designed to improve working conditions for the operators, and this can be presented as an important aspect of change.

In order to have change perceived as a positive experience, in most circumstances the advantages of the new have to be seen to be demonstrably greater than the old. For example, in the case of water-based inks the advantages – of having a cleaner process, with no noxious solvent smells and noisy extractors, with easy water wash-up and screen reclamation and a lower risk of fire – would have to be set positively against the learning curve required in using the new ink system, which does take time to get used to.

If we are to set about changing attitudes we must begin by realizing that resistance to change is best overcome by intelligent and sensitive

human resource management. Investing time in training and the demon-
stration of the new techniques is a cost which has a proportional
pay-back. Providing an opportunity for the production team to discuss
the new system with the technical representative, or to see the system in
operation in the production environment where first-hand feedback can
be obtained from those with practical experience of the system, are ways
in which attitudes to change can be modified. If the benefits of the new
are to be perceived as real benefits they should be presented by those
whose experience carries the credibility of common experience. To have
sales persons demonstrate a new product or process is often not as
effective as actually seeing it in production. The first-hand language of
production is often far more convincing than the smooth sales pitch, no
matter how well polished. The more care and effort put into introducing
change, the more readily it will be adopted by those most directly affected.

Since so much of our experience is now determined by the dynamics
of change it is sensible to encourage staff, especially production staff, to
take an interest in the technological developments in the process. Access
to product information and trade journals provides an opportunity for
production staff to keep up to date with developments in the industry and
encourages a sense of involvement. Visits to trade shows are also very
important in encouraging more open-minded attitudes and an interest in
the changes taking place.

Membership of trade associations such as the SPA and the Screen
Process Technical Association (SPTA) provide vital links across the
industry. Both organizations provide the opportunity for members to
meet and discuss developments and strategies. Joint lecture programmes
are organized on topics of specific or general interest, and these too
provide valuable opportunities to update knowledge and to address
important issues of concern. The Screen Printing and Graphic Imaging
Association International (SGIA) provides a comprehensive service to the
international screen printing community with conferences and work-
shops dealing with a wide spectrum of current issues. The statistical
reports, research documents and news bulletins produced by such organizations provide useful mechanisms for up-dating staff and raising the
general awareness of what is going on in the industry, both in the UK and
in other parts of the world.

Formal training programmes, whether provided by colleges, training
agency centres or the suppliers, also offer important opportunities for the
development of positive attitudes in employees. For example, sending a
sales representative, a manager and two production staff to do a short
course in quality management might seem extravagant. The reaction
might be: why send all four when the training is most relevant to only
two of them? The answer is that the experience of working together in
an area which concerns the future of the company is important for all
members of the group. The experience will create a sense of common

worth and importance and may provide a valuable opportunity to develop what is known as 'peer bonding' – a strong sense of common interest within the working relationship. This is often developed much more readily in work-related activities undertaken away from the workplace (especially if they involve a residential experience) which set a challenge for those attending, i.e. evaluating a new process and reporting back to management on its relevance to the company, its products and services.

I remember some years ago, when capillary films were first introduced, a representative from a major supplier assured me that capillary films 'would never take off'. How wrong he was! We live in a world where we must consider all possibilities, dismiss nothing and actively seek the new. In the information age we need to be better informed than ever before. We need to recognize that information is central to the security we have until now enjoyed, in an industry which has experienced uninterrupted growth since its inception, even through the darkest days of economic recession. We need to understand that change is a condition of modern life. If we are to survive in the world of work we must learn to become more flexible, adaptable and alert to the changes going on around us. It is no longer sufficient to be simply good at what we do; we must be better at it and able to learn more quickly how to be better.

Screen printing applications 12

Screen printing is the most versatile method of all the printing processes in use today. It is used both as a graphic and decorative medium and as an industrial process in the manufacture of a vast range of products. This chapter will outline some of the more distinctive and interesting aspects of its many and varied applications.

To begin we should consider the structure of the industry, since the applications of the process tend to be divided into fairly distinctive product areas or market sectors. Fine art printing is treated as a separate specialist application, since many of the techniques used in this field are exclusive and have no place within the mainstream of commercial screen printing.

The major commercial sectors are:

- Graphics
- Garment printing
- Textiles
- Glass and ceramics
- Industrial
- Electronics.

Graphics applications

The graphics sector is by far the largest and most diverse sector of the UK screen printing industry. It includes a wide range of applications, some of which are specialist in nature, such as the security printing of lottery tickets and credit cards. The major areas in the sector include: point-of-sale and display; posters; packaging and merchandising; self-adhesives; signs and vehicle marking.

Companies in the sector range from small sole-proprietor print shops producing small run work (typically 50–500 runs) to large screen printers providing a total service from design to installation. There are many small to medium size companies employing 5–15 people.

SUBSTRATES

In point-of-sale and display applications the most common substrates are paper, board, corrugated board, self-adhesive vinyl and rigid vinyl. Most posters are printed on machine glazed (MG) poster paper. A number of printers specialize in the production self-adhesive stickers and labels, often employing narrow web machines with UV drying and in-line finishing units.

The use of screen printing in packaging and merchandising has grown considerably in recent years, with many packaging companies investing in screen printing plant. There is a wide range of substrates, ranging from corrugated board and coated or uncoated box board to rigid vinyl and cellulose acetate. One of the main advantages of screen printing is the versatility of the printing machinery, which can accommodate a wide range of formats and stock thicknesses. The other main advantage is in the quality of vivid three-dimensional colour reproduction which can be achieved – an important factor in buying print for point-of-sale and display. The designer and print buyer are looking for visual impact and quality colour printing, both of which can be achieved in the screen print.

Other specialist printers include those involved in the production of screen printed signs and vehicle markings. Companies who specialize in these applications usually offer large format printing, since much of the work requires the accommodation of large-scale graphics (image areas of 4.5×1.5 m, or 15×5 ft), often with multisheet four colour process on self-adhesive and rigid vinyl, fluted polypropylene and acrylic sheet materials. Some sign printers also specialize in screen printed metal signs for the road and rail transport industries.

INK SYSTEMS

The most commonly used inks in graphics applications are the solvent-based ink systems for paper, board and vinyl substrates. UV and the new water-based UV systems are finding increased acceptance by the larger graphic printers, using fully automatic flat-bed and cylinder lines, especially where two colour presses are employed. The specialist sign printers also use acrylic inks, two pack catalytic and stoving enamels for use on metal signs. Evaporation drying water-based inks are being used by some graphics printers. Not surprisingly they have found most acceptance in the education sector, where the focus on environmental concerns is given a high profile and the absence of production pressures allows time to work through the learning curve required with these new systems.

PRINTING MACHINERY

The machines used in graphic applications range from simple hand-benches to multicolour, multiprocess, in-line reel-to-reel label printing machines. The most common machines are perhaps the semi and fully automatic flat-bed machines, some of which are used in the production of large format multisheet work. High speed cylinder machines are also used in the production of point-of-sale, display and poster work. Screen printed packaging and merchandising are also printed on large format flat-bed and cylinder machines. Sign and vehicle livery printers use hand-bench and large format semi-automatic machines, some of which are custom built to accommodate the very large print formats required.

DRYING SYSTEMS

The most common drying system used in the graphics printing sector is jet air, followed by UV and infra-red. In some situations combination dryers are used, providing a choice of jet air and UV.

DEVELOPMENTS

The rapidly developing area of digital design and pre-press will require printers to have the capacity to handle work in digital format. It is also likely that the market will favour those printers who can operate in a fully integrated way with their clients by communicating electronically with them through ISDN or modem links.

Digital proofing systems will eliminate the need for screen printed proofs and will supersede conventional dry toner systems like Chromalin. The new stochastic screening systems will improve the quality of four colour process work and encourage more printers to offer this as a service. The pressures created by the revolution in digital design and pre-press are likely to increase the need for effective direct-to-screen imaging systems. Printers who are unable to handle work in a digital format may find that they will lose clients to those printers who can.

The rapidly developing area of digital colour printing will have an impact on some areas of the graphics sector; indeed it is already establishing a place in the large format sign and vehicle livery market with systems like the 3M Scotchprint. The system is capable of digital imaging directly on to 3M Controltac self-adhesive film, with enlargements up to 160 times the original artwork. Systems such as the Gerber Edge are also finding applications in the short run sign and label printing markets. As with most new technology, the initial cost is high, as market share increases and the cost comes down, making it a more competitive alternative.

Printers in the graphics sector should be alert to the developments that are now taking place in digital colour printing technology. The pace of development here is very rapid in quality, speed and substrate versatility. Failure to consider the positive market gain potential in this technology may result in a lost opportunity to secure new markets and to consolidate current market share with the additional services it can provide. Once the mass-marketing machine realizes the flexibility and responsiveness provided by the 'on demand' facility of digital printing, there is little doubt that a growing demand for its services will begin to emerge.

Garment printing

The garment printing sector has developed rapidly in the UK and in Europe over the last 20 years. Its technology and much of the culture which has spawned this growth come from the USA. The T-shirt was 'born in the USA', as the song has it. It is as much a part of the American culture as the baseball cap and the hamburger. It is part of the CocaCola culture; it is pop art and as such has become globally accepted as the post-modern uniform of the classless society, as acceptable on the waterfront at Cannes as it is in a third world shanty town.

From its modest beginnings as a means of promotional advertising, the printed T-shirt has evolved into a complex fashion statement. Much of this has been encouraged through the marketing machine of the popular music industry. During the 1960s and 1970s the T-shirt took on a new significance, since the image it carried could convey important cultural and social messages about the identity of the wearer. For example, the T-shirt of the concert identifies the wearer with a complex range of values and attitudes associated with a particular group. The 'seen it, heard it, bought the T-shirt' phenomenon has been created by the massive marketing power of the pop music world. It has also been adopted in other areas of mass entertainment, as part of a whole added-value merchandising process. Other examples of its use have been in the promotion of big, global causes – also interestingly associated with pop music events, such as the Live Aid and Band Aid concerts of the mid 1980s.

There has always been an important element of fashion associated with these promotional functions. This aspect has been exploited by some designers who have produced 'designer T-shirts', created by named fashion designers, printed in limited editions and sold to the 'élite' at high fashion prices. Now the T-shirt is designed and produced as a fashion garment for the mass market. It no longer has to promote anything, other than the particular tastes in colour and formal design of the person who wears it.

The T-shirt as an item of clothing also says other important things about the person wearing it. As a garment it is associated with casualness, coolness, youthfulness, health, vigour and fitness. It is this aspect of the printed T-shirt which has lead directly to the development of the imprinted sportswear and leisurewear market. There is a direct link between the T-shirt and the culture of health and fitness which has become so important to Western society in recent years. Clothing which has had a very specific functional purpose in the past, such as the tracksuit or sports training footwear, has now taken on a highly developed fashion value, which is being exploited by designers and manufacturers. Screen printing provides an important method for decorating cut-piece goods and finished garments. It is the ideal process for the short-run fashion market and for promotional imprinting on ready-made sportswear. It is also used in high volume printing for the mass fashion market of the high street chain-stores.

SUBSTRATES

Cotton, polycotton blends and synthetic fabrics such as Lycra are used in garment printing. Most garment printers buy from the large wholesalers who will stock a range of makes and various qualities, from famous names such as Screen Stars, Fruit of the Loom, Hanes and Jersees, to wholesaler branded imports and promotional standard products. They will stock T-shirts, polo shirts, sweatshirts, tracksuits, football and rugby shirts, athletic vests, nylon jackets, and baseball caps and jackets. Major suppliers will stock a full range of colours and can offer special batch dying to order. The famous name brands also produce discharge dye ranges for use with discharge dye systems.

Quality

The quality of garment will have an important influence on the printing process and the final quality of the printed product. It is always wise to source good quality garments from reliable suppliers. Famous names may be more expensive but the quality is guaranteed. As in all things there is often a balance to be struck between quality and price. If the job is a budget promotion for a local charity event then such things as fabric weight, linting and wash resistance may not be important factors. However, always be wary of any products that are of unknown origin or manufacture. If in doubt, subject them to rigorous random testing. When sourcing new garments always check quality of assembly by tugging at the seams; look for evidence of loose stitching or gaping; check the quality of the neck. If the order is a large one, test samples for dye migration, wash resistance and shrinkage; keep samples to reference the quality of the bulk order; also ensure that the supplier is able to provide the quantities needed and can guarantee continuity of supply.

Most suppliers will accept returns of substandard shirts but some may refuse printed returns. If a fault is discovered in the assembly of the shirt or on the non-printed side, most good suppliers will replace them.

Cotton and polyester

T-shirts are made from 100% cotton or from cotton polyester blends. Most quality 100% cotton shirts are preshrunk. Cotton fibres are long and porous in nature and when spun and knitted into a fabric they have a particularly soft and warm feel. They also have the property of trapping air and absorbing moisture. For these reasons they are often regarded as superior to the 50/50 cotton/poly blends, simply because they are cooler and more comfortable to wear. Synthetic fabrics tend to have a smooth, rather hard feel and do not have the same absorbency and insulative quality as cotton fabrics. However, they do provide fabrics with good wash and wear resistance. The 50/50 cotton/poly blend is a good compromise between durability and comfort.

The quality of a T-shirt will be determined by the quality of the cotton from which it is made. The highest quality cotton comes from the US and Egypt. It may also be sourced from Pakistan, India, China and Africa. The quality of the cotton is determined largely by the manufacture of the yarn, which is made by spinning the cotton fibres into lengths. Before it is spun the cotton is cleaned by 'carding' the fibre through fine metal combs; this helps to remove any foreign matter, seeds or short, tangled fibres. The more rigorous the carding, the fluffier and softer the fibres will be. High quality cotton is 'double carded'.

After carding, the fibres are combed to remove any short fibres. They may then be drawn together with synthetic fibres to form a blend or spun with other cotton fibres to form a 100% cotton yarn. There are two types of yarn. The first is known as 'open-end' yarn and is used in most standard-weight shirts. The second involves an additional fibre softening process and is known as 'ring-spun' yarn. The latter results in a softer, fluffier fabric. It provides an excellent printing surface for fine detail work such as four colour process but its tendency to lint on washing can cause colours to fade. It is always good practice to provide washing instructions, advising the customer that the garment should be washed inside out.

Jersey, rib or interlock

T-shirts are made by knitting the yarn in a circular structure to provide a tubular form which eliminates the need to have side seams. There are three different types of stitch used in knitting T-shirt fabrics.

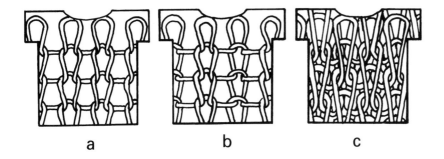

Fig. 67 Knitting styles (see below).

(a) Jersey or 'plain knit' produces a smooth-surfaced fabric with a fine linear pattern ('wales') on the outside and horizontal rows ('courses') on the inside.
(b) Rib knit produces a fabric with 'wales' on both sides, every other 'course' loop falling on the back of the knit. This produces a more elastic cloth than jersey.
(c) Interlock knit is a combination of jersey and rib knitting. It is less elastic than either, but produces a superior run-resistant fabric which is smooth on both sides. It is used in the production of high quality fashion garments, children's wear and top quality T-shirts.

Weight

Another important quality factor is the weight of the fabric. This depends on the yarn number (the thickness of the yarn) and how tightly or loosely it is knitted. T-shirts are usually made from 24–36 single yarn (the higher the number, the thinner the yarn): most lightweight T-shirts are made from 26–28 single yarn, midweights 22–24 and heavyweights from 20 downwards. However, the weight of the shirt can also be influenced by the knit. In some cases a 28 single shirt can have more courses and wales than a 22 single shirt and yet be heavier in weight. Generally speaking, the higher the number of courses and wales, the heavier the fabric will be.

Sweatshirts and fleece garments

Originally used for athletic tracksuits, fleece fabrics are now used for a whole range of sportswear and leisurewear. The fabric is made from a special heavyweight jersey knit in which three different types of yarn are used: face, tie-in and backing yarn. The tightly woven face yarn is used on the front of the fabric to provide high abrasion resistance; the tie-in yarn is used to connect the face to the backing yarn; the backing yarn is loosely woven in place and softened by a napping process in which needles are used to pull small fibres of the backing yarn loose to produce a deep, soft, fluffy surface.

Other fabrics

There are many other types of fabric used in the manufacture of garments for imprinting; each has its own specific qualities and technical requirements. For example, in sublimation transfer printing the requirements are for fabrics with a high synthetic content; the higher the content the more successfully the subliming dyes will transfer. The most commonly used are 100% polyester or nylon.

INK SYSTEMS

A number of different ink systems are used in garment imprinting. Some of them are printed directly on to the garment; others are printed on special transfer papers and subsequently heat-transferred on to the garment in a special transfer press.

Garment printing inks may be classified in three broad categories:

- Plastisols
- Water-based
- Sublimation transfer.

In each of these broad categories there may be a range of ink types and specific finishes. For example, there are several different ink types and media which are classified as plastisols. As these are by far the most commonly used inks for garment printing, they will be dealt with in some detail.

PLASTISOLS

Plastisol inks are made both for direct printing and heat transfer applications. They are formulated on thermoplastic vinyl resin systems, dispersed in plasticizer, which fuse (cure) to a form a solid, flexible plastic film when subjected to heat. The curing temperature is between 149 and 160°C (300–320°F). Pure plastisols do not contain any solvents; they are 100% solids. They are generally of a soft, viscous, buttery consistency and produce a thick ink film deposit. They are only suitable for printing on to absorbent, porous materials, such as cotton or cotton/polyester blends. They may be printed directly on to the garment or on to heat transfer

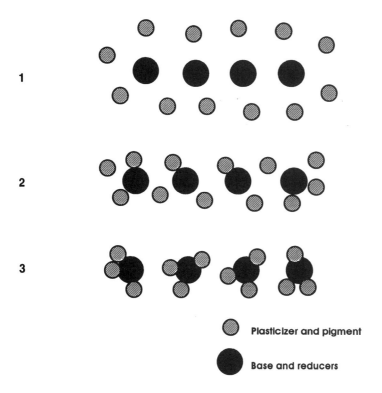

Fig. 68 The curing phases of plastisol ink.
1. Wet ink film.
2. Flashed/semi-cured or gel state.
3. Fully cured ink.

paper and subsequently transferred to a garment in a heat transfer press. In the latter application the transfer print is partially cured, ('soft cured') to between 82 and 121°C (180–250°F) to provide a surface-dry, stable print. During the transfer process the semi-cured plastisol film releases from the siliconized transfer paper and fuses on to the garment, reaching its full-cure temperature in the process.

Plastisol inks will only start to dry when they reach these soft-cure temperatures, below which they will remain in a paste form indefinitely. Washing up or cleaning the image area is usually done with white spirit.

There are many types of plastisol ink. Each type is formulated to provide particular properties and finish characteristics, such as high opacity, reduced film weight, soft hand, translucence, increased abrasion resistance, high elasticity, etc. Although there are general-purpose plastisol inks which can be used in most applications, the range of special effects and quality of finish demanded by the imprinted garment market over recent years has encouraged the ink makers to produce an increasingly diverse range of products. It is not possible to treat the whole range here, nor indeed to deal with the subject of garment printing in the detail it deserves. However, the main types of ink will be outlined and their main functional characteristics indicated.

General-purpose plastisols

These inks provide a smooth, creamy consistency and are suitable for printing on to most light coloured garments; they may also be used on dark garments when a 'first-down' white is printed. They are available in a wide range of colours but do not have the opacity or sufficient colour strength to be used directly on dark grounds. Examples are: Union Ink's Ultrasoft from John T. Keep & Sons Ltd, and Easiprint EZ from Sericol Ltd.

High opacity plastisols

In recent years there has been an increasing fashion trend for bright whites and brilliant colours, including four colour process, printed on black or dark grounds. High opacity plastisols are formulated to provide high undercolour obliteration. The inks contain especially fine milled pigments and special opaque fillers, producing brilliant colours which can be printed directly down on to dark grounds without loss of colour saturation or luminosity. Special low-bleed formulations are also available for use with synthetics and synthetic blends where the dyes used to dye the garment tend to leach out into the ink during or after curing. (A classic example of this is when a white on a red shirt turns pink as the red dye bleeds into the plastisol.) Examples are: MP Super Opaque from Wilflex; Union Ink's Maxopaque LF from John T. Keep & Sons Ltd; Texopaque Aqua XE from Sericol Limited, who provide a range of opaque plastisols which can be thinned and washed up with water.

First-down white

These inks, sometimes referred to as flash-cure whites or underbase whites, are formulated to provide a low-temperature cure. They are used for printing on dark grounds to seal the fabric surface and to provide a white ground for subsequent overprinting, often with four colour process work. Their low-temperature cure allows them to be 'soft cured' in seconds under a 'spot curing' or 'flashing' unit. The semi-cured ink film provides a stable, smooth surface, preventing 'pick up' or slurring in subsequent printing. This is particularly important when printing fine half-tone work, where mid tones can quickly become 'muddied' by excessive dot gain; printing on to a sealed surface improves dot shape and maintains the sharpness of the printed image. Examples would be Wilflex Eurowhite 11150 from Euroflex Ltd, or Aquaflash from Sericol Ltd.

Athletic plastisols

These inks are specially formulated for printing on to stretch fabrics and garments which will require high levels of wear and abrasion resistance. The inks provide high levels of elasticity and superior adhesion. They dry to a glossy finish. The most common applications are in cyclewear, aerobics garments, swimwear and wet suits. The addition of chemical bonding agents will improve wash and chlorine resistance. Flexitex FE, from Sericol Ltd, and Union Ink's Athletic, from John T. Keep & Sons Ltd, are good examples.

Water-borne plastisols

These inks contain a small amount of water, which acts as a solvent. The water helps to reduce the ink film deposit, since it evaporates during the curing process. The resultant finish is softer and more natural than conventional plastisol, which tends to have a rather rubbery feel to it. Some designers specify that the garment must have a 'soft hand', i.e. the image must not form another surface on the garment. Aquasoft, from John T. Keep & Sons Ltd, and Texiscreen Aqua AJ, from Sericol, are examples.

Special effect inks

A number of special effect inks and additives can be used with plastisol inks. For example, there are inks and additives which provide a raised finish to the ink film. These 'puff' inks contain a chemical which produces a gas that foams in the ink film as it cures. The result is an ink film with a soft, high-build relief finish, giving a really effective three-dimensional quality to the print. Some designers have exploited this quality with stunningly creative effect. The inks are often used on children's T-shirts and sportswear.

'Glitter' inks contain large particles of foil-coated plastic. These inks are printed through very coarse screens with low mesh counts (typically 12 HD) to allow for the free passage of the glitter pigments. Glitter inks are used primarily on high fashion garments and are most effective on dark grounds.

WATER-BASED TEXTILE INKS

There are a number of water-based textile inks, technically referred to as pigment dyes, on the market. They are formulated on water-in-oil or oil-in-water emulsion systems. Some, like the Brico Halizarin pigment dyes from Hayes Chemicals, are supplied in the form of a pigment concentrate and a PVA binder. The pigment concentrates are mixed with the binder by the user. The colours are all intermixable in the binder. The binder contains white spirit which helps to prevent the pigment/resin system from drying in the screen.

The inks are available in a wide range of colours, including fluorescents, metallics and special pearlized colours. The standard colours are translucent and may be overprinted to provide strong, clean undertones. Opaque colours can be made by using a special opaque binder. The addition of opaque white will make pastel shades which can be printed on to dark grounds. Care must be taken in screen selection, as opaque colours tend to clog the screen mesh.

Water-based textile inks can be air dried. Chemical curing catalysts can be added to these inks to make them wash resistant. In most industrial applications they are fixed or cured by baking them in a gas dryer. Small lengths and short T-shirt runs can be fixed by ironing the print after it has air dried; the iron should be set at the cotton/polyester temperature setting. Garments can also be fixed in a tumble dryer, set on maximum and fixed for a period of 15 minutes.

Unlike plastisols, water-based inks penetrate the fabric fibres, providing strong colouration whilst retaining a softer hand to the fabric. They can be ironed and dry cleaned, and some suppliers claim they have greater wash resistance than plastisols. These properties make them especially suitable for fashion garments and yard-goods (high volume web-printed fabrics). Water-based inks are particularly useful for printing towelling material, since the inks will penetrate deep into the fabric structure without changing its soft feel.

However, water-based inks do tend to 'dry in' and clog the screen, and when this occurs the dried ink can be difficult to remove. Screen meshes between 43 and 63 threads/cm are recommended; the higher the mesh count, the greater the tendency for drying in to occur. Furthermore, because these inks contain both water and solvent, the stencil system must be a dual-cure type, with resistance to both water and solvent. For long and repeat run work, stencils should be reinforced with a waterproofing treatment after which it will not be possible to reclaim the screen.

As with all ink systems requiring controlled drying or curing, it is necessary to carry out extensive workshop tests to establish print recipes and fixing or curing conditions. Subjecting the print to rigorous wash/rub resistance and ironing tests is an important part of this process. As each ink/dye system is formulated on a different selection and mix of raw materials, such tests must be carried out whenever a new system is used. Examples of pigment dye systems are: Hydrodye, from John T. Keep & Sons Ltd; Riviera, from Gibbon Marler; and Brico Halizarin Dyes, from Hayes Chemicals.

HEAT TRANSFER SYSTEMS

There are a wide range of materials available for heat transfer printing and garment application. They provide a relatively simple method of garment decoration which allows the end user the flexibility to decorate on demand. Printing transfers rather than shirts is less costly, since the transfer comprises simply paper and ink and takes up less space in storage. The main transfer systems are:

- Plastisol transfers (hot-peel and cold-peel)
- Foil transfers
- Flock transfers
- Sublimation transfers.

Hot-peel plastisol

The 'hot-peel' or 'hot-split' transfer is printed on a special high grade transfer paper (T-55, often called soft-trans or trans-55). In this process the transfer paper is peeled away from the garment directly after it is removed from the transfer press, whilst it is still hot. This allows the ink film to split, leaving a film of ink on the paper and providing the image on the garment with a softer feel and an appearance close to that of a direct printed image.

Cold-peel plastisol

The 'cold-peel' or 'cold-split' transfer is printed on a standard transfer paper (T-75, also known as French paper). It has superior 'hold-out' properties, allowing 100% ink film transfer under the transfer press. As its name implies, the transfer is peeled away from the garment after it has cooled. This provides a very flat, smooth, high-build effect on the garment. It is mainly used for small designs, such as logos and promotions. It is not used for large transfers since the thick ink film seals the fabric, preventing it from 'breathing', which can make the garment uncomfortable to wear.

Foil transfers

Foil transfers are very popular on black or dark coloured garments. They can provide stunning images, with brilliant reflectance. They are made by applying a special metallic foil either to a direct printed plastisol image, or from a hot-foil block, i.e. a relief metal plate placed under the heat-transfer press.

Flock transfers

Flock transfers are applied in a very similar way to foil transfers. Special flock-coated transfer papers are used. They consist of a release paper, coated with a fine layer of synthetic fibres, having the appearance and feel of velvet. They are available in a range of colours and in white. Designs are reverse-printed on to the flock paper and subsequently overprinted with a heat-transfer adhesive, which may also be used on its own with coloured flock transfer papers. The transfer is then placed face down on the garment. When heat and pressure are applied in the transfer press, the adhesive image bonds the flock to the surface of the garment. When the transfer has cooled the paper carrier is peeled away, leaving the flocked image on the garment.

Sublimation transfers

Sublimation transfer inks are made from special dyes which have the property of 'subliming'; that is, changing from a solid state into a gas and back into a solid again without passing through the liquid phase. They are only suitable for fabrics with a high (above 65%) synthetic content.

The inks are printed on to a glazed transfer paper stock, with the image in reverse. This is then placed in contact with the fabric, usually in a heat-transfer press or, in the case of yard goods, by passing the fabric and transfer paper through heated rollers. Under heat and pressure the dyes penetrate the synthetic fibres and bond with them.

Sublimation inks provide strong, bright colours but are only suitable for transfer on to white or light-coloured fabrics, since they are highly translucent. In addition to fabric applications they may also be used for specially coated metal and ceramics. They are commonly printed by offset-litho and screen printing, but are also printed by non-impact methods. Colour copiers may also be used with special sublimation transfer papers. Although the transfers produced by such methods are comparatively expensive they do provide an ideal method of direct colour imaging, either from flat copy or from computer disc, on to a wide range of substrates. They provide an ideal method for one-off prints or short runs for special events. Most of the major ink suppliers offer textile transfer systems. Subliscreen Aqua HQ, from Sericol Ltd, is a good example of a sublimation dye transfer system. The Magic Touch, a company in St. Albans, supplies a sublimation transfer system for non-impact printing. The system allows images to be transferred on to a wide range of surfaces, including textiles, plastics, glass, metal and ceramics.

MACHINERY

The machinery and equipment used in garment and textile printing is determined by the nature of the application and the volume of production. This can range from small hand-printing tables and carousels to large fully automated and highly specialized multicolour (up to 14 colours) flat-bed, rotary and oval printing units, some of which will print on both sides of the garment or duplex print the fabric.

DRYING SYSTEMS

The most common drying systems used in garment and textile printing are those employing infra-red radiation or gas conveyor dryers. The latter have become more popular in recent years, since it is claimed that they provide greater energy efficiency and are more control-responsive. On the other hand, infra-red dryers can be less costly to purchase.

DEVELOPMENTS

Garment printing has become a highly sophisticated and technologically informed area of the screen printing industry. The quality standards have advanced considerably in recent years with the development of high tension meshes and improved understanding of the critical relationship between mesh tension and image definition on the garment.

Developments in low cost colour imaging, desk-top scanning and proofing systems, ideally suited for the low resolution work required by the garment printer, has meant that more and more garment printers will be able to offer process colour work 'in house', working from artwork supplied in digital format as well as in the conventional transparency or flat artwork forms. There is still much to learn about the specific problems and requirements presented by four colour process printing on textile substrates. As the technology is relatively new, and as yet no standards exist for textile applications, there is considerable scope for research and development in the whole area of quality control in process colour printing.

The development of non-impact printing systems will continue to find application in the instant print market. Digital colour printing may also find a growing application as a rapid proofing device for the garment printer. In high volume textiles, the Iris printer from Scitext is used to provide digital proofing on to fabrics and other substrates.

The development of direct-to-screen systems like the Gerber ScreenJet will find application in the garment printing sector. The relatively low-resolution imaging capability of the inkjet printer used in such devices (typically 300 dpi) falls within the image resolution requirements of most garment printers. Quality in inkjet printing technology is improving all the time, which can only be of further benefit to the pre-press function.

The development of computer-driven embroidery machines is presenting a challenge to certain sectors of the conventional garment printing market. However, as the market is driven very much by changing fashions, this may be a passing trend, or it may create a further opportunity for the garment printer to provide increased added value to the printed product in both the promotional and fashion markets.

Industrial printing

Industrial screen printing is the most diverse and diffuse sector of the screen printing industry. It consists very largely of in-plant printing applications, which in many cases form but one element of a complex manufacturing process. So diverse are the applications within this sector that it is not possible to treat them all. However, there are three main areas which can be described as distinctive applications within this industrial sector:

- Container printing
- Nameplate and instrumentation
- Compact disc printing.

CONTAINER PRINTING

Screen printing on to glass and plastic containers is a well established area of the screen printing industry. There are a few companies who provide a container printing service. However, most of the 600 or so companies engaged in container printing are involved in manufacturing, i.e. blow-moulding, filling, packing and bottling. Here the printing process usually forms an integral part of the production line.

Screen printing is used to label or to decorate containers because it can quite easily be integrated into a production line. It also provides a durable printed image which forms an integral part of the container, rather than a label which can become damaged or detached from the container.

Substrates

The main substrates used in container printing are glass and blow-moulded plastics, vinyl, polyethylene, polypropylene and polycarbonate. Most plastics require some form of pretreatment before they are printed to provide a 'key' for the ink to adhere to the surface. In some cases this will involve corona discharge treatment, where the bottle is passed through an electrical field which positively charges the surface of the plastic, making it receptive to the wet ink film. In other cases the container is 'flamed' (rotated in a gas flame) prior to printing. This softens and 'opens' the surface of the plastic, allowing the wet ink to fuse with the surface as it is printed.

Inks for container printing

A number of different types of ink are used in container printing and the choice of ink will be determined by the type of substrate. For example, glass bottles are usually printed with glass enamels or with thermo-setting inks; whereas PVC containers will require a vinyl based ink; and a one-pack catalytic ink may be used when printing polyethylene. UV-curing ink systems are also available for printing on to plastic containers.

The product specifications for most screen printed containers are extremely demanding. This is because the container has to meet a wide range of product, manufacturing, distribution and user requirements. Screen printed plastic containers are often used for products such as detergents, bleaches and household cleaners which contain highly 'aggressive' chemical components. In production, in distribution and in use the ink film will be subjected to abrasion and stressing and must remain durable and resistant throughout its life.

Some plastics can present adhesion problems and must be correctly pretreated before they are printed. Rigorous product testing must be undertaken whenever a new substrate, ink system or product is printed. Rigorous testing is also necessary on the production line to ensure that quality standards are being met, as variations in the quality of the substrate can seriously impair the performance of the ink system, causing ink adhesion failure, cracking and embrittlement. Without a thoroughly established in-line quality systems approach, such faults can be difficult to detect and may not manifest themselves until months later when the retailer or customer returns the product.

Container printing machinery

The machinery used in container printing is most frequently designed on the cylinder machine principle. The printing unit is usually integrated within the production line, so that containers are transported to and from the print station(s) automatically. Where the surface decoration and labelling design permits, 'split-screen' multicolour printing is often employed. Analogous to 'split-duct' printing in offset-litho, the screen is divided into separate colour sections, each with its own ink supply and squeegee. This allows for two or three separate colours to be printed simultaneously on the container from a single screen/print station.

This sector of the industry is similar to that of container printing in that it comprises a mix of in-plant and specialist printers. The applications are also diverse, ranging from instrumentation and labelling of domestic electrical appliances, such as washing machines, dishwashers and cooking appliances, to the printing of precision scales and graticules for scientific instruments.

Substrates

Substrates used are also diverse. They include: a wide range of plastics; glass and ceramics; stainless and coated steel and aluminium.

Inks

The choice of ink systems is determined by the substrate type and the application. Vinyl and acrylic-based inks are commonly used for plastics, as are UV-based inks. Two-pack catalytic inks are used for metal and glass. Specialist ceramic and glass colours are also used for these applications.

Machinery

Flat-bed printing equipment and machinery is widely used in this sector. This ranges from small format manual vacuum tables for prototyping or short run printing, to fully automated, computer-controlled precision printing lines in high volume production. Some industrial nameplates and labels are produced on reel-to-reel machines. Most major suppliers will build precision machinery to the customer's specifications.

COMPACT DISC PRINTING

The development of the compact disc has brought about a revolution in the printing and communications industry. It has also created a new market segment in the industrial screen printing sector. First used in the audio entertainment market, compact discs are now a rapidly growing market in the media and communications industry. The areas of educational and home computing provide huge potential for market growth, with CD video, laser discs and CD ROM increasing the size of the market as more applications are introduced.

The development of re-writable CDs together with developments in telecommunications and the 'information superhighway' create a considerable growth potential for CD printing, which has hitherto been the province of communications giants such as Nimbus and EMI. As the technology becomes more and more accessible, more publishers and producers will enter the domain, producing an ever wider range of products and thus creating an increased demand for screen printing.

Substrates

Compact discs are made from rigid vinyl. They are printed with UV inks, using specially designed multicolour printing units. The machines operate on the carousel principle, the discs being fed from hoppers into a rotational jig which transports the discs through a series of printing and UV drying stations.

DEVELOPMENTS

The application of robotization and computer-controlled production is already well established within the industrial screen printing sector. Developments in non-impact printing technology will find an application in proofing and prototyping for nameplate and industrial label printing. Developments in flexographic printing and in waterless litho may also have some impact on the printing of CDs, where the demand for high volume, high quality colour printing is growing. However, it is likely that screen printing will remain the major process in this sector for the foreseeable future.

Screen printing has been used as a medium for surface decoration since its invention in the early part of the 20th century. Today it is used in the decoration of glass and chinaware, ceramic tiles, glass shower panels and doors, plastic laminate surfaces, wallpaper and floor coverings and in the production of simulated leather materials for footwear, clothing and upholstery.

Surface decoration

Again, the range of applications is too wide to be treated here. The main segments of the sector will be outlined and major differences in the market and the application of the process will be indicated.

GLASS AND CHINAWARE

Improvements in materials and technology have led to a growth in screen printed decoration on glass and chinaware. There are two principal methods: direct printing and transfer or decal printing.

Direct printing is used for decorating cylindrical items such as glasses, jugs and mugs. It is also used for printing on to flatware such as plates, using special screens designed to fit within the curved form of the object.

Transfers, or decals, as they are often called, have been used to decorate china and porcelain since the 18th century. Formerly, much of this work was printed by dry-offset, using a clear printed base and coating this with dry ceramic colour ('frit'). The offset process is time consuming and often difficult to control. With the development of finer-ground ceramic pigments, new screen meshes and improved stencil systems it has become possible to produce high quality, fine detail ceramic transfers by screen printing. At the top end of the market, commemorative designs are printed in up to 25 half-tone separations, using 133 and 150 lines/inch screen rulings. The work produced is in many cases superior in quality to that formerly produced by dry-offset – so much so that the majority of this work is now screen printed.

Substrates

Direct printing is carried out on glass and various types of china and earthenware. Transfers for ceramic and glass decoration are produced on special water-slide transfer or decal papers. Essentially these consist of a stable paper base, coated with a water-soluble release coating. The design is printed on to the coated paper. It is then overprinted with a clear lacquer or 'covercoat', which acts as a temporary support for the image during the transfer process. When dry the printed image is transferred to the object by soaking the transfer in water. This causes the water-soluble subcoating to dissolve, allowing the image to be slid away from the paper base and transferred to the ceramic or glassware object.

Inks

The inks used in glass and ceramic decoration are mainly either the two-pack catalytic type or specialist glass and ceramic colours. The latter are manufactured by specialist suppliers, such as Degussa or Johnson and Mathey. They are made from very abrasive, finely ground glass particles, combined with inorganic pigments. This 'frit' is mixed with an organic resin and reduced with a solvent (usually white spirit) to produce a printing paste.

Stainless steel screen meshes are often used in these applications, as they provide superior wear resistance and printability, reducing the clogging tendency associated with paste inks containing large pigment particles. Direct emulsion and capillary direct film stencils are also widely employed, since they provide optimum quality in terms of durability and fine line/tone reproduction.

Machinery

Industrial screen printing machinery of the type used for containers is commonly used for direct decoration of ceramics and glassware. Transfers are usually printed on standard semi-automatic flat-bed or cylinder machines, using space-rack or wicket drying.

FLAT GLASS DECORATION

Screen printing is used to decorate a range of flat glass products. It is used in printing decorative UV coatings around the edges of car windows and windscreens, to provide a protective mask for the urethane rubber adhesive that fixes the glass in place. It is also used to produce the light-reduction barriers on the glass of sun-roof panels. Rear-window heater panels are screen printed with a special 'cer–met' (ceramic–metal) ink. The maker's name or logo is often printed on the glass.

Other applications include oven doors and halogen hot plates, glass shower panels, mirrors and games machines. These products often involve multicolour designs, using translucent or matt finish coatings to simulate etched glass or sandblasting effects.

Inks

The inks for flat glass decoration are of a specialist nature. They may be ceramic frit-type inks or two-pack catalytic inks. Some are silver-based, others provide conductivity or have etchant properties. The drying method will be determined by the ink type; common systems include IR and gas dryers.

WALL AND FLOOR COVERINGS

Ceramic wall and floor tiles are screen printed by direct methods. In this application the inks, screen mesh and stencil systems are the same as those used for hollow-ware decoration. Other printing methods include dry flexography and non-impact screen printing, where the dry ceramic frit is applied to the tile.

Screen printing is also used in the production of wallpaper and vinyl floor coverings. The type of ink will be determined by the nature of the substrate. Matt-finish synthetic thin film inks are used for the production of paper coverings, and vinyl inks for vinyl-coated papers and vinyl floor coverings. Puff-finish plastisols are also used, as are flocking techniques.

Machinery

Machine design varies according to the application and volume. For example, short-run specialist designs on carpet tiles will be produced on a simple hand-operated vacuum table, whereas high volume production of cushion vinyl flooring will be produced on a web-fed, multicolour, rotary screen printing machine. Specialist hand-printed wall coverings are produced on long flat-bed tables, similar to those used in printing textile lengths, whereas high volume puff-finish vinyls are printed by rotary screen.

Drying

The drying system will be determined by the ink type and the machine configuration. Jet air drying and gas drying are commonly employed.

DEVELOPMENTS

Developments in this sector follow the general trends in the screen printing industry. Concerns for the environment have encouraged research and development into safer, more environmentally acceptable inks for ceramic and glass printing. Ecotoxic pigments such as cadmium and lead are being phased out as alternative pigments are developed. Sublimation transfer systems for ceramics and glass have been introduced, allowing proofs to be generated direct from digital artwork, via an electrostatic printer. Such systems will provide new opportunities for the instant print market and also the possibility of instant proofing for the direct ceramic and glassware printer.

Electronics The applications of screen printing in the electronics industry are complex and highly specialized. The sector continues to form an important part of the screen printing industry, being the third largest sector after graphics and industrial printing.

Many different applications of screen printing are used in the production of electronic circuits and switch devices. What follows is a brief description of the main product groups:

- Printed circuit boards (PCBs)
- Hybrid and thick film circuits
- Surface mounted technology
- Membrane switches.

PRINTED CIRCUIT BOARDS

Conventional PCBs

Conventional screen printed circuit boards, also known as 'single-sided' circuit boards, are made by printing the circuit track pattern on to a copper-clad glass-fibre board, using an acid-resistant ink. After printing, the board is treated with an acid etchant which dissolves the exposed copper cladding, leaving the etch-resist pattern intact. The resist is removed by solvent treatment, leaving the conductive copper circuit track on the non-conductive glass-fibre base. The board is then coated with solder ready for the electrical components to be surface mounted.

Plated through-holes (PTHs)

Plated through-hole circuits are produced on double-sided copper laminate glass-fibre boards. The manufacturing process involves fives stages:

1. The boards are first drilled to allow circuit connections to be made from one side of the board to the other.
2. The board is then electroplated with a thin layer (0.5 microns) of copper, which coats the entire surface of the board, including the walls of the drilled holes. This provides electrical conductivity through the board.
3. A negative circuit image is printed on both sides of the board with a plating resist, which protects the non-circuit areas.
4. The printed board is electroplated in the uncoated areas, producing a thicker copper layer to form the conductive tracks and pathways in and around the through-holes.
5. In the final stage, the electroplating resist is removed and the very thin copper background layer is etched away, leaving a thick plated circuit on both sides of the board, with conductive paths passing through the drilled holes from one side to the other.

The advantages of PTH circuits are that they provide improved electrical contact and durability, allowing for more complex and compact circuit design.

Copper and solder are the most common plating materials, but precious metals such as silver, gold and platinum are also used. Different sections of the circuit may be given deposits of different metals: the copper circuit may be coated with solder, whereas the edge connectors may be plated with nickel and gold.

The production of PTH boards is complex and therefore costly. Alternative methods of production, using photodeposition techniques, are also used in place of screen printing, especially where extremely fine and high density circuit tracks are required.

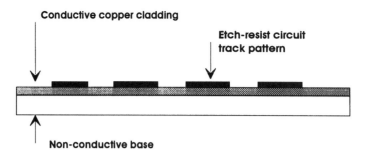

STAGE ONE

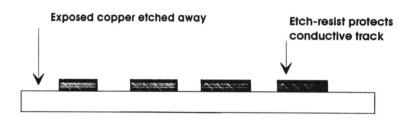

STAGE TWO

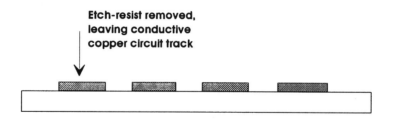

STAGE THREE

Fig. 69 Stages of production for conventional PCB manufacture.

Multilayer circuits are produced by a complex multistage process involving PTH technology. Typically they consist of 4–12 circuit layers, with integrated connectors linking components through the entire circuit 'sandwich'.

Flexible circuits

Flexible circuits are used in the manufacture of all kinds of electrical equipment from washing machines to aerospace components. Open the bonnet of any modern motor vehicle and you will find flexible circuit and switch technology.

Flexible circuits are made by print-etch techniques, using thin copper-laminated polyester and polyamide foils. The etch-resist circuit pattern is web-printed on to the foil, which subsequently receives in-line etching and solvent treatments.

HYBRID THICK FILM CIRCUITS

Hybrid circuits are made using a combination of screen printed conductive ceramic–metal (cer–met) inks, often containing gold, silver or platinum, and thin film dielectric resists. Such devices can involve complex thick film, multilayer, multistage processing, in which screen printing is used to produce different conductive and non-conductive elements of the circuit, or they can be simple thin film devices, comprising a simple circuit conductor track with resistor pads.

In either case production involves printing on to a small format ceramic or metal base, usually 12–50 mm across. By printing precision controlled deposits of metal and dielectric resists, it is possible to build up complex electrical components with precise electrical performance values. For example, resistors with values in the range of 0.5 to 5 ohms ($0.5–5\ \Omega$) can be produced in this way.

After printing the circuit is fired in a kiln, much in the same way as ceramic and glassware are fired. This fuses the cer–met inks to the base, producing a durable integrated circuit. These may then be combined with other components and integrated into larger conventional PCBs.

SURFACE MOUNTED TECHNOLOGY (SMT)

This is an area of screen printing which continues to grow in volume both in the UK and worldwide (see Stewart Partridge, *The Impact of Non-impact*, SPA (UK) Ltd, 1994). The process allows for the selective deposition of controlled layers of solder cream on to the circuit board, thus considerably reducing its weight and bulk. The growth in the market for this application is the result of increased consumer demand for small, lightweight electronic devices such as personal stereos, CD players, mobile phones, video cameras and notebook computers. The main users are communications giants like Motorola, Philips and Sony, circuit board assembly companies and contract manufacturers (see Stewart Partridge, *ibid.*).

Methods of application other than screen printing involve computer-controlled syringe deposition and stencilling. The latter method is gaining in popularity and may replace conventional screen printing as the preferred method of solder cream application.

MEMBRANE SWITCHES

This is an area of the electronics sector which has developed rapidly during recent years. The products are of high value and involve complex multilayer, multistage production. Screen printing is used not only in the manufacture of the circuit and switch components but also in creating the visual appearance and graphics of the switch panel, often involving high definition, reverse-printed, multicolour printing with opaque masks (dead front graphics) and translucent colour panels for interactive back illumination.

Fig. 70 Sectional diagram of membrane switch. (Courtesy of Autotype International Ltd.)

Membrane switches are manufactured from multiple layers of high stability polyester film. The switch component comprises two layers, each printed with a silver-based conductive ink. Special insulating dielectric inks are then printed over the circuits at strategic points to prevent them from 'shorting out' when the two layers are pressed into contact. The two circuits are then mounted one above the other with polyester film 'spacers' interleaved between them. The reverse-printed, textured polyester graphics panel, displaying the switch information, is then mounted on the top. When pressure is applied at a particular point on the graphics panel, contact is made between the two circuit layers beneath and the switch is operated.

INKS

The ink systems used in the manufacture of printed circuits and membrane switches are specialist products. Acid and plating resists must provide a finish that is resistant to scratches and chemicals; they must have very specific flow characteristics so as to provide a full, even coating without pinholes, whilst maintaining good edge definition and minimal edge flow-out.

The inks used to produce conductive paths are based upon the noble metals – silver, gold and platinum. They are often combined with graphite to produce specific electrical resistance. These inks are costly and used only in the manufacture of high value products such as hybrid circuits and membrane switches.

Solder resists and legend printing inks are usually two-pack epoxy resin-based systems. They must provide high levels of adhesion, surface hardness and durability.

MACHINERY

The equipment and machinery used in the electronics sector varies widely in format and configuration. In most cases the machines used for high volume, high specification products are precision engineered, facilitating controlled register repeatability of +/– 2 microns, with fully automatic CCD camera register alignment, and automatic squeegee alignment and bias control. Web presses are utilized in the production of flexible circuits, where resist printing, etching and resist removal are all in-line processes.

The choice of drying system will be determined by the ink type. The most common systems are IR, UV and gas oven.

DEVELOPMENT

Many of the technological advances in screen mesh manufacture and in stencil systems have been encouraged by the expanding and increasingly demanding electronics market. Indeed many of the advantages enjoyed by the modern screen printer are there as a result of developments in this field of application.

Developments in computer-based design systems will have little impact, since they have been used in the electronics industry for many years. The main challenges to the sector are coming from alternative primary imaging processes, such as direct laser imaging on dry film. This involves the lamination of a photopolymer circuit resist film which can be subsequently imaged using an argon laser to produce 25-micron lines. There are technical problems still to be overcome and the current high cost means that only a limited number of systems are installed worldwide.

The control of environmental pollution will also impinge heavily upon this sector of the industry. Considerable quantities of ecotoxic chemicals are produced in the manufacture of printed circuits. The controlled use and disposal of these waste products will incur additional and rising costs. The development of alternative materials, processes and technologies for recovery or recycling will play a major role in the future of the electronics sector.

The art and craft of **13** screen printing

Screen printing has been used as a purely creative medium by artists since the beginning of the century. Early examples of hand-painted 'selectasine' block-out prints, dating back to 1930, are exhibited at the Victoria and Albert Museum in London. The process was first developed as a fine art medium by a group of commercial artists who worked under Hyman Warsager, director of the Works Progress Administration Federal Art Project, set up at the Reproduction Division of the US Air Force, at Lowry Fields, Colorado, in 1929. This group of artists experimented with the process, striving to achieve the qualities of painting in their prints.

They called the prints 'serigraphs', to distinguish them from commercial printing. The qualities achieved in these early prints are quite remarkable. They were printed with oil-based opaque inks, in 10 or 12 colours, using highly developed dry brush techniques to produce the painterly effects of what look like gouache paintings.

However, it was not until the 1960s that screen printing really began to develop as a fine art medium. During the 1960s and 1970s there was an explosion in the market for limited edition screen prints. The flexibility of the process, with its hard-edged, flat colours, was the perfect medium for the production of pop art. Many artists used the process to print directly on to canvas and create screen paintings.

One of the best-known exponents of this technique was the American pop artist, Andy Warhol. There is little doubt that his screen printing on to canvas has done more to popularize the medium among young artists than the work of any other artist this century.

Although technically speaking the quality of printing is very crude and uncontrolled, Warhol used the process with great visual force and power. The images are huge, often exploiting the opportunity for the repetition commonly associated with the world of consumer advertising. They force the commercial context of the supermarket upon the viewer, challenging us to consider the art of the everyday in the context of the art gallery and by analogy the nature of art and experience itself.

Many of the paintings use the element of accident, flooding, misprinting and drying-in to increase the power of the visual statement. Often this relates to the visual impact created by the degradation of the image as it repeats. In the famous Marilyn paintings, the crude application of cosmetic colouring, printed out of register, again forces the viewer to see the image as manufactured and artificial, yet at the same time as an extraordinarily powerful and complex 20th century symbol.

There is little doubt that the printing process contributed greatly to the development of Warhol's work. Indeed, it is through his engagement with the process that he finds the appropriate form for the expression of the visual ideas which are the focus for his creative motivation.

The methods and techniques used by Andy Warhol were standard commercial screen printing techniques, which might be found in any large format sign or banner printers. The screens were made by means of standard photostencil systems, often with the use of paper masks to blank off areas of the image or to lay down simple blocks of flat colour.

Many artists use conventional materials and processes in the creation of limited edition prints. However, there are also many techniques and methods which are used only in the context of fine art printing. In this chapter some of these techniques will be outlined, to give an indication of the diversity and range of effects which can be achieved by those who use screen printing as a purely creative image-making medium.

Much of what is said here will concern the use of screen making materials, particularly in the context of the hand or autographic techniques of drawing, painting and hand-cutting stencils. The chapter also deals with wax-release and mono-printing techniques.

Hand-painted stencils   The techniques of making stencils by drawing or painting directly on the screen (sometimes referred to as serigraphy, a word derived from the Greek meaning silk drawing) has been used by artists and printmakers since the very early days of the process. Although a number of different techniques and materials can be used, there are essentially two basic methods: block-out and wax-resist.

THE BLOCK-OUT METHOD

One of the earliest methods of making stencils was the selectasine process. With this technique the print is made by an elimination process, blocking out the open portions of the screen after each printing and gradually building up a picture by overprinting. Various screen blocking mediums can be used: solvent-based cellulose for water-based inks, or water-based fillers for solvent-based inks. Direct stencil emulsion can also be used as a water resistant screen filler, provided that it is exposed to UV light prior to printing.

Plate 2   Point-of-sale advertising.
Window display advertising provides eye-catching colour and variety in the high street, an important element in most advertising campaigns. Self-cling and self-adhesive vinyls are often used in this context. (Courtesy of Sericol Ltd.)

Plate 1   Point-of-sale advertising.
In-store advertising and merchandising provide a large market for the graphic screen printer. Common substrates used include MG poster paper, display board, corrugated board, and rigid and flexible vinyl. (Courtesy of Sericol Ltd.)

Plate 3   Large format vehicle livery.
Large format vehicle livery is often printed on to self-adhesive vinyl, using an ink/substrate system which provides guaranteed weather resistance. (Courtesy of Autotype International Ltd.)

Plate 4 Garment printing.
Garment printing machines can provide fully automated, computer-controlled operation with as many as 14 print stations, including integrated flash curing. Here, the screens are raised for inspection, showing an 'all-over' design on a black shirt. (Courtesy of Things Ltd.)

Plate 5 Rotary screen printing.
Vinyl floor coverings, wall coverings and fabrics are printed by rotary screen printing methods. Here, vinyl floor covering is being printed. The web passes up from beneath the floor, through the print head and up into the dryer above. Ink is pumped from the container on the left directly to the squeegee blade inside the rotary screen. (Courtesy of Stork BV.)

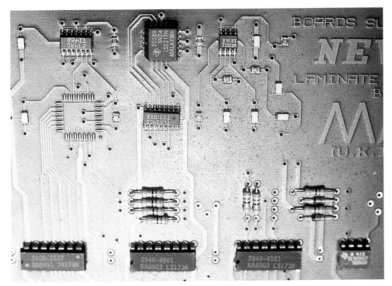

Plate 6 Printed circuit board.
Precision screen printing is used in the production of electronic circuits. Here on this PTH circuit board, the circuit track is seen as a pale green line, protected by a coating of solder-resist. The surface-mounted components can be seen attached to the board at various points, with the connectors soldered to the through-holes in the board. (Courtesy of Autotype International Ltd.)

Plate 7 Industrial printing products.
A wide variety of products are printed in industrial screen printing applications. Printing on to irregularly shaped objects, such as containers and facia panels, can require the use of special screens and product jigs. Companies like Rondec have specialized in this field for many years. (Courtesy of Rondec Screen Process Ltd.)

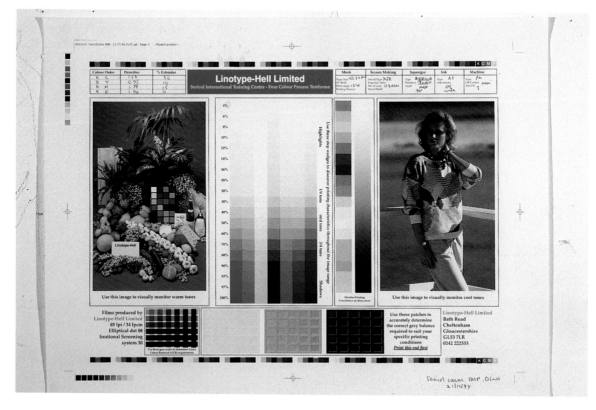

Plate 8 Linotype-Hell Ltd four colour test forme.
Using a colour control test forme helps to establish
colour reproduction data which can be used to establish the scanning, screen making and printing parameters required in producing consistent results in
four colour process printing. The colour bars on the
forme are used to measure colour density, dot gain,
trapping and slurring. (Courtesy of Sericol Ltd.)

Plate 9 The block-out technique.
(a) An open area is created on the screen, using adhesive tape as a filler-mask. Here, masking tape has been used to give a ragged edge to the image area; cellulose tape will provide a sharp-edged mask. Screen filler is applied to the screen, blocking the area around the tape mask. When the filler is dry the tape mask is removed. Water-based filler is used for solvent-based inks. When working with water-based media, water-resistant direct stencil emulsion can be used as a screen filler – the screen must be exposed to ultraviolet light before printing.

(b) Each layer of the image is selectively created in the remaining open area of the screen. Here, the final detail image is created by painting out the remaining open area of the screen with filler.

(c) The finished print: *Out!*, by John Stephens.

Plate 10 The wax subtraction technique.
(a) The image is created by drawing in the open area of the screen with soft wax crayons. The coloured wax blocks the screen mesh.

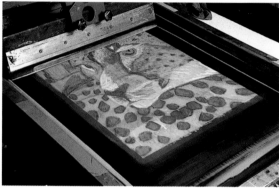

(b) The completed image is then printed with a colourless extender base, a medium rather like matt varnish. The white spirit in the extender base dissolves the wax and releases the colour as the print is taken. Successive prints can be taken from the image with decreasing levels of colour saturation.

(c) The finished print (*Cheetah*, by A. Braithwaite, LCPDT) should be sealed with a further coating of extender base.

Plate 11 Mono-printing with Rowney System 3 Acrylics.

(a) Water-based acrylic colours, mixed with a screening medium, can be applied direct to the screen. The colours are thixotropic and have a gel-like consistency which makes it relatively easy to control their placement. A wide range of colour-laying techniques can be used: colour can be squeezed through pipettes or syringes to provide fine line drawing or applied with a broad brush or cranked palette knife to create richly textured, expressive marks.

(b) The finished print (*My Valentine*, by Laurence Stephens) accurately records the painterly effects of brush marks and colour blending, created in the screen painting. This acrylic mono-print was overprinted with a key line, drawn with a No. 3 Litho Crayon on Autotype True-Grain film.

Plate 12

(a) *Passages*, by Ian Wilkinson, a print originated from separations drawn directly on True-Grain film. The image has been created using a range of media to provide the rich and expressive mark making of the painted image. The print was produced at Curwin Chilford Prints. (Courtesy of Autotype International Ltd.)

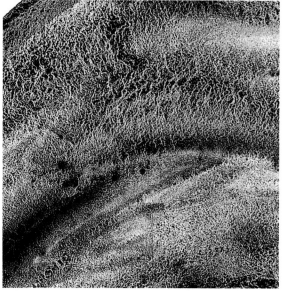

(b) A section from the blue separation of the *Passages* origination, showing the incredibly fine tonal values which can be achieved with True-Grain. (Courtesy of Autotype International Ltd.)

The screen blocking medium can be painted, dry brushed, scumbled, sprayed or splattered on to the screen, using tape masks to create shapes. Of all the screen making techniques, this is the simplest and most direct form.

THE WAX-RESIST METHOD

It is possible to make stencils by drawing or painting directly on to the screen mesh with a soft wax crayon (No. 3 Litho crayon) or liquid litho drawing ink (tusche) or bitumen paint, thinned with white spirit.

For the best effects a fine screen should be used. Silk is particularly

1.

2.

3.

Fig. 71 Wax-resist method.
1. An image is drawn or painted on to the screen with a No. 3 litho crayon, or lithographic drawing ink.
2. The screen is filled with a water-soluble screen filler, usually reduced by 30% with water.
3. When the screen filler is dry the wax medium is removed with a solvent.

good because it is blocked very easily by the graphic medium; its rough surface is much more responsive and expressive than the slippery surface of conventional polyester or nylon. Synthetic mesh with a count of 120/140 threads/cm would be most suitable.

When the painting or drawing is complete the screen is blocked out with a water-based liquid filler. The wax drawing medium resists the filler and when the filler is dry the drawing medium is dissolved out of the screen mesh with a solvent (usually white spirit). This in turn creates the screen openings to form the printed image – a faithful reproduction of what has been drawn on to the screen.

It is possible to produce a very wide range of textures and tone effects with the techniques described above. Soft-edged, painterly rendering can be achieved by using the painting techniques of dry brushing, scumbling, stippling and spattering the resist on to the screen. Similarly, litho drawing ink can be used in a painterly manner, whereas wax crayon may be used to produce rich and varied textures by rubbing it into the mesh over a textured surface such as coarse-grained wood or textured plastic. Special texture plates can be made from heavily textured fabrics, pasted down on to boards. Artists and printmakers using these techniques will collect a whole range of different surfaces to extend their mark-making palette.

When using water-based inks, water-resistant photostencil emulsion should be used with the wax-resist instead of using screen filler. The emulsion may be applied in the same way as the screen filler, but the screen must be exposed to UV light after the wax-resist image has been washed out. This could be done by simply leaving the screen exposed to daylight for several hours. After exposure the screen coating will be water resistant and suitable for use with water-based inks.

WAX-SUBTRACTION METHOD

With this method an open image area is first created on the screen by tape and filler techniques. The image is then drawn directly on the screen in this area, using soft coloured oil crayons. Again, it is best to use a fine screen with a mesh count of 120–140 threads/cm.

When the image is complete a translucent extender, based on white spirit, is printed through the screen. The solvent in the extender softens and dissolves the coloured wax crayon image, forcing it through the screen mesh to create a subtly changing range of coloured versions of the drawing made in the screen.

Further applications of crayon may be applied as the colours weaken and fade. It is important to add small amounts of extender, sufficient for only two prints, so that fresh medium can be applied for each print, since the medium on the screen quickly becomes degraded by the dissolving wax colours. Care should be taken in handling and stacking the prints, as the dissolved wax will easily mar. The finished prints should be sealed with a further coating of matting base to prevent the soft wax from smudging.

MONOPRINTING

Monoprints are one-off screen paintings, using the screen as a temporary support surface for the image. An open area is created in the screen, using tape and filler techniques. Colour is then applied in this area, using a range of tools, including pipettes, plastic palette knifes, bushes or atomizers. Gel-type inks with a thixotropic rheology are best for this application, since they provide more control on the screen. Daler Rowney make a water-based acrylic screening base which can be used with their System 3 acrylic colours. This system has two main advantages over conventional screen printing inks. The colours are artist's colours and may therefore be used for painting or printing. They provide excellent screen stability, allowing the artist time to create a complex image on the screen without the image drying in the mesh before it is printed. Artist-grade acrylics such as Cryla, Liquitex and Lasco provide high quality, light-fast single pigment colours which can also be used with acrylic screening medium to produce prints of archival standard.

Textured films and UV blocks

The Cambridge-based fine art printers, Curwin Chilford Prints, in association with Autotype International Ltd, have pioneered the development of new materials for fine art printing. One of these materials is True-Grain, a grained polyester drafting film which can be drawn or painted on to produce very fine-grained tone images and autographic colour separations. Master printer Kip Gresham has developed a range of different media for use with the film, providing the artist with a wide choice of very fine tonal effects. Among the media used are:

- Pencils, from 2B to 4B; 9B graphite sticks; graphite dust, which can be rubbed into the textured surface of the film to produce soft smudged tonal effects.
- Charcoal; compressed charcoal; Conté cayon; black oil pastel; litho crayons; chinagraph pencils.
- Water-soluble pencils and crayons, such as:
  - Black Caran D'Ache colour pencil;
  - Black Neo Color II water-soluble crayon;
  - Berol Karismacolor, Karisma Graphite Aquarelle
- Pentel waterproof and water-soluble marker pens.

Many interesting and varied effects can be obtained by smudging and mixing the materials with water and solvents. The media may easily be manipulated and worked over, erasing unwanted areas.

CREATING WASH EFFECTS

The textured surface of True-Grain allows washes to be created by trapping tiny particles of pigment as the wash dries out. The best effects are obtained by choosing materials which allow the pigments to separate out of suspension as the liquid dries. Adhesion may be achieved by adding a few drops of diluted clear PVA to the wash.

Water-based washes

The following water materials provide good results when thinned with water.

- Plumtree Black Liquid Opaque with diluted PVA
- Lamp Black Powder Pigment with diluted PVA, or brushed into the wet film, with diluted Foto-Flow
- Ivory Black Powder Pigment, dusted into diluted PVA
- Indian Ink with diluted PVA
- Chinese Ink with diluted PVA
- Chinese Stick Ink with water
- Rotring Film Ink with water
- Korn's Litho Stick Tusche dissolved in water with Rotring Ink
- Graphite Dust mixed with PVA and Photo-Opaque

Solvent-based washes

Screen inks, such as Sericol's Colorjet Black, can be used to create wash effects when mixed with solvents such as screen wash or oil-based retarder, which causes the pigment to separate on the film. With this technique, the film is wetted with the solvent and the thinned ink is painted on to the wet surface. Reactivator sprays like Sericol's Actisol can be used, or plant mist sprays.

Health and Safety Note

Proper attention must be given to health and safety practices whenever volatile solvents are used, especially where they are applied in a spray or atomized form. Solvents should only be used in a well ventilated area. A fume mask, safety goggles and gloves should be worn to provide appropriate personal protection. Precautions should also be taken against the potential fire hazards presented by volatile solvents. This will include the safe disposal of any contaminated materials used in imaging processes.

These unique wash effects were screen printed from artwork made on True-Grain

Plumtree opaque in water and PVA.

Compressed charcoal stick.

Lamp black and lamp black gouache.

Karisma graphite aquarelle pencil.

Colourjet black into oil bound retarder.

Lamp black gouache.

Fig. 72 Wash effects of True-Grain. Courtesy of Autotype International Ltd.

UV BLOCKS

Autotype's UV Block, a clear UV-blocking medium, can be pigmented and painted on to the film to provide the most intricate yet completely UV-blocking photomasks. One of the main advantages of this medium is that the artist can visualize the work as each coloured overlay is produced.

The best results have been achieved with 110T screens and Autotype's Alpha Star indirect gelatine-based film, which provides the very wide exposure latitudes required for the range of exposures needed. It is not uncommon for a single image to be produced in a range of tonal separations, using over- and underexposure techniques to create different levels of tonal detail in the stencil.

When working with these materials it is essential to conduct a series of stepped exposure tests to establish the exposure values of the light source in relation to the sensitivity parameters of the stencil emulsion (see Chapter 5, Conducting a stepped exposure test).

Knife-cut stencils   Knife-cut stencils provide a very simple and direct method of working when hard-edged, large-scale work is required. Because knife-cut stencils can be made by cutting to a keyline original, costly origination and photographic work can be short cut.

PAPER STENCILS

Knife-cut stencils can be made from paper. Thin, translucent crystal parchment or light bank paper is most suitable. Thin acetate or polyester is equally effective for water-based inks.

The stencil is cut by placing a sheet of protective acetate over the art work and tracing the image area with a sharp stencil knife. When the stencil has been cut and the non-image areas removed, the art-work and stencil are placed under the screen, which should be pre-masked in readiness for the stencil. The screen is then lowered and a print is taken. As the ink is pulled across the screen the stencil will adhere to the underside of the screen.

When using paper stencils for very simple block areas, the stencil may be taped to the back of the screen. In this case, it is important always to ensure that the stencil is evenly attached to the underside of the screen, since it may become creased during printing if the stencil is not flat.

KNIFE-CUT LAMINATES AND FILMS

There are three types of commercially available knife-cut stencil material in current use:

- Paper laminates
- Water-adhered films
- Solvent-adhered films.

PAPER LAMINATES

These duplex paper stencil materials are a development of the paper stencil. They were first marketed in America by I.F. de Autremont in 1930. The original material was made from two layers of parchment paper, temporarily fixed together with paraffin wax. The lighter upper layer had an adhesive coating of plasticized shellac, which could be softened and pressed into the underside of the screen mesh by ironing with a hot domestic iron.

This material, originally called Profilm, is available from major suppliers like Sericol, Coates Screen, or John T. Keep & Son. It is now sold under the brand name of Stenplex Amber (Profilm) and is amber in colour. The heat-adhered, shellac-coated laminate has very good adhesion to silk screen mesh, but its adhesion to synthetic mesh materials is rather poor. It is also unsuitable for use with inks containing aggressive solvents, such as the ketonic solvents used in vinyl inks. It does have a limited use for printing short runs with water-based textile inks.

For general graphic printing there is a paper laminate which has a water-soluble adhesive coating and greater resistance to solvent based inks. This material is green and is supplied under the name of Stenplex Green (Greenfilm).

Cutting the stencil

A sheet of stencil material is cut, slightly larger than the area of the stencil. This is then taped or pinned over the original, making sure that it is flat and firmly fixed in place. The image is then traced out with a stencil knife. The knife should be held in an upright position, using just enough pressure to cut through the upper layer of the laminate. Heavy cutting which scores or cuts through the underlayer of waxed paper should be avoided as this will cause problems when the stencil is adhered to the screen mesh.

When the entire image area has been traced it is peeled away from the waxed paper support, leaving the stencil opening clear. The cut stencil profiles should be checked at this stage for any defects, such as torn fragments of tissue left behind after peeling the image area. It is important to examine the stencil edges very closely.

Adhering the stencil

The stencil is placed on a mounting pad – two sheets of straw or display board, cut slightly larger than the stencil, yet smaller than the inside dimensions of the screen will provide an ideal support. It is important to have the mounting pad the right size, since it must:

- provide a firm support for the entire stencil; and
- allow for intimate contact between the underside of the screen mesh and the adhesive coating of the stencil material.

Stenplex Amber (Profilm) is adhered to the screen by placing the screen over the stencil and pressing the stencil area with a domestic iron, set for silk or synthetics, using a thin sheet of paper (newsprint or bank paper is good) to diffuse the heat and keep the bottom of the iron free from shellac.

As the shellac coating melts into the mesh the stencil will darken in colour. When the entire surface of the stencil takes on this appearance and is even in colour, the screen can be raised and turned over to remove the waxed support sheet.

Stenplex Green (Greenfilm) is applied in a similar manner but requires the application of an aqueous alcohol adhering solution (1 part water to 3 parts methylated spirit). The adhering solution is best applied by dampening a small area (20 cm^2) of newsprint and pressing this over the stencil area with a domestic iron, set on silk or synthetics.

The stencil will darken in colour when it is adhered to the mesh. The appearance of pale shiny areas indicates that the stencil is not fully adhered and a further application of solution is necessary. Care must be taken in applying more adhering solution as the stencil can very easily be overwetted, resulting in a loss of adhesion and in excessive swelling of the stencil paper. Overwetting will cause a loss of dimensional stability which can be very considerable on large stencils (in excess of A2).

Removing the stencil

The removal of the stencil will depend on whether the adhesive coating is spirit-soluble shellac, as is the case with Stenplex Amber, or a water-soluble PVA coating as with Stenplex Green.

Stenplex Amber is removed after cleaning away any remaining ink with an appropriate solvent. The screen is placed over a pad of newspaper. It is then saturated from above with methylate spirit and left to soak for

10–15 minutes. When the shellac has dissolved the screen can be raised; the stencil paper should transfer to the newspaper below. Any remaining shellac must be quickly removed from the screen with a wiper, soaked in methylated spirit. On no account should the screen be allowed to dry during this process, as this will cause the shellac to harden permanently in the screen mesh, making its removal very difficult to achieve.

Stenplex Green is removed by washing the screen in warm water, after all the ink has been removed with screen cleaner. The water soluble adhesive will dissolve, quickly releasing the stencil paper from the screen. Any residual adhesive will wash out immediately after the stencil paper peels away.

Troubleshooting

Adhesion failure is caused in most cases by the presence of grease, either in the screen mesh (due to insufficient degreasing) or on the surface of the stencil (due to contamination during cutting and handling). Failure can also result from applying too much moisture, or mixing the wrong ratio of alcohol/water adhering solution.

Stencil wrinkles are usually due to overwetting with adhering solution. The stencil paper swells and stretches as it takes on moisture then shrinks violently when the heat from the iron is applied. Wrinkling can also result from a delay between applying the adhering solution (via the newsprint) and applying the heat. It is very important to dry the moisture out of the screen mesh as quickly as possible, as success depends upon the instantaneous wetting and drying of the micro-thin adhesive coating.

Difficulty in removing the backing paper is usually the result of adhesive seeping between the laminate interface at the image-forming edges of the stencil and fixing them together when heat is applied. The fault is caused by scoring or cutting through the backing paper and by overwetting with adhering solution. If the stencil is gently dampened from the back with adhering solution the backing paper will usually release after a few moments, leaving the stencil edges intact. The backing paper should never be pulled away against the cut edges of the stencil as this can cause damage to the stencil profiles; it should always be removed by peeling along the cut edges.

WATER-ADHERED FILMS

Paper laminate stencils are unsuitable for close register work because they lack the required dimensional stability. Modern knife-cut films which have high stability plastic bases have been developed to cope with the demands of close register multicolour work. Among the most commonly used materials are the water-adhered films. Examples are Autocut Amber, made by Autotype International Ltd, and Ulanocut, made by the Ulano Group of Companies.

The material is composed of a precision film coating of water-soluble PVA (polyvinyl alcohol) supported on a 75 micron (0.075 mm/0.003 in) polyester base. The base material provides excellent dimensional stability and allows the film coating to be re-laid after peeling, making cutting corrections an easy matter. The film is tinted to provide good visual clarity. It is translucent enough to give a clear view of the original, and has a matted surface finish to prevent glare.

Cutting

Water-adhered films must be cut on a firm cutting base, using a sharp stencil knife blade. The polyester base is very sensitive to denting, which can occur when too much pressure is used on the stencil knife. If the film base is scored or dented the stencil may fail to adhere to the screen at that point. The image-forming edges of the stencil may also dissolve during adhesion, producing what are known as 'burnt edges'.

Adhering

The stencil is fixed in the conventional way, using a raised mounting pad to bring the surface into intimate contact with the underside of the screen. Water is applied through the mesh, using a fine mist spray (the type used for house plants). The stencil film will darken in appearance as it is wetted. When the entire stencil has been treated, the excess moisture is removed by blotting the screen with newsprint and rolling the entire area with a sponge paint roller.

Drying

The screen must be dried with warm air. It is best to place the fan so that the current of warm air is directed through the mesh to the damp stencil. Drying usually takes about 15 minutes to complete, depending on the size of the stencil. When the stencil is dry, the film base should peel away quite freely. If there is any resistance to peeling, this will indicate that the stencil is not yet dry and must be left for a further drying period.

1.   2.

Fig. 73 Adhering a water-adhered stencil.
1. Wetting the stencil.
2. Blotting the stencil.

Removing the stencil

After the ink has been removed from the screen with an appropriate solvent, the stencil can be removed by washing the screen with warm water. The stencil is completely water soluble and will dissolve away after a few minutes washing.

Troubleshooting

Adhesion failure is usually caused by inadequate screen preparation – failure to pretreat and/or degrease the screen correctly prior to adhering the stencil. The surface of the film may also become greasy due to excessive handling during cutting. If grease is present it will act as a barrier, preventing the stencil emulsion from contacting the screen mesh threads.

Pale spots or patches are usually caused by incomplete wetting of the stencil. They will almost always disappear when the screen is rewetted and blotted again. Care should be taken not to overwet the stencil as this can cause loss of edge definition.

Burnt edges are usually caused by denting or scoring the film base; they may also result from excessive wetting during adhesion.

SOLVENT-ADHERED FILMS

These stencil films are made for use with water-based inks. They have excellent dimensional stability, being unaffected by changes in temperature or humidity. Examples include: Solvent Green, made by Autotype International Ltd, and Sta-Sharp S3S, made by the Ulano Group of Companies.

Solvent-adhered films consist of a nitrocellulose film coating, on a 75 micron (0.075 mm/0.003 in) polyester base; vinyl-based films are also produced. The nitrocellulose stencil coating is soluble in ketonic-based solvents, and films are supplied with a specially formulated adhering liquid. Like the water-adhered films, the stencil coating is tinted to provide maximum visual clarity, and has a matted surface finish to prevent glare.

Cutting

This film has exactly the same cutting characteristics as the water-adhered materials, and must be cut with the same care and attention to prevent scoring or denting the film base. The polyester-backed films allow for re-laying, so that corrections can be made to cutting errors.

Adhering

The stencil is adhered in the conventional way, using a raised mounting pad to provide good stencil/screen mesh contact. The adhering liquid is applied from the top of the screen with a lintless cloth, and then dried with a second cloth, working over the entire stencil area from one end to the other. It is good practice to use local ventilation to remove the evaporating solvent from the screen, as this reduces the drying time of the stencil.

Drying

When the entire stencil has been treated, it is left to dry in front of a cold fan for 5 minutes. After this the backing film should peel away quite freely.

Removing the stencil

After removal of the ink or printing medium, the screen is placed on a pad of newspaper. Screen wash or a universal screen cleaning solvent is then applied over the surface of the screen. After a few minutes the stencil will release from the screen on to the pad beneath. Any stencil residue that remains in the screen when it is lifted away from the pad can be removed with a clean cloth and a little solvent.

1.   2.

Fig. 74 1. Adhering a solvent-adhered knife-cut stencil.
  2. Removing a solvent-adhered stencil from the screen.

Troubleshooting

Solvent-adhered stencil films are subject to the same cutting and adhering requirements as water-adhered films, and thus remarks made earlier in this respect apply here also.

The stencil dissolving into the mesh is usually caused by overwetting with adhering liquid and/or using too much pressure when removing the excess liquid with the dry cloth. The stencil coating may be drawn through the screen and into the cloth, and then transferred into an open area of the screen, causing image blocking.

Health and Safety Note

Whenever volatile solvents like methyl alcohol or acetone-based solvents are used, proper attention must be given to health and safety practices. In particular, such solvents should only be used in a well ventilated area. A fume mask and gloves should be worn to provide appropriate personal protection. Precautions should also be taken against the potential fire hazards presented by volatile solvents. This will include the safe disposal of any contaminated materials used in adhering and removing knife-cut stencil materials.

Whilst the old saying that 'a bad craftsman always blames his tools' may be as true of bad stencil cutters as it is of any other crafts person, it is also true that a good stencil cutter is only as good as the knife that is used.

Stencil-cutting tools

   If the stencil knife is to allow its user to cut with precision and speed, it must conform to the following general requirements:

- The blade must be kept sharp, with an oblique profile, providing a good cutting point.
- The blade should be neither too long nor too short. If it is too long it will be awkward to handle, and if it is too short it may obscure the work during cutting.
- The handle of the knife should be barrel-shaped, and no thicker than a pencil. The barrel shape allows the knife to be twisted between the thumb and forefinger when negotiating curves.
- The knife should be correctly weighted and balanced so that there is the minimum pressure on the blade when cutting.

There are a number of stencil knives on the market; the best of them will exhibit the features listed above. Some of the better knives have replaceable blades, and these may also be honed on a fine oil stone to keep their cutting edge sharp.

The American company Ulano have been pioneers in the design of stencil and masking-film cutting instruments. One of the first precision tools they developed was the Ulano Swivel Knife.

This knife is built to very exacting design specifications. It conforms to all the requirements described above. In addition it has a precision engineered swivel blade facility. The tiny chuck which houses the blade rotates in a ball-race sleeve, inside the barrel shaped handle. The blade may also be locked in a fixed position if required. When unlocked it provides a smooth swivel action which enables the blade to be guided effortlessly around the contours of the most intricately curved design. Skilled users can cut stencils and photomasks accurately and rapidly with a tool like this.

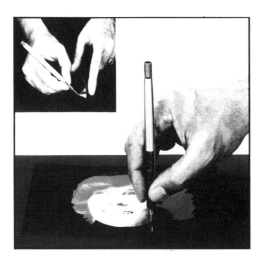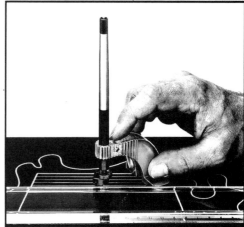

Fig. 75 Ulano 'Swivel Knife'.

Stencil cutting is a skill which has to be learned rather than taught. The teacher can only point out certain elementary aspects of the skill; its development requires diligent and patient practice.

A very effective way of developing this skill is to practise cutting the large letter forms found in the headlines of the daily newspaper. Regular practice, first cutting the headlines and then working on the smaller type faces in the subheadings and advertisements, will very quickly develop the precision, dexterity and confidence which characterizes skilled stencil cutting.

Before cutting commences, the sharpness of the blade should be tested. The blade should be sharp enough to cut right through the upper layer of the stencil material with the minimum of pressure applied to the knife.

The knife should be held in an upright position, so that the cutting point is clearly visible. If the knife is allowed to lean, it will produce a stencil which has an obliquely formed shoulder, causing inaccuracy and stencil breakdown.

The first attempts at stencil cutting are usually rather tense and awkward, producing faltering curves. As practice continues the hand should become more relaxed and confident in negotiating the design contours, producing smoother curves with greater continuity of form.

It is good practice to examine the back of the stencil after it has been cut. Any evidence of scoring or denting will indicate excessive knife pressure, which is usually caused by tension in the hand as difficult areas are traced. The key aspect here is to keep the hand as relaxed as possible whilst exercising maximum control of the blade.

COMPUTER STENCIL-CUTTING SYSTEMS

Developments in computerized plotting devices which drive stencil-cutting tools have been used in the screen printing industry for some years now. They were first introduced into the sign printing sector, where large

Fig. 76   The cutting head. (Courtesy of Signus Ltd.)

format line images are commonly produced using knife-cut stencil techniques.

The machines are a direct development of the technology used in computerized drafting systems. Artwork is produced in digital format. This is then electronically manipulated, translated from tone to line, enlarged, reduced, or even colour-separated. The software now available offers very powerful design and origination tools, allowing the printer to provide the customer with a visual proof of the image as it would appear in situ – on a range of vehicles, for example, or in the shopping mall.

When the design is completed it is transmitted to the plotter which will drive the cutting tool across the stencil or mask film according the data received from the computer work station.

Recent developments in non-impact printing have been taking place alongside the development of computer cutting technology. The ability to cut a vast range of type faces in sizes ranging from 12 pt to 1200 mm high, and to incorporate multicoloured graphics at the same time, makes this equipment much more than a simple stencil-cutting device. It provides a good example of the impact of high technology on the craft side of the industry and is a clear indication of the change which has now taken place in the industry – which brings me back to where I began.

There is much more that can be said and written about this diverse and rapidly developing process. Here I have tried to indicate something of its range and its complexity. My concern is that those who are new to the process will have gained some insight about the techniques and applications. For those already familiar with the technology and the art I trust that there will also be something of interest and of value in these pages.

Appendix: Contacts

Professional bodies and information sources

Screen Printing Association (UK) Ltd
7a West Street
Reigate
Surrey RH2 9BL

Federation of European Screen Printers
Association (FESPA)
7a West Street
Reigate
Surrey RH2 9BL

British Printing Industries Federation
11 Bedford Row
London WC1R 4DX

Pira International
Randalls Road
Leatherhead
Surrey KT22 7RU

Screen Printing and Graphic Imaging
Association International
10015 Main Street
Fairfax
VA 22031
USA

Trade publications

Screen Process
(Monthly)
Batiste Publications Ltd

Pembroke House
Campsbourne Road
Hornsey
London N8 7PE

Screen Printing
(Monthly)
ST Publications Inc.
407 Gilbert Avenue
Cincinnati
OH 45202
USA

Printwear & Promotion
(Six issues per year)
Batiste Publications Ltd
Pembroke House
Campsbourne Road
Hornsey
London N8 7PE

Images
(Six issues per year)
CN Publishing
9a Kings Road
Flitwick
Bedfordshire MK45 1ED

Screen and Display
A and E Morgan
Old Aerodrome Farm
Aston Down
Chalford
Stroud
Gloucestershire GL6 8HR

Environmental management

Confederation of British Industry (CBI)
Centrepoint
103 New Oxford Street
London WC1A 1DU

Department of Trade and Industry
Environment Business Unit
151 Buckingham Palace Road
3rd Floor
London SW1W 9SF

Environment Council
21 Elizabeth Street
London SW1W 9RP

The Environmental Management Standard
British Standards Institute (BSI)
Information Department
Linford Wood
Milton Keynes MK14 6LE

Her Majesty's Inspectorate of Pollution
Romney House
43 Marsham Street
London SW1P 5DT

National Society for Clean Air and
Environmental Protection
136 North Street
Brighton BN1 1RG

UK Centre for Economic and Environment
Development
3E Kings Parade
Cambridge CB2 1SJ

Croners Environmental Management
Croner Publications
Croner House
London Road
Kingston upon Thames
Surrey KT2 6SR

Environmental Consultancy
University of Sheffield
Endcliffe Holt
343 Fulwood Road
Sheffield S10 3BQ

Environmental Data Services
Finsbury Business Centre
40 Bowling Green Lane
London EC1R 0NE

Greenpeace Business
Greenpeace
Canonbury Villas
London N1 2PN

Greenprint
Innovation Way
Barnsley
South Yorkshire
S75 1JL

Technical Publications Ltd
The British Library
100 High Avenue
Letchworth
Herts. SG6 3RR

Colleges and training centres

Many local Further and Adult Education
Colleges offer classes in screen
printing. The approach is usually art and
design or craft based. For guidance on
registered NVQ centres and the NVQ in
Screen Printing contact Michael Turner, Screen
Printing Association (UK) Limited, 7a West
Street, Reigate, Surrey RH2 9BL.

Barking College of Technology
Department of General and Visual Studies
Dagenham Road
Romford
Essex RM7 0XU

The Europrint Centre
Innovation Way
Barnsley
South Yorkshire S75 1JL

Castlereagh College
Northern Ireland School of Printing
Montgomery Road
Belfast BT6 9JD

Matthew Boulton College of FE/HE
School of Printing, Art and Design
Sherlock Street
Birmingham B5 70B

Blackburn College
St Paul's Avenue
Blackburn BB2 1LH

Brunel College of Arts and
Technology Faculty of Sciences and
Visual Arts
Davy House
Ashley Down
Bristol BS7 9BU

Cardiff Institute of Higher Education
School of Two-dimensional Design
Penarth Road
Cardiff CF1 5AJ

Cardiff Institute of Higher Education
School of Print and Foundation
Studies
Australia Road
Cardiff CF4 3DA

Colchester Institute
School of Art and Design (Printing)
Sheepen Road
Colchester CO3 3LL

Dunstable College
Kingsway
Dunstable LU5 4HG
Napier University

Department of Print Media, Publishing and
Communication
10 Colinton Road
Edinburgh EH10 5DJ

Falmouth College of Art
Faculty of Design Studies
Wood Lane
Falmouth TR11 4RA

College of Building and Printing
60 North Hanover Street
Glasgow G1 2BP

Gloucester College of Arts and
Technology
Faculty of Design and Technology
Brunswick Road
Gloucester GL1 1HS

Guildford College of FE and HE
Creative Studies Division
Stoke Park
Guildford GU1 1EZ

Leeds College of Technology
Printing Studies Programme
Calverley Street
Leeds LS1 3HE

South Fields College
Faculty of Art, Design and Technology
Aylestone Road
Leicester LE2 3HE

City of Liverpool Community College
Design, Print and Publishing Centre
105 Boundary Street
Liverpool L5 9YT

London College of Printing and Distributive
Trades
School of Printing Technology
Elephant and Castle
London SE1 6SB

Kent Institute of Art and Design
Oakwood Park
Maidstone ME16 8AG

City College Manchester
Manchester School of Printing
Moor Road
Wythenshawe
Manchester M23 9PQ

Manchester Metropolitan University
School of Print Media, Department of
Communication Media
All Saints
Manchester M15 6BR

Cleveland College of Art and Design
Green Lane
Linthorpe
Middlesbrough TS5 7RJ

Newcastle College
School of Art and Design
Ryehill Campus
Scotswood Road
Newcastle upon Tyne NE4 7SA

Nene College
Faculty of Art and Design
St George's Avenue
Northampton NN2 6JD

South Nottingham College
Department of Printing
Charnwood Centre
Farnborough Road

Clifton
Nottingham NG11 8LU

Plymouth College of Art and Design
School of Printing
Tavistock Place
Plymouth PL4 8AT

Berkshire College of Art and Design
King's Road
Reading RG1 4HJ

University of Reading
Department of Typography and Graphic
Communication
2 Earley Gate
Whiteknights
Reading RG6 2AU

Staffordshire University
Department of Design
College Road
Stoke-on-Trent ST4 2DE

West Herts College
Faculty of Visual Communications
Watford Campus
Hempstead Road
Watford WD1 3EZ

Dublin Institute of Technology
College of Technology
School of Printing and Graphic Communication
Bolton Street
Dublin
Eire

Suppliers

Key: **A** inks; **B** inks and sundries;
        C equipment/machinery;
        D screen mesh; **E** screen covering;
        F screen making; **G** substrates;
        H films and photo emulsion;
        I imaging systems.

Abbess Dryers
Brookside Works
Abbess Roding
Near Ongar
Essex CM5 ONY
C

Acheson Colloids Co.
Prince Rock
Plymouth
Devon PL4 OSP
A

Active Supply Company Ltd
33 Diamond Ridge
Camberley
Surrey GU15 4LN
C E

Adelco Screen Process Ltd
Units 16–18
Highview
High Street
Bordon
Hants GU35 OAX
C

Adhesive and Display Products Ltd
Huntsman House
Mansion Close
Moulton Park
Northampton NN3 1LA.
G

Adhesive Paper Products
Red House Road
Croydon
Surrey

CR0 3AQ
G

Advance International
Suite 2
110 Frimley Road
Camberley
Surrey GU15 2QN
C

Autotype International Ltd
Grove Road
Wantage
Oxon. X12 7BZ
H I

J.W. Bollom & Co. Ltd
(John T. Keep & Sons Ltd)
PO Box 78
Croydon Road
Elmers End
Beckenham
Kent BR3 4BL
B C D E F H

G. Bopp & Co. Ltd
Block C
115 Brunswick Park Road
New Southgate
London N11 1LJ
D

B&P Graphics Systems
Unit 3
Chertsey Business Centre
Riversdell Close
Chertsey
Surrey KT16 9AS
I

Brittains (TR) Ltd
Ivy House Paper Mills
Commercial Road
Hanley
Stoke on Trent ST1 3QS
G

Brittons Printing Inks Ltd
Eddington Lane
Herne Bay
Kent CT6 5TR
A

Coates Screen Ltd
Cray Avenue
St Mary Cray
Orpington
Kent BR5 3PP
B C D E F G H I

Colenso Screen Services Ltd
Unit 3
Fairoak Court
Whitehouse
Runcorn
Cheshire WA7 3DX
B D F

Colours Ltd
Unit 25
JFK Industrial Estate
Dublin 12
Eire
A

Dean Valley Ltd
Lower House Mills
Bollington
Macclesfield
Cheshire
SK10 5HP
G

Deca Products Spinks
Unit 6
Vaughan Road
Heaton Norris
Stockport SK4 2PQ
B H

Euroflex Screen Print Supplies Ltd
Unit 4
Orbital One Trading Estate

Green Street
Green Road
Dartford
Kent DA1 1QG
B

Fabprint
Railway Lane
Littlemore
Oxford OX4
C

Folex Ltd
18–19 Monkspath Business
Park
Shirley
Solihull
West Midlands B40 9NY
H

Fotec AG
PO Box 1123
Eigenheimstrasse 22
8700 Kuesnacht
Switzerland
H

Fox Graphic Machinery Ltd
KG House
Kingsfield Close
Gladstone Industry
Dallington
Northampton NN5 7QS
C

George Hall (Sales) Ltd
Hardman Street
Chestergate
Stockport SK3 OHA
B C D H

Granthams Graphic Technology
Corporation Street
Preston PR1 2UQ
I

Johnson Matthey Print
Burslem
Stoke-on-Trent ST6 3AT
I

Kimoto UK Ltd
40A, Jasmine Grove
Penge
London SE20 8JP
H I

H.G. Kippax & Sons Ltd
Upper Bankfield Mills
Almondbury Bank
Huddersfield HD5 8HF
C

Klemm Equipment & Services
Postfach 170361
D4800 Bielefeld 17
Germany
C

Marabu (UK) Ltd
Unit 17
Capel Hendre Industrial Estate
Ammanford
Dyfed SA18 3SJ
B

Mografo A/S
Klovermarken 120
DK 7190 Billund
Denmark
I

Natgraph Ltd
Dabell Avenue
Blenheim Industrial Estate
Nottingham NG6 8WA
C

Nor-Cote International Inc.
7 Warrior Park
Eagle Close
Chandlers Ford Industrial

Estate
Chandlers Ford
Hants SO5 3NF
B

Printall Display Ltd
Unit 5
Three Stars Trading Estate
Ten Acre Lane
Egham
Surrey TW20 8RJ
B D E F G H

Printing and Graphic Machinery Ltd
Millboard Road
Bourne End
Bucks. SL8 5XE
C

Projecon Ltd
4 Gooseacre
Radley
Abingdon OX14 3BL
I

Registerprint Machinery Ltd
Redlands
Marlpit Lane
Coulsdon
Surrey CR3 2UH
C I

Screen Printing Machinery Ltd
1 Sugar Lane
Stratford
London E15 2QN
C I

Sericol Ltd
Westwood Road
Broadstairs
Kent CT10 2PA
B C D E F G H

Silk Screen Europe
Delaunay House
Scoresby Street
Little Germany
Bradford BD1 5BJ
C

R.A. Smart (Screen Suppliers) Ltd
Clough Bank
Grimshaw Lane
Bollington
Macclesfield
Cheshire SK10 5JB
B C D F G H (textile specialists)

Tripette et Renaud
ZI Du Val De Seine
20 Avenue Marcellin Berthelot
92396 Villenuve La Garenne
Cedex
France
C

Trumax Ltd
Tower Road
Warmley
Bristol BS15 2XL
C

Index

CSL

Coated Screens Limited

QUALITY PRODUCTS AND SERVICES
FOR SCREEN PROCESS PRINTING

OUR PRODUCT RANGE

- **Pre-Coated Screens**
- **Precision Screen Fabrics & Frames**
- **Photosensitive Films & Emulsions**
- **Cleaning & Preparation Chemicals**
- **Studio Materials & Masking Films**
- **Printing Sundries & Equipment**
- **Inks & Solvents**

OUR SERVICES

- **Screen Recovering**
- **Artwork**
- **Stencil Making**
- **Technical Support**

Orchard House, Church Lane, Wallington, Surrey SM6 7ND.
Tel: 0181 773 2331 (5 lines) Fax: 0181 669 6417

SPA,
Working for its Members and the Screen Printing Industry

Whether you are a Printer or a Supplier to the trade, the Screen Printing Association is there for you - ready to help and serve you on any Industry related enquiry - including technological advances.

We do not flood Members with unnecessary information - we seek to help you do what you do best and reduce the burden of administration - from A - Z.

If you would like to know more about the SPA and its activities without obligation, just call or fax us on Tel: 01737 240792 - or Fax: 01737 240770 Screen Printing Association (UK) Ltd, Association House, 7a, West Street, Reigate, Surrey RH2 9BL

Specialists in the Printing & Decoration of Components

Do it RIGHT!

First Time ... and every time!

Product Decoration Services have a well established history of providing a comprehensive quality service to many household name manufacturers. If you have a printing related problem, save time and money by getting in the specialists to sort it out quickly and effectively.

Process Improvements

PDS will carry out an assessment of your printing facility and produce a report which will highlight areas where improvements can be made. These are nearly always no or low cost recommendations.

Trouble Shooting

Most production problems can be resolved quickly with production resumed within hours. As a print manager it is all too easy to become so engrossed in the symptoms that the cause is missed. PDS will look at the problem without prejudice.

Training

Training programmes are developed to suit your needs. Combining focused theoretical sessions with practical "hands-on" training on your own equipment.

Project Management

If you have an unusual or innovative application, are new to printing or curious as to the alternative methods of decorating your product, we can help. We can advise you on the advantages of each process, equipment available, costs, print rates, etc., right through to overseeing installation and commissioning of equipment.

To discuss what we can do together to make your print department a profitable part of your business, contact us. We have no ties with any manufacturer and all advice will only be in your best interests.

Product Decoration Services
Innovation Way, Barnsley, South Yorkshire, S75 1JL, ENGLAND
Tel: +44 (0)1226 249590   Fax: +44 (0)1226 294797
Email: 100615.3570@compuserve.com